BALI
CHRONICLES

BALI
CHRONICLES

Fascinating People *and* Events *in* Balinese History

Willard A. Hanna
Introduction by **Adrian Vickers**

PERIPLUS EDITIONS
Singapore • Hong Kong • Indonesia

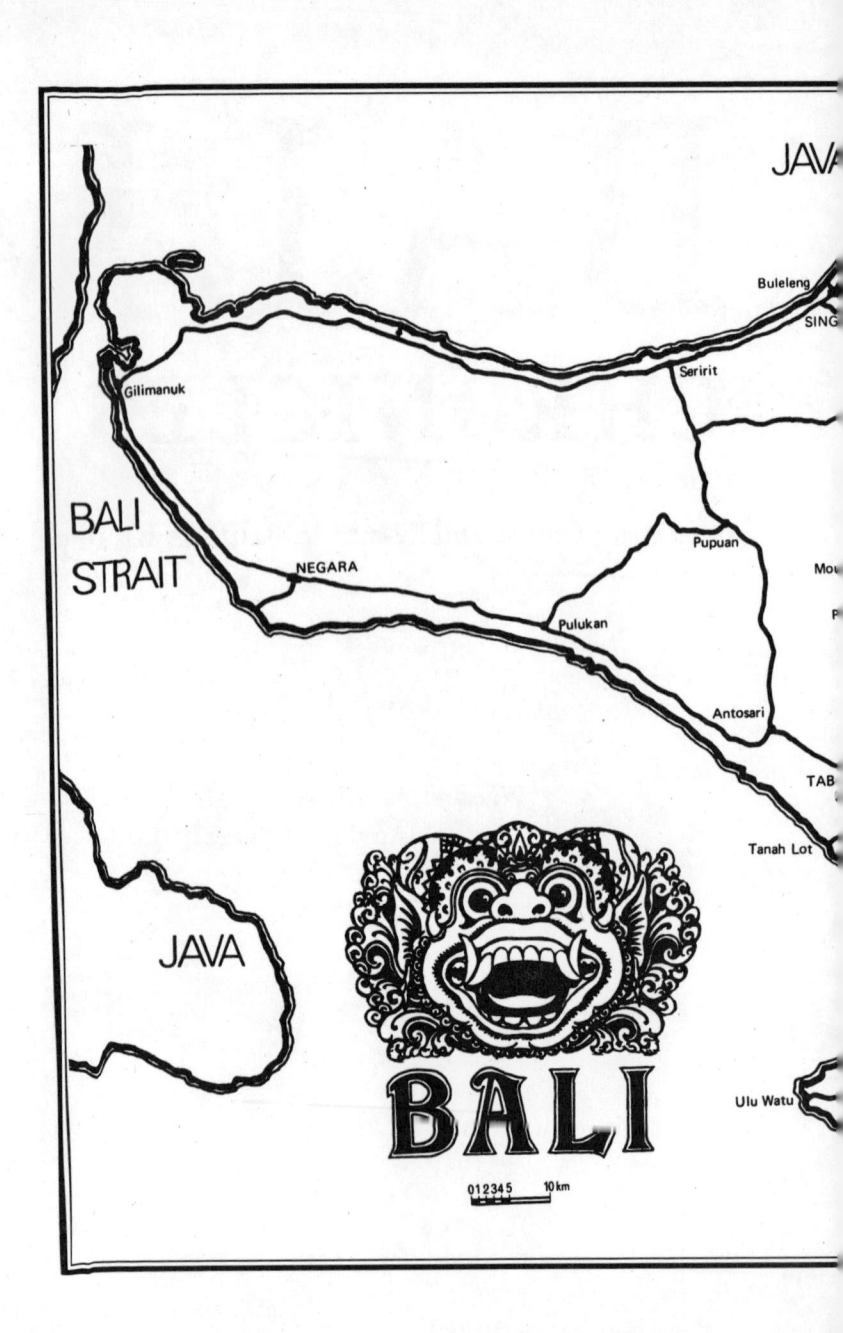

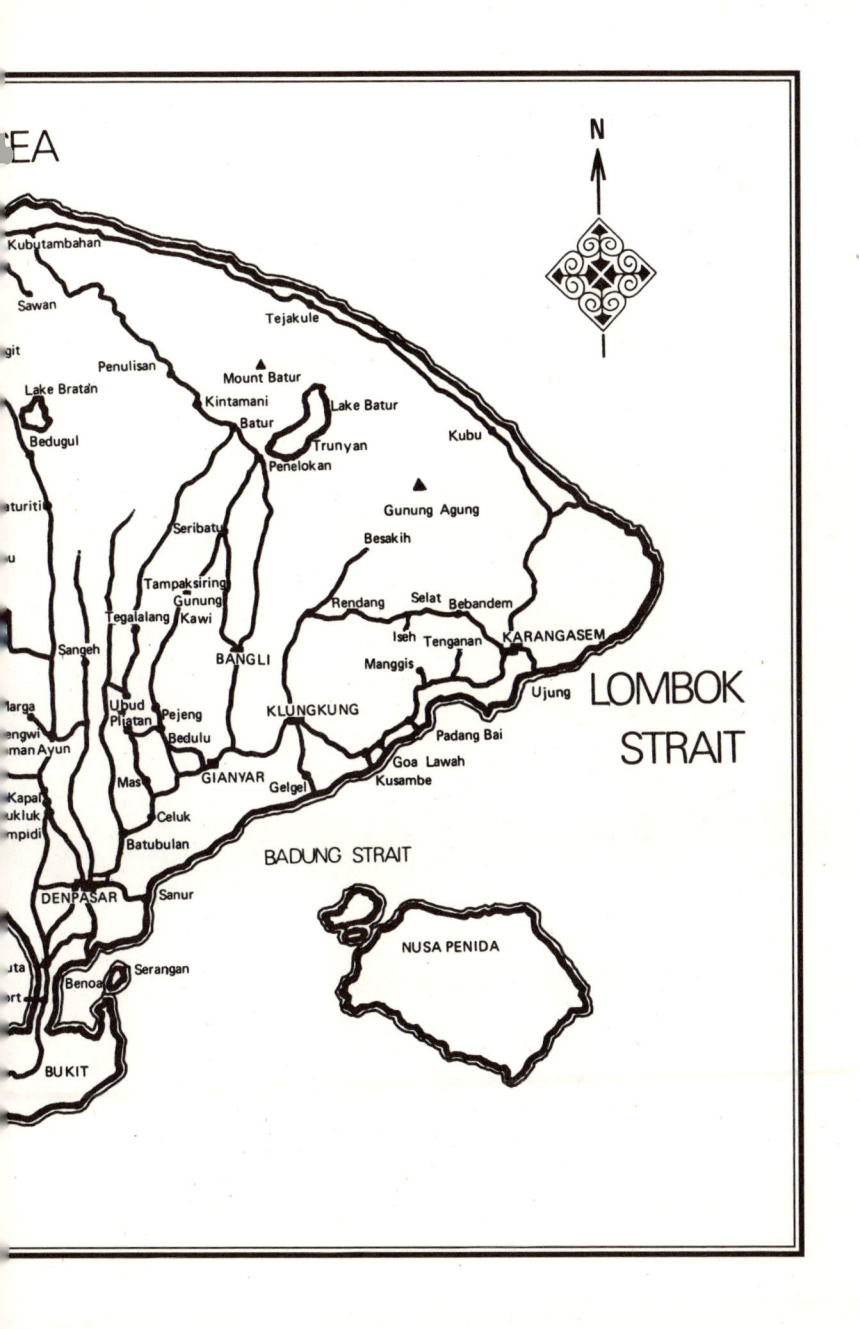

Published by Periplus Editions (HK) Ltd.

www.periplus.com

Copyright © 2004 Institute of Current World Affairs

First published as *Bali Profile: People, Events, Circumstances (1001–1976)* by American Universities Field Staff, New York, 1976
First Periplus edition, 2004

Distributors
Indonesia
PT Java Books Indonesia
Jl. Rawa Gelam IV No. 9
Kawasan Industri Pulogadung
Jakarta 13930, Indonesia
Tel: 62 (21) 4682 1088; Fax: 62 (21) 461 0206
crm@periplus.co.id
www.periplus.com

Asia Pacific
Berkeley Books Pte. Ltd.
61 Tai Seng Avenue #02-12,
Singapore 534167
Tel: (65) 6280-1330; Fax: (65) 6280-6290
inquiries@periplus.com.sg
www.periplus.com

Japan
Tuttle Publishing
Yaekari Building 3rd Fl, 5-4-12 Osaki
Shinagawa-ku, Tokyo 141 0032, Japan
Tel: 81 (3) 5437-0171; Fax: 81 (3) 5437-0755
sales@tuttle.co.jp
www.tuttle.co.jp

North America, Latin America & Europe
Tuttle Publishing
364 Innovation Drive
North Clarendon, VT 05759-9436 U.S.A
Tel: 1 (802) 773-8930; Fax: 1 (802) 773-6993
info@tuttlepublishing.com
www.tuttlepublishing.com

17 16 15 14 13   5 4 3 2   1306MP

Introduction

Those of us who began our research on Bali in the 1970s had only one English source on which to rely for any sense of Balinese history: Willard A. Hanna's *Bali Profile: People, Events, Circumstances 1001–1976*, reprinted here as *Bali Chronicles*. I first came upon it on the shelves of a Balinese scholar, Madé Kanta, and after months of patiently combing the bookstores of Bali came upon a worn copy for the princely sum of Rp 7,000. It still remains one of the favorites that I dip into every now and then for a taste both of a different sense of Bali and for the flavor of the time in which it was produced.

The book that you have before you began life as a series of American Universities Field Staff Reports. Having been published first in that form, where leading anthropologists of Bali such as James A. Boon and Clifford Geertz referred to them, they were then republished in 1976 as a single volume under the title *Bali Profile*. Not all of the original reports seem to have been incorporated into this single volume, which concentrates on colonial processes by which the Dutch took power over Bali and the neighboring island of Lombok. The fact that the chapters were originally separate reports accounts for the slightly disjointed nature of the whole. With his good knowledge of Dutch, Willard A. Hanna produced a similar set of studies on Ambon that remains one of the key introductions to Eastern Indonesia.

Bali Chronicles contains two types of views of Bali. It is not a history as such—it lacks the footnotes, the archival research and the questioning approach to sources of an historian. Rather, it presents a set of largely Dutch views of the island, as Hanna himself notes in his Foreword, but tied to the view of the early period of the New Order government of President Suharto (president from 1967 to 1998).

What Hanna has done is essentially to produce clear and entertaining summaries of a set of very different Dutch writings on the island, as well as of Balinese control of Lombok. He has not tried to reconcile the discrepancies between these views, let alone to check them against Balinese sources, as shown by the bad spelling of Balinese names taken directly from these sources. Nevertheless, we get a good sense of the different European participants in Balinese history, the Dutch government contract-maker Huskus Koopman, the Danish trader Mads Lange, the Controleur—or district officer—P. L. van Bloemen Waanders, and the parliamentarian H. H. van Kol. Further archival research would have fleshed out the character and motives of these participants: the fraudulent manner in which Huskus Koopman tricked various Balinese rulers into signing over sovereignty, Mads Lange's involvement in the arms trade, and H. H. van Kol's advocacy of socialism. And we do not have enough sense of the attitudes and motivations of many of the Balinese actors. Many of them, particularly the members of the Karangasem–Lombok dynasty, remain victims of bad Dutch publicity.

Even for those who can read Dutch, such a compilation is of some value. But then Willard A. Hanna has attempted to reconcile the written views of Bali with the sense of history provided by Balinese and other participants: Bobby Mörzer Bruyns, one of the founders of Bali's tourist industry; Jimmy Pandy, who helped restart the tourist industry after World War II, the Indonesian Revolution, and the Post-Revolutionary conflicts; former governor I Gusti Bagus Oka and Ibu Gedong, major figures in fixing Bali's cultural identity; and Ide Anak Agung Gde Agung, former Foreign Minister of Indonesia and head of the royal family of Gianyar.

Through Mörzer Bruyns and other oral sources we get a good sense of the characters involved in the founding of the tourist industry of Bali. Hanna combines his summary of their accounts with useful statistical and social information. His overall account of early twentieth-century Bali is a rosy one, viewed through the nostalgic rose-colored glasses of its participants. Unfortunately, the majority of Balinese, for whom life in the 1930s involved poverty and hardship, would not agree with the view that "Life in Bali in the 1930s was agreeable not only for affluent foreigners but also for the Balinese."

It is especially through the controversial Ide Anak Agung that Hanna provides an early New Order view of Bali. As a major opponent of former President Sukarno, Ide Anak Agung's political views shine through this book's negative account of the Sukarno period, and even in the conservative account of the period of Balinese participation in the Indonesian struggle for Independence of 1945–49. Many more Balinese were enthusiastic, even passionately devoted, supporters of Indonesia's first president than the book indicates. Here Hanna and Ide Anak Agung were very much of a like mind; Hanna coming from Cold War America had no time for the Left's ideas of Land Reform or People's Art, while Ide Anak Agung, as a very modern traditional ruler, was on a side of politics that was simultaneously conservative and liberal. His political grouping, identified with the leadership of the wise Sutan Sjahrir, was conservative because of its opposition to radical reform, particularly of wealth and privilege, but adopted a liberal and internationalist perspective. Ide Anak Agung's own cosmopolitan life and outlook exemplified this.

This book's highlighting of the kingdom of Gianyar at the expense of the other former Balinese kingdoms needs to be taken with a grain of salt, since Gianyar was the newest of the Balinese kingdoms, and had neither the status of the high kingdom, Klungkung, nor the prestige of Gianyar's main twentieth-century rival kingdom, Karangasem. The autobiography of one of Karangasem's royal sons, Dr A. A. Madé Djelantik, *The Birthmark: Memoires of a Balinese Prince* (Periplus), makes a useful counter reading to the pro-Gianyar views of *Bali Chronicles*.

At a time when the Balinese are desperate to restore tourist numbers to the days before Indonesia's political crises and the catastrophic bombings of October 2002, it seems strange that Hanna was so worried about what would happen when Bali's tourist visits reached the 300,000 mark. This is another reflection of the views current at the time the book was written: that Bali required a strategy to preserve its culture against tourism. In retrospect, this strategy, which had its origins in the research of Balinese writer Nyoman S. Pendit on the international sociology of tourism, ignored a number of issues. First, culture is not a fixed or unchangeable "thing," but rather an adaptable series of perceptions and social representations. In Bali's case, tourism has helped to reinforce a separate sense of Balinese identity, and given Balinese players in Indonesian society the means by which to support their island's idea of uniqueness. As Hanna points out, the dilemma for Bali has always been one of how to support a dense population with limited resources, and tourism is the chief means to provide such support. Bali, in that sense, has been a model of success for other islands, and even nations, to emulate.

The real problem for Bali, one that was not so clear in the priorities of the 1970s, is preserving nature rather than culture. Rather than reaching the predicted level of 500,000 visitors per year in 2000, Bali achieved over 1,000,000 per year, but at the expense of its ecology. Despite excellent planning processes, government authorities were left at the mercy of rampant development too close to beaches, in ugly ribbons of small shops, and throughout areas that were originally planned as "green belts." The result has been polluted and eroded beaches, shortages of water, and a deterioration of the quality of life for most Balinese. The challenge of the twenty-first century will be to restore tourism while making Bali livable.

Hanna's sense of concern for Bali, and his devotion to the island, shines through in each part of the book, no more so than in the last section, with its potted version of Balinese religion and culture. Falling back on stereotypes of "the Balinese," as any such summary will, this section is most in need of updating. No longer can we say "the Balinese family lives in a spacious, walled compound which is part of an enclave of compounds," for example, since the majority of Balinese live in crowded conditions in cities, although in many cases the villages that Hanna encountered in the 1970s have been incorporated into urban sprawl in a way that maintains many earlier aspects of social organization.

This is a book of its time, a description of Bali's interaction with the West, but a book that deserves re-reading. Willard A. Hanna has left us a book that should be enjoyed as a collection of voices, sometimes dissonant, often self-serving, but always fascinating.

Associate Professor Adrian Vickers
University of Wollongong
January 2004

Contents

Acknowledgments

I wish to make grateful acknowledgment to the writers listed in the Bibliography at the end of this book and to a certain few individuals who have knowingly or unknowingly contributed most generously to my store of information about Bali: Ide Anak Agung Gde Agung dan Isteri, last Radja of Gianjar, and his wife, Vera, whose personal reminiscences and companionship have proved more revealing than any books; the late Professor I Gusti Gde Raka, the pioneer student of the Balinese economy, who patiently explained it to me; former Governor I. G. Bagoes Oka and Gedong Bagoes Oka, the mentors of Bali's cultural conservationists; James Pandy, a connoisseur of Balinese life and art; A. Mörzer Bruyns, whose vivid recollections of prewar Bali should form the basis for his own memoirs; J. H. Ritman, who introduced me to the Dutch liberal point of view regarding Bali and other regions of Indonesia; G. A. Schotel, the doyen of the Western business community in Bali in the 1930s, who helped me with hard-to-get facts and figures.

Foreword

Contemporary Balinese Dilemma

This book relates the story of Bali, its rulers, its people, and its encounters, often traumatic, with the Western world. Spanning the entire period since the beginning of recorded island history, it gives intimations of the long-term sources of the contemporary crisis which now confronts the Balinese with the grim choice between economic decay in obscurity or cultural decadence on the floodlighted stage of international tourism.

There already exists a wealth of literature on Balinese art and thought and the singularly beautiful Balinese way of life which often seems to outsiders like a lavishly costumed pageant continuously and merrily played out against a superbly scenic tropical backdrop. Except for several Balinese court chronicles, impenetrable to most foreigners, and a few other works, mainly in Dutch, by Western writers of the nineteenth or early twentieth century, there is almost nothing of any consequence with regard to Balinese history, economics, and politics, or the roots of the present dilemma. It is the aim, therefore, of this account to provide a background sketch of historic events, to trace the complications of domestic and international politics, to depict the changing economic scene, and to introduce the key characters, Balinese and Western, of the island drama of the last millennium as it now comes to an especially significant new climax. Since all else in Bali cues to the cultural tradition, there is also a chapter dealing with the basic conceptual elements of a life-outlook best described as Balinism.

The exposure, however brief, may provide insight into the still living manifestations of a richly textured medievalism which is now threatened with extinction. Paradoxically and tragically, it is the very policy now being designed for the purpose of cultural conservation which poses the greatest threat. The plan is to promote "Cultural Tourism" as the one and only really promising new industry. Under this strange new device Bali now deliberately invites a late twentieth century invasion of jumbo-jet borne barbarians. The rather fanciful concept seems to be that flights of joy-seekers from overseas crave not just exoticism but also aestheticism and will generously pay the costs of Bali's coming reincarnation as a prosperously modernized but still uniquely artistic island entity.

Even by resort to more enlightened developmental planning it may already be much too late to revitalize an archaic system which is as anachronistic in the twentieth century as it was appropriate to the sixteenth and has been miraculously preserved almost intact through many previous disasters. Perhaps Cultural Tourism really will result in the transfusion of cash and the acquisition of skills which will enable the Balinese, guided in some esoteric manner by their own true genius, to survive and to flourish within a culture-centric society precariously perched on the rim of the materialistic world. The artistically endowed Balinese are now so economically impoverished, however, that they seem not indisposed to engage in a folklorical sort of exhibitionism in return for their visitors' admission fees. A spectacle so transparently shabby can scarcely be expected to yield transcendental rewards.

It lies just beyond the scope of this book to present any very extended analysis of Bali's modern dilemma or any deeply reasoned forecast of the consequences of Cultural Tourism or any suggestion of alternatives. But the basic factors can be quickly identified. Up until about the year 1900 the island's agricultural economy was able to support the masses of the Balinese people in such rustic affluence that they enjoyed the plenty and the leisure to indulge themselves fully in the elaborate and costly ceremonialism which is the island's most distinctive characteristic. It also enabled a large class of highly privileged lay and religious rulers to create palaces, courts, and temples richly ornamented with works of astonishing artistry or craftsmanship. All this was possible because the land was and is wonderfully fertile; there is abundant rainfall; the climate allows for two or three food crops each year; the farmers are skillful and industrious; and Balinese agriculture, especially its rice culture, is the envy even of the ingenious Javanese. The ordinary Balinese, furthermore, is gifted with quite extraordinary powers of observing and representing the wonder and the mystery of the world about him; it is as though nature itself compels artistic self-expression.

Since 1900 Balinese circumstances have altered quite drastically, not only because of the imposition island-wide of Dutch colonialism but also because of natural developments which long went almost unremarked. The population has at least doubled within this century, while land holdings have shrunk to less than one acre per family with the finest irrigated rice lands having to be divided and sub-divided. The rice crop is still abundant, but it is far from adequate to meet the demands of a population which would contentedly eat enough rice to make up 90% or more of its total protein and caloric intake but is now compelled to rely more and more upon not very highly esteemed cassava and sweet potatoes. Although coffee, copra, cattle, and pigs provide important cash earnings, Bali's economy shows a dangerously increasing excess of imports over exports, and the provincial government is largely dependent upon central government financing. An island which was rice-rich in the past and lavished its wealth upon cultural display is rice-poor today and is about to be reduced to catering its culture as cocktail canapé for tourists.

In yet more specific terms, Bali now has a population of over 2.2 million and is rapidly growing toward a total of 4.4 million by the year 2000. It is unable to support more than one million persons in anything approximating the degree of comfort and pleasure it afforded in times past. The annual per capita income is probably about $75. It would require a quadrupling of the rice harvest (from 200,000 to 800,000 tons) or the entertainment of some 300,000 visitors (there were 100,000 in 1973) to raise the income to $175; both together might raise it to a more respectable and acceptable $275. But the rice crop is not susceptible to any such escalation, sudden or gradual, and the prospect of 300,000 tourists is not especially reassuring with regard to the spiritual integrity of the future Balinese farmer turned tourist tout, the student graduated to become beach boy or bar girl, or the musicians, dancers, and actors who adapt their performances to the standards of the discotheque and nightclub. Aside from the development of tourism there seems to be no other possibility of stimulating economic growth on a scale remotely commensurate with the need. Coffee, copra, cattle, and pigs now bring in something like $4–6 million each year; but imports of textiles, foodstuffs, and other essential goods total at least $10–15 million. Arts and crafts yield $1 million; 100,000 tourists now spend $12.5 million. Provincial government revenues come to only about $500,000; provincial and central government expenditures on island administration and development amount to $6 million. Out of this very unsatisfactory fiscal mix, as reflected in official but not very reliable statistics, solvency is not the predictable end product.

The Balinese population, meanwhile, is being exposed to modern education—230,000 pupils at the primary level, 45,000 secondary school students, and 2,500 registered in the provincial university. Such schooling unfits the youth for life as farmers; it equips them to observe the difference between their own status and that of the foreign visitor. The latter will spend in a single day at the Bali Beach Hotel or one of the newer, even more luxurious establishments, what it costs a university student to maintain himself for six to twelve months. The government, which is spending a modest one to two million dollars per year on education ($2.00 per head at the primary level), is laying out an equivalent amount on new systems of communication. New roads and other facilities are calculated to serve the people; even more specifically and immediately, however, they accommodate the tourists, who are the carriers of discontent. In seeking suitable employment the educated young Balinese now turns, gratefully or reluctantly to the tourist industry so that a newly opening hotel has been known to receive 10,000 applications for 500 positions.

The Bali provincial government, like the Indonesian national government, is attempting to implement policies of basic reform and rehabilitation which will serve to repair the enormous damage done to the nation by the reckless policies of the Sukarno years, when Bali in particular was subjected to shameful neglect and exploitation. The policies of the new Suharto regime are epitomized in the popular slogan and acronym KISS, signifying *Koordinasi, Integrasi, Simplifika-si dan Stabilisasi*, or, alternatively, *Sinkronisasi*. KISS, by extension, also implies a whole macaronic catalogue of other much acclaimed principles, such as *rationalisasi* and *modernisasi*, *anti-inflasi* and *anti-korupsi*, *desentralisasi* and *deburocrasi*, *rehabilitasi, rekonstruksi, reor-ganisasi, revaluasi, restrukturasi,* and *reorientasi.* In the very formulation of new concepts to guide policies and programs, the new Indone-sians, the Balinese among them, are forced to reach out beyond their own linguistic context in the creation of a new semantics as the basis of rethinking, talking, planning, and acting. In seeking new *inspira-si* and *identifikasi*, they are thus impelled at one and the same time to construct and to conduct a whole new *dialog* for a new *pendina-misan dan kevitalan politik, ekonomis dan sosial.*

The Bali *dialog* now inevitably comes to a focus upon Cultural Tourism as contrived and christened by visiting French experts and subject to the mystical interpretation of the Balinese themselves. Some Balinese quite openly despair of explaining how tens and hundreds of thousands of frenetic sightseers are suddenly to be transformed into contemplative connoisseurs. Cultural Tourism, others suggest, means "tourism for Bali, not Bali for tourism." The intent, in short, is to max-imize the advantages (profits) and minimize the hazards (social and cultural pollution) and thus to preserve Balinese values while still acquiring desperately needed foreign valuta. If the Balinese them-selves are to continue to enjoy their traditional way of life, work, and worship, they can do so, it seems, only if they invite outsiders to share the pleasure and delicately to pay the costs, a felicitous combination of circumstances which seems improbable. Bali, the paradise island of the Pacific, is now self-consciously converting itself into a tourist paradise. It may quite soon be neither if droves of tourists should shatter the very enchantments which they seek. KISS may very soon have to be re-spelled to read as an unpalatable KISSW, signifying an unwelcome overlay of *Waikikianisasi.*

It is prudent, however, to point out that certain highly discriminat-ing visitors of the 1920s and 1930s, who first made the island's magi-cal charm well known to the outside world, warned even then that it was already too late for later comers to experience the real, unspoiled Bali. It was not then in fact too late. It is not too late now. Given Bali's demonstrated capacity over the centuries for continuous and creative self-renewal, it still may not be too late in 2000. But a stampede of half a million tourists each year seems the formula for extinguishing, not rekindling the luminous culture which is Bali's glory.

CHAPTER 1

The Dewa Agung and the Radjas
(Pre–1800)

Island Setting and Cultural Background

The island of Bali is celebrated for the peculiar splendor of its Bali-nese-Hindu culture, a highly developed and artistically embellished system of life and worship which was arrested in the sixteenth century at the very moment of its finest flowering and preserved into modern times with little perceptible loss of vitality. This life of medieval pageantry is still the living tradition of an island population made up of extraordinarily handsome and gifted people. The island itself is a Pacific enclave of such pristine natural beauty as to be suggestive, as Pandit Nehru poetically put it, of "the world's last morning." No one can very satisfactorily explain just how this miracle happened—how it was that one idyllic little island created and sustained a rich civilization that was in certain significant respects as anomalous in former times as it is anachronistic today, but one which has never until recently been tainted with artificiality.

The most plausible conjecture with regard to Bali's good fortune is that the island and the islanders profited enormously from a quite fortuitous combination of involvement and detachment. Bali was exposed to the great early civilizing influences of Southeast Asia, but up until very late in the colonial era it was insulated against the intrusion of rude white barbarians. The island, furthermore, is as fertile as it is scenic, and the islanders are industrious as well as artistic. It must be conceded that ancient evils such as superstition, slavery, and suttee long persisted, but there have also been compensations.

One of these has been the animistic conviction that the divinities of nature are more disposed to be protective than vindictive.

Bali lies just one mile off the eastern tip of Java on the direct trade route between the spice islands of the Moluccas and the Asian entrepôts which long distributed their cloves, nutmegs, and mace to a spice-hungry world. From early times the island was visited by Indian, Arab, Chinese, Japanese, Bugis and other Eastern traders who brought with them not only their goods but their manners and customs. But once the island was really inhabited, Bali and the Balinese did more to repel than to attract any considerable number of later settlers. Along most of its sea coast Bali enjoyed the natural protection of high cliffs and continuous coral reefs. The nearby seas were notorious for sudden storms; they were also known to be shark- and barracuda-infested. The Balinese people themselves were physically vigorous and likely to be ferocious in battle. They regarded the seas as the abode of demons and monsters and were little inclined either to explore them or to extend aid and comfort to alien voyagers. One of the beliefs of the island was that whatever and whomever the waves tossed up on the shore were destined to become the property of the kings, shipwrecks being meant for plunder and castaways for enslavement. Bali therefore remained little known to the outside world and not especially inviting to better acquaintance. The early Asian and the later European seafarers preferred generally to sail on past Bali to other islands which offered surer, safer profits.

Notwithstanding their suspicion of what the seas bore them, the Balinese were quick to accept certain outside influences, which they ingeniously adapted to their own requirements, meanwhile devoting themselves to the development of their lovely and fruitful island. They began the planting of rice at least two millennia ago and achieved a scientific and artistic standard of cultivation unmatched in the region. At least a millennium and a half ago they began to transmute their native animism by adopting Hindu rites; by the sixteenth century they had achieved a distinctive civilization matched in miniature if it did not indeed surpass anything in India itself or Indianized Southeast Asia. The microcosmic Balinese-Hindu world survived intact up until the nineteenth century and did not then really shatter when it felt the full impact of Dutch colonialism. Even in the twentieth century the illusion if not the actuality of the traditional Bali still persists.

The early history of Bali is a matter of theoretical reconstruction of the precise origins of the population and the evolution of the society. The Balinese are clearly a blend of the various Mongoloid peoples who moved through mainland into insular Southeast Asia long before historic times. Their well-integrated society is the creation of an animistic, agricultural people inspired by vigorous priests and princes. The first great outside influence upon the early Balinese was exercised by Indian or Indianized traders and travelers who brought with them the Hindu learning. Bali shared very generously in the great wave of Indianizing influences which spread throughout most of Southeast Asia in the latter half of the first millennium. In politics and religion the Indians introduced the key concept of the God-King, whose capital reflects the splendors and perfections of Heaven and whose people prosper only so long as the ruler conducts himself in conformity with natural and divine law. Every Balinese ruler therefore had his monumental *kraton* or *puri* (palace) from which he exercised spiritual and temporal power through a hierarchy of courtiers and priests who not infrequently deposed an evil ruler and replaced him with a better.

Hinduization and Javanese Influences

The conversion of primitive Bali into a Hinduized society was the result not of conquest and colonization but rather of the contagion of civilization. The rulers found in Indian culture the religious and administrative practices which exactly served their purposes, and the people responded with such enthusiasm as to prove the appropriateness of the choice. India provided the literary, the artistic, the social, as well as the theological and political model for an evolving Balinese society. The Balinese exercised their own creative adaptations while still retaining much of the Indian original. Even today Bali preserves manifestations of early Hinduism, among them manuscript copies of certain epics, which have since disappeared in India itself.

The Hinduization of Bali was a process of many centuries. The most pervasive influence was exercised not by India itself but by nearby Java, which had been subject even earlier than Bali to an even more extensive Indianizing process. The documented history of Bali during this period is mainly a catalog of names of obscure royal personages and imprecise references to forgotten events. Modern archaeologists have reconstructed the approximate historical sequence from fragmentary inscriptions in Sanskrit or classical Balinese on various objects of stone and metal, most of them temple treasures. By an amazing exercise of erudition they have matched up names, dates, and events to create a chronological outline which meshes with a rather more detailed table similarly constructed for the island of Java and other regions.

One thus learns that certain Hinduized rulers invoked certain Indian deities in commemorating their own succession to the throne, in building or endowing a temple, in winning a battle, or in celebrating other events. It is clear that by the year 1001 (or perhaps 991), when the first reasonably well authenticated historic event occurred, Bali was already very extensively Hinduized. In that year, presumably, was born Airlangga, the son of a Balinese King, Dharmmodayanawarmmadewa (also known as Udayana, and sometimes identified with King Udayadityavarman of Cambodia who was exiled in about the year 1000, perhaps to Bali), and his Javanese queen, Gunapriyadharmapatni (also known as Mahendradatta). In his early youth Airlangga was sent for education and marriage to the court of the Emperor of Java. When the Emperor was himself overthrown in the course of civil wars, Airlangga was invited to succeed him. He devoted himself to rebuilding the empire and in so doing he added his home island of Bali to the Javanese domain, ruling it through a regent who was no doubt an uncle, brother, or cousin. Airlangga thus inaugurated a period of close Javanese–Balinese political and cultural contacts which continued, to Bali's very great advantage, for well over three centuries. The relationship was not without its conflicts. The Balinese several times asserted their autonomy and the Javanese Singasari emperors, or their successors, the Modjapahit, as often reasserted their own hegemony. Balinese rulers, in whose veins flowed varying proportions of Balinese and Javanese blood, were always implicated in dynastic rivalries which Modjapahit was not infrequently called upon to settle. The Javanese ruler Kratanagara, for instance, found it necessary to pacify and reunify Bali in the year 1262 (or

1284), as did the great General Gadjah Mada in 1343. Modjapahit imposed more and more of its own institutions upon its far from unreceptive dependency. Eventually, when the Modjapahit Empire itself collapsed in 1515, migrations of refugees from Java to Bali resulted in still more massive cultural transfusion.

Modjapahit Conquest and Early Rulers

With the Modjapahit period Balinese history begins to assume clearer content and pattern although much remains legendary. Gadjah Mada constituted Bali a province of the empire with a Modjapahit governor. Kapakisan, the first incumbent, and, according to Balinese legend, the offspring of a stone Brahma and a heavenly nymph, became the founder of a line of princes who ruled the island more as supporters than as subordinates of the Javanese state. Kapakisan and his successors sometimes used the Javanese title of Susuhunan (Great Sultan, or Emperor), but more commonly the Balinese title of Dewa Agung (Great Deity), thus more than merely implying that they ruled independently and by divine right. Kapakisan built his *kraton* (Javanese term) or *puri* (Balinese) in Samprangan and ruled firmly but justly over the whole of the island. He was succeeded by his son, Krsna-Kapakisan, about whom nothing is known except his name. Krsna-Kapakisan was in turn succeeded by his own son, I Dewa Samprangan, about whom nothing is known which does him credit.

I Dewa Samprangan, the third Dewa Agung, was so given to vanity, frivolity, and venality that his counselors encouraged his young son, I Dewa Ktut, to build a separate *kraton* in nearby Gelgel and gradually to usurp the powers which his father was too dissipated to exercise. I Dewa Ktut succeeded in restoring royal authority and prestige. He is especially celebrated for having journeyed to Java to participate in a solemn imperial council called together by Emperor Hayam Wuruk (r. 1350–1380) to consider the gathering troubles which were already shaking his empire and were to overwhelm and destroy it a century later.

The fall of Modjapahit signaled the rise of Mataram, a new Javanese empire built out of small kingdoms newly reinspired and reinvigorated by the advent of powerful Islamic influences. Many thousands of Modjapahit Hindu priests, nobles, soldiers, artists, and artisans fled from Java to Bali to escape their Muslim conquerors. In Bali they gave fresh impetus to an already strongly Hinduized culture which was thus able to enrich and maintain itself while in Java the Hindu tradition was almost submerged under the Islamic overlay. But Hindu Bali and Muslim Java became implacable enemies. The East Javanese state of Blambangan, separated from Bali by a mile-wide strait which was both difficult and dangerous to cross, became a buffer region. The Balinese claimed and occasionally half conquered Blambangan, Mataram often threatened but usually failed to mount a counter invasion, and for centuries Balinese–Javanese relations remained readily inflammable.

Dewa Agung as Emperor and Symbol

At the end of the fifteenth century, then, the Dewa Agung and his remote court at Gelgel, who suddenly fell heir to the still glittering legacy of the vanquished and vanished Modjapahit Empire, achieved previously undreamed of splendor and authority. The sixteenth century was destined to be Bali's golden age. Under Batu Renggong, who became the Dewa Agung in about the year 1550, the various Balinese principalities were welded together into a strongly centralized kingdom. Batu Renggong followed up his successes at home by launching military expeditions abroad. He conquered Blambangan, where he installed a vassal ruler and supported him against Mataram's counterattack. Then he turned his attention eastward to the islands of Sumbawa and Lombok, which he both conquered and colonized. Political and military triumphs of Batu Renggong's reign were more than matched by a cultural renaissance. The Balinese transformed the Modjapahit influences to conform to their own special needs and abilities. They created what is in fact the contemporary Balinese culture, endowing it with that special element of Balinese genius, the secret of eternal renewal of youth. The Balinese still share with the Javanese many common traditions of language, music, dance, sculpture, and literature, but the gap between Hindu Bali and Muslim Java is almost as wide as that between youth and old age. The older, the Balinese-Modjapahit culture, paradoxically preserved its freshness and animation, while the younger, the Javanese-Mataram society, grew both sober and somber. It is the riddle and the miracle of Bali that from the embers of Modjapahit Java should have been ignited the fires which still burn bright in the neighboring islet.

Emergence and Divergence of Eight Radjadoms

Gelgel's golden age flickered during the reign of Batu Renggong's son, Radja Bekung, and died out under his grandson, Di Made. Radja Bekung engaged in an ill-advised adventure in Blambangan which all but provoked a full-scale invasion by Mataram of Bali itself. He lost the respect of the other Balinese princes, who became openly defiant, and he played host to the first Dutch visitors, whose arrival eventually proved to have been an omen of evil. But it was Di Made who suffered the undeniable, the irreparable reverses. He lost Blambangan, Sumbawa, and Lombok, and he lost also the allegiance of the other princes. Di Made's successor, Gusti Sideman, abandoned the *kraton* of Gelgel, which was clearly under a curse, built a new one in nearby Klungkung, and sought to rule as grandly as had his predecessors. But it was already too late. The Dewa Agung was to be less prominent thereafter than various of his presumed vassals. Klungkung therefore never matched Gelgel in glory, but Bali's silver

A vintage portrait of all eight Balinese kings gathered in the Gianyar palace grounds, ca. 1930.

age, which set in when Klungkung was founded, saw the island-wide dissemination of the Gelgel culture.

The Dewa Agung and his court in Klungkung continued to symbolize Hindu imperial grandeur but never again imperial power. The other princes became the Dewa Agung's rivals and even his enemies; their own *punggawa* (chiefs) at times presumed to virtual autonomy; the *pendanda* (priests) sometimes assumed almost independent temporal power over villages and groups of villages which fell theoretically within the domain of the radjas. The ruling families, princely and priestly, were polygamously intermarried and easily provoked to blood feuds. Divination, prophecy, and mere superstition were factors of comparable significance to jealousy, intrigue, and military conflict in conditioning personal and state affairs. As the domain and the authority of the Dewa Agung diminished, there emerged a dozen more or less clearly defined little independent radjadoms. Eight of these still survive as geographic and political entities (now administrative districts). They are: Gianjar, Badung, Bangli, and Tabanan in addition to Klungkung in the South-Central region, and Buleleng, Karangasem, and Djembrana in the North, the Northeast, and the Northwest respectively.

The history of these eight Balinese radjadoms of modern times—and those of adjacent Lombok—is closely linked to that of Dutch colonial penetration. It is a story which remains as yet to be very accurately reconstructed from fragmentary and conflicting records, many of which are still lost in Dutch and Indonesian archives. Some inspired student may one day search out the sources in order to write what could be a classic of East–West relations as revealed in the vivid Balinese microcosm. For present purposes and with present resources, it must suffice merely to identify the protagonists and to establish the progression by reference to radjas and radjadoms.

The Dewa Agung and his radjadom of Klungkung survived but did not flourish, for the Dewa Agung himself was powerless and his kingdom was minute. Little Gianjar rivaled Klungkung as a center of traditional Balinese culture and even presumed at times to military might. But until the latter part of the nineteenth century, Gianjar was never at the focus of Balinese events, and neither were the neighboring states of Bangli, Tabanan, or, except for brief intervals, Badung.

These states shared with Gianjar and Klungkung the fertile rice lands of the southern slopes of the central mountains and shared also the rich culture which rich rice lands nourished. Mengwi, a state of the center, enjoyed occasional prominence but overreached itself and was partitioned among its neighbors (1891), surviving today only in the loyalty of the people to the family of the traditional ruler and to the state shrines. The Dewa Agung's military and political powers passed first to Buleleng, the large northern state which was the first focus of foreign commerce and international competition; next to Karangasem, the large eastern state which came to dominate also the island of Lombok; and eventually to the Dutch. Buleleng and Karangasem, sometimes friends, sometimes enemies, generally under the rule of members of the same royal family, were to become the two power factors of modern Bali.

Gusti Pandji Sakti, who came to the throne at the end of the seventeenth century, was primarily responsible for Buleleng's assertion of island hegemony. By skillful political and military maneuvers he extended his own authority throughout most of Karangasem and Djembrana, exacted deferential treatment from the southern states, and concentrated next upon Blambangan. He listened sympathetically to an appeal from Mas Purba, the heir-apparent to the throne of Blambangan, who sought military aid in ousting a rival and resisting Mataram pressures. Gusti Pandji Sakti sent an expedition to Java (1697), which placed Mas Purba more or less securely on the throne, but succeeded more convincingly in establishing his own claim to succession to the Dewa Agung's former power. But Gusti Pandji Sakti's son-in-law, Gusti Agung Sakti, the ruler of Mengwi, presently usurped his father-in-law's own kingdom of Buleleng (1711). He went on to consolidate his position by another adventure in Java, where Mas Purba had wavered in loyalty and flirted both with Mataram and the Dutch. The joint radjadom of Buleleng–Mengwi flourished for the better part of the eighteenth century but then separated again and forfeited power to Karangasem.

Karangasem began its rise to prominence by seizing the opportunity to champion Balinese interests in Lombok at a time when Buleleng was preoccupied by exploits in Java. Upon slipping from Balinese control in the time of Di Made, Lombok had fallen under the domination of Sumbawa and Goa (Makassar), sometimes one, sometimes the other, sometimes both. It had been subjected by and through these states to strong Islamizing influences. The paramount radja was converted to Islam along with various of his court; aided if not in fact compelled by soldiers from Sumbawa and Goa, the radja then attempted to expel the large Balinese Hindu population already living in the island. The new Muslim clique in Lombok had to contend meanwhile with very troublesome little rebellions among the warlike Sassak tribespeople, who made up the greater part of the population. Karangasem found this situation conducive to its own endeavors to bring Lombok once again under Balinese control, an objective which, after half a century of intermittent effort, it quite clearly accomplished. By the mid-seventeenth century Lombok was parceled out among four weak little radjadoms, each ruled by a Balinese prince who owed his allegiance to Karangasem.

It may be of help in fixing in mind the main currents of Balinese history to do as many of the Balinese themselves do, which is to accept a much abridged version of events from Modjapahit times onward and to dwell upon a simplified pattern of conflict mainly between the North and the South. According to popular Balinese account, the Modjapahit conquest of Bali and collapse in Java occurred in quick succession and the leading characters in the former, Gadjah Mada and Arja Damar, accompanied Bra Widjana, the fallen Madjapahit Emperor to Gelgel to re-establish his court. In appreciation for his distinguished services, Bra Widjana named Arja Damar as Prime Minister and assigned him extensive lands to be divided among himself and his followers. Arja Damar received, in fact, virtually the whole of the lush rice growing area of the south which then constituted the states of Tabanan and Mengwi, from which later split off Badung and Bongli. To Gadjah Mada went the large but not so desirable central mountain region and the coastal areas beyond, out of which, presently, were created the radjadoms of Buleleng. Karangasem, and Djembrana. Gadjah Mada's services in the Bali campaign had not been deemed especially meritorious, for he had idled away his time in various pleasures leaving it to Arja Damar to fight the major battles and to lead the main invasion forces southward from Buleleng. Thus there originated the jealousies and rivalries of two different sets of rulers, those of the South, who stemmed from Arja Damar, and those of the North, who stemmed from Gadjah Mada. The latter all but openly repudiated their allegiance to the Dewa Agung in the mid-eighteenth century. The former continued to pay homage and tribute, however meager, up until the late nineteenth or very early twentieth century.

Decline of Dewa Agung's Authority

The conspicuous decline of the Dewa Agung's own power and prestige, according to this reading, dates from approximately the year 1750 when there occurred a series of incidents which shocked all of Bali. The Radja of Karangasem, an ascetic sage of repulsive physical habits and appearance, generally so engrossed in meditation that he let his excrement drop where it might, paid a visit of homage to Klungkung in the course of which he greatly shocked and outraged the Dewa Agung. When the Radja set out again for home, the Dewa Agung gave orders that he should be ambushed and assassinated, and the Radja was accordingly murdered. His three filial sons immediately sought to take vengeance. They raised an army and marched into Klungkung to invest the *puri*. Some residue of respect for tradition deterred them from either killing or deposing the Dewa Agung or even depriving him of much of his realm. But they made virtual declaration of independence and returned home to rule Karangasem without much further regard for the Dewa Agung's authority. The eldest son succeeded as radja; presently, he conquered Buleleng, where he made his younger brother radja, and then Lombok, which he assigned to the other. From that time on, Karangasem, Buleleng, and Lombok were more often hostile than amenable to Klungkung. But at the time of the Balinese–Dutch wars of 1846–1849, both Karangasem and Buleleng, but not Lombok, solicited and reciprocated the Dewa Agung's support.

The long and the short versions of centuries of Balinese history, much of which, technically, is pre-history, converge upon one famous personage, Gusti Gde Karangasem, Radja of Karangasem at the turn of the nineteenth century, the gadfly of the Dewa Agung and the kingpin of a new coalition. Once having made himself master of Buleleng as well as of Lombok and having made his brothers the radjas, he next added Djembrana to his domain. He did so over the vigorous protest of Badung, which had recently treated that state as an appendage of its own but had tolerated the rule of a Bugis prince from Makassar named Kapiten Patimi. Karangasem put rude pressures upon other states as well and stirred up widespread resentment and resistance.

By this time the patterns of Balinese power and politics were becoming almost incomprehensible even to the Balinese, as is still further indicated by the sudden emergence in the late eighteenth century of the state of Gianjar as a rival to Klungkung and a military threat to Buleleng, Karangasem, Mengwi, and Bangli. Buleleng itself presently rebelled successfully against Karangasem (1823), and the Radja of Karangasem, Gusti Gde Ngurah Lanang, was forced to flee to Lombok. There he built a new *puri* and attempted to impose central authority over the mutually jealous little Lombok radjadoms, which welcomed his defeat in Bali as an invitation to defiance; he sought at the same time to force his onetime vassals in Bali itself yet once again to recognize him as ruler. Gusti Gde Ngurah Lanang thus did much to create the insular and inter-insular turbulence which the Dutch found conducive to the imposition of Western rule.

CHAPTER 2

Western Intruders
(Pre–1800)

Early Portuguese and Other European Visitors

Up until the time that the Dutch seriously interested themselves in Bali, which was at a very late date in their colonial history, Western contacts with the island were infrequent and transitory. The early Portuguese explorers, adventurers, merchants, missionaries, and conquerors, who reached Malacca in 1509 and the Moluccas in 1511, all but by-passed Bali in their eager rush to acquire riches, souls, and territory. So did the Spaniards. The Magellan expedition (1519–1522) sighted an island, probably Bali, which it identified as "Java Minor," but apparently no one went ashore. Fernando Mendez Pinto, the great Portuguese navigator and Munchausen-like narrator, may have visited Bali briefly in about the year 1546, but the evidence is not clear. Various others of the pioneer Portuguese and Spanish no doubt sighted Bali if they did not actually explore it, and they made due notation of the island (under various names: Boly, Bale, Bally) on the early charts. Sir Francis Drake called briefly in 1580 and Thomas Cavendish perhaps visited Bali itself as well as its East Java dependency of Blambangan in 1585, but they left no written record.

The Portuguese were the first to entertain any designs upon Balinese trade and territory. The Malacca government fitted out a ship to dispatch to Bali in 1585 with soldiers and merchants, building materials and trade goods, the intent being to build a fort and to open a trading post. The ship foundered on the reef off Bukit and most of the ship's company were drowned. Five survivors found their way to shore, where they were impressed into the service of the Dewa Agung, who treated them on the whole quite kindly, providing them with homes and wives, but refused to permit them to return to Malacca.

Houtman Expedition of 1597; Shore Party in Kuta and Gelgel

In 1597, twelve years after the ill-fated Portuguese enterprise, Cornelis de Houtman, the earliest of the Dutch explorers and traders in the East Indies, paid a visit. The record of his expedition—an official report and a detailed personal letter by one of the ship captains—constitutes the first substantial body of information about the island available to the Western world. Although its two-year voyage had been punctuated by mutiny, murder, piracy, brigandage, and such ill-natured haggling over prices of local produce that it failed ever to find cargo, the expedition's conduct in Bali was almost blameless. Cornelis de Houtman, the braggart and scoundrel to whom the leadership had fallen after the mysterious demise en route of several predecessors, was so moved by the beauty and wealth of the island that he indulged in an unaccustomed but characteristically inappropriate flight of poetic fantasy and christened it Jonck Hollandt (Young Holland). It was a description so evocative of misapprehension as to lead later Dutchmen to fancy that in introducing Dutch civilization and commerce they were guiding the islanders toward their manifest destiny.

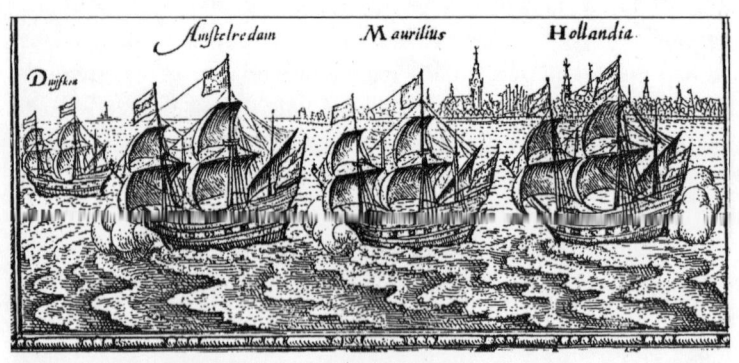

Detail from an engraving showing the four ships in the "First Fleet" under Cornelis de Houtman, from G. P Rouffaer and J. W. IJzerman (eds), *De Eerste Schipvaart der Nederlanders naar Oost-Indië onder Cornelis de Houtman, 1595– 1597*, The Hague, 1915–29.

The three surviving ships of the expedition, the *Hollandia*, the *Mauritius*, and the diminutive pinnace, the *Duifje* (Little Dove), with company of 89 men (out of the original 249), arrived by relays in Balinese waters—the *Mauritius* on December 25, the *Hollandia* on January 27, the *Duifje* shortly thereafter. The *Mauritius* anchored first off the coast of Djembrana, the *Hollandia* first at Kuta; the *Duifje* for a time shuttled in between; all three presently assembled in the safer waters of Padang Bai.

Four members of the Houtman company spent most of the period February 9–14 on shore, mainly in Kuta, but they made one trip to Gelgel and went on one expedition into the countryside, along with Balinese escorts, to hunt wild birds. They had been sent ashore to negotiate with the Balinese rulers for opening of trade, an enterprise which came to nothing since the Balinese could offer only a very limited quantity of spices and the Dutch, as usual, were too parsimonious in their bids for other goods. The four men on shore actually gave little thought to trade but occupied themselves in quite agreeable and informative intercourse with the hospitable Balinese. The rulers treated them as honored guests—also as prized hostages, Houtman himself having already seized three Balinese whom he was holding on shipboard—and made many occasions to elicit information about European life and customs. They were especially skillful about exacting gifts, most notably a chart of the world which the Dutch repeatedly promised and only belatedly delivered, declining, however, to sell the Dewa Agung the big ships' guns which he was eager to buy.

Arnoudt Lintgens, Captain of the *Hollandia*, was the ranking member of the shore party. Emanuel Roodenburg, a sailor from Amsterdam, was the messenger between sea and shore and the carrier of Houtman's gifts; Jan the Portuguese, a Mestizo "slave" who had come on board at Bantam as interpreter, participated in all the more significant encounters; and Jacob Claaszoon, an ordinary seaman from Delft, gained historical fame along with Roodenburg by jumping ship just as the expedition was about to set sail back to Holland.

Lintgens, Roodenburg, and Jan the Portuguese were guests of the *Kijloer*, the chief official of the *Conick*, that is, the Dewa Agung. Both the Dewa Agung and the *Kijloer* were then in residence in Kuta, where they were readying an expeditionary force of 20,000 men to send to the relief of their Javanese dependency, Blambangan, which was under siege by the Susuhunan of Mataram.

The Dewa Agung, whom Lintgens described as a tall, dark, stout, vigorous man of about forty, astounded the Dutch with his wealth, power, and magnificence. He lived ordinarily in a huge palace in the walled town of Gelgel, surrounded by his harem of 200 wives, his troupe of 50 misshapen dwarfs (their bodies deliberately deformed to resemble the grotesque figures of *kris* hilts) and his many noblemen, who ruled in his name over the 300,000 persons who then populated the island. His state *kris*, said Lintgens, was especially notable for the splendor of its jewels and the weight (two pounds) of its intricately wrought golden hilt. The handle of his state parasol was equally showy, and in his palace were to be found many other *krises*, lances, parasols, vessels of gold and silver, and miscellaneous treasures such as would be the envy of any king in Europe. When the Dewa Agung ventured outside his palace, he was accompanied by a procession of scores of lance and banner bearers and rode either in a palanquin or in a cart drawn by two white oxen which he himself drove. He held

The king of Bali in his carriage pulled by two white buffaloes, as seen by the Dutch in their first expedition to the East Indies, from Cornelis de Houtman, *Verhael vande Reyse ... Naer Oost Indien*, Middleburgh, 1597.

the love and respect of his people and his courtiers and was famous for the clemency of his rule, having only recently, it was said, spared certain conspirators who had plotted against his life, commuting their sentence from execution to exile on a nearby islet.

Audience with Dewa Agung and Lesson in Geography

Once it was determined that the visitors would bear gifts and exactly what those gifts would be, the *Kijloer* escorted the three—Lintgens, Roodenburg, and Jan the Portuguese—to an audience with the Dewa Agung in his Kuta palace, where all of the high nobility had assembled as witnesses. The Dewa Agung was delighted with the gifts: a large gilt-framed mirror, a print of a ship resembling the *Mauritius* (which he had viewed from the shore), several lengths of plain colored velvet (not as fine as the flowered velvet which had already been presented to the *Kijloer*, of which the Dewa Agung was jealous), six pieces-of-eight (the "coins of the Dutch"), a rifle, and the much coveted chart. The rifle had to be demonstrated at once, much to the satisfaction of all of the court; but it was the chart which was the real sensation. The Dewa Agung, reported Lintgens, regarded it as evidence of the "subtilty of our nation;" when he found a globe pictured in one corner he was even more astonished and insisted that the Dutch must bring him one on their next visit. He himself proposed to write a letter of appreciation to the Dutch King and to send him a *kris* and a dwarf, none of which are mentioned again in the records.

The Dewa Agung called at once for a lesson in world geography, and Lintgens was happy to oblige. The lesson started with the islands of Southeast Asia, the Dewa Agung expressing great disappointment to find that Bali "showed so small." Next came the Empire of the "Great Turk," which mightily impressed him. Finally came the European continent, Lintgens being required very clearly to explain about the Netherlands and the port of Amsterdam and then the route by which the expedition had traveled to the East. Upon being queried by the Dewa Agung which was the larger, China or Holland, Lintgens replied by tracing boundaries of the Netherlands so imaginative as to include Scandinavia, Austria, and a generous portion of Imperial Russia.

The audience developed into a prolonged interview in which the Dewa Agung demanded detailed information about the King of Holland (Prince Maurits), his age (30), his marital status (single, much to the King's amazement), his armies (50,000 foot soldiers, 30,000 cavalry, and 150 pieces of heavy artillery), his commerce (700 large ships a day visiting Amsterdam), the Dutch climate (with elucidation of the strange phenomenon of ice), and much, much else, including personal information about his immediate callers and other members of the expedition, the nature of the vessels and their guns. Since, said *the Kijloer*, the Dewa Agung made a point of surrounding himself with foreigners and requiring all newcomers to visit him and perhaps also to remain in Gelgel, he was especially pleased to learn that the expedition had brought with it two young boys from "St. Louwerens Island," whom, said Lintgens, he might see if he wished.

Entertainment by *Kijloer*; Interview with Portuguese Merchant
Before and after the audience with the Dewa Agung and a subsequent visit to Gelgel, Lintgens, Roodenburg, and Jan the Portuguese were entertained in the splendid Kuta and Gelgel palaces of the *Kijloer*, who served lavish feasts (one being brought in by twelve of the Dewa Agung's wives) and was fully as curious as was the Dewa Agung himself with regard to European customs, including the system of justice and the punishments meted out to thieves and murderers. The *Kijloer* informed his guests about previous European visitors—the English (presumably Sir Francis Drake), and the Portuguese. One morning he suddenly produced for their inspection Pedro de Noronha, a merchant from Malacca who had been in the service of the Dewa Agung ever since the shipwreck of 1585. Pedro told them something of his life story, inquired about conditions in Portugal, and allowed that although he had been eager at first to return to Malacca he was now quite content to remain in Bali together with his Balinese wife and their two children. He had been forbidden, nevertheless, to establish any contact with the Houtman expedition until the *Kijloer* himself introduced him.

For reasons which the record does not make clear, Cornelis Houtman himself seems to have gone ashore only once, a few days before setting sail again for Holland. There he met with the brother of the Dewa Agung, engaging in desultory conversation and the consumption of fruits and sweets while his Balinese hostages were being brought ashore so that Lintgens and his companions would be permitted to go back on shipboard.

Desertion of Roodenburg, Claaszoon, and Jan the Portuguese

The Houtman expedition departed from Bali on February 20, without Roodenburg and Claaszoon, who had vanished. They had remained ashore to enter the service of the Dewa Agung, perhaps of their own volition, perhaps not, most probably quite willing to be induced to forgo the rigors of the voyage back to wet, cold, gloomy, little Holland in preference for the pleasures of equatorial Bali. In any event, they both settled in Gelgel, took Balinese wives, learned the Balinese language, and attended upon the Dewa Agung. When the next Dutch expedition appeared, that of Jacob van Heemskerck in 1601, Roodenburg joined it as interpreter and translator, also as general informant and advisor. According to vague contemporary accounts, Heemskerck appears to have shown his appreciation for Roodenburg's services (and unspecified services of Claaszoon) by "buying them free." Roodenburg (but not Claaszoon) subsequently reappeared in Holland as a humble clerk in an Amsterdam office, an unlikely sequel to his Bali idyll.

Heemskerck Expedition of 1601; Roodenburg as Interpreter; Dewa Agung's Letter to Prince Maurits

The Heemskerck expedition left no such detailed records as those of its predecessor, but Heemskerck himself was a more perceptive and sympathetic visitor than Houtman and served as his own ambassador. He carried a letter from Prince Maurits which he presented in person to the Dewa Agung together with the usual presents, thus eliciting a gracious letter of acknowledgment from "den conick van Bali" to "den conick van Hollandt." The Dewa Agung advised the King of Holland that he was pleased to comply with his request for permission to open trade and stated, further, apparently in reply to a suggestion of political relationship, that he concurred that Holland and Bali should "be one." Heemskerck (or Eemskerck) promptly dispatched the original letter in Balinese together with the Dutch translation by Roodenburg (or Rodenburch) back to Holland as evidence of the success of his mission. The somewhat obscure text of the translation read as follows:

7 July 1601

God Be Praised

The King of Bali sends the King of Holland his greetings. Your Admiral Cornelis van Eemskerck has come to me, bringing me a letter from Your Highness and requesting that I should permit Hollanders to trade here as freely as the Balinese themselves, wherefore I grant permission for all whom You send to trade as freely as my own people may when they visit Holland and for Bali and Holland to be one.

This is a copy of the King's letter, which was given to me in the Balinese language and which Emanuel Rodenburch has translated into Dutch. There was no signature. It will also be sent from me to you.

Cornells van Eemskerck

The Radja also presented van Heemskerck with a typical token of royal favor—a beautiful Balinese female slave. Van Heemskerck seemed unaccountably indisposed to accept, at least until Roodenburg explained that to decline would be impolitic. Neither van Heemskerck nor his successors proved reluctant to accept the Radja's far from naive consent to reciprocal trading conditions as a charter for one-way trade or his offhand endorsement of Dutch hopes for unity as acknowledgment of an alliance. Although nothing much came of the contact for almost two and one half centuries, it was on the basis of this document that the Dutch assured themselves that they had special rights in the island.

V.O.C. Factory and Free Burghers from Batavia

The Netherlands (or United) East India Company, known in the East as the V.O.C. (Vereenegde Oost-Indische Compagnie), manifested little interest in Bali even though it took vigorous and often violent measures to establish itself firmly in the Moluccas, Java, and Sumatra. It does seem to have opened some sort of trading post in about

A Balinese slave of Batavia, ca. 1700, from Cornelis de Bruin, *Voyages de Corneille le Brun...*, Amsterdam, 1718. The proliferation of new Balinese kingdoms and the power of kings was clearly related to the number of peasantry obtained as slaves by a local lord.

the year 1620, but there is very little indication of subsequent activities or of any continuing European presence. The first merchant, Hans van Meldert, was instructed to purchase "rice, beasts, provisions, and women," but he aroused such suspicion and hostility on the part of the radjas that he was very soon recalled, having acquired, it seems, as the total result of his enterprise only one consignment of fourteen female slaves. For the next two centuries, Balinese commerce was mainly in the hands of Chinese, Arab, Bugis, and occasional Dutch private traders. These latter were the Batavian "free burghers" who came to be tolerated on the fringes of the Company's Batavia Castle and were permitted to deal in goods which the V.O.C. itself found either profitless or objectionable, although it did at times quietly and indirectly participate. In the case of Bali this meant mainly slaves and opium.

Trade in Slaves and Opium; Missions of Oosterwijk and Bacharach

The very skimpy records of Dutch contacts with Bali during the seventeenth and eighteenth centuries relate mainly to the appearance in Batavia and in Bali of various slavers and opium-runners, the acts of mutiny, piracy, and treachery which their activities provoked, and the inconsecutive and ineffectual efforts of the V.O.C. officials either to ban or control and restrict the trade. Other records refer to the rapidly growing Balinese community in Batavia itself—by the end of the eighteenth century a total of about 1,000 Balinese members of the Dutch colonial army, some 1,500 free Balinese residents, and very numerous Balinese slaves. This entire community traced its origins either to slaves sold as soldiers, who earned their freedom after five to ten years of faithful service, or household slaves, who were commonly freed by their masters or declared free upon the death of their masters, open sale generally being prohibited. The free Balinese population of Batavia was fourth in size of all the racial sectors, the first being the *Mardyckers* (Portuguese who lived like Malays), second the Dutch, and third the Chinese. The total population of the city was then about 30,000, half slave and half free.

Balinese Community in Batavia; Senopati; Balinese–Javanese Wars

The most famous member of the Balinese community in Batavia was Senopati, a Balinese in fact only by association, a folk hero of the late seventeenth century whose history is half legendary. Senopati seems by birth to have been a Javanese prince, but he fled to Bali in early youth to escape from the cruelty of his uncle, the Susuhunan. Settling in Djembrana, he became the foster son of the Chinese *sjahbandar* (harbor master). Later, in a spirit of pure adventure, he permitted himself to be sold as a slave and shipped to Java. In the course of the voyage he earned the admiration and gratitude of the slaver by fighting off pirates, but upon reaching Batavia he consented nevertheless to be sold into the family of a wealthy Dutch merchant. He served his Dutch master faithfully up until the time that he fell into a complicated set of difficulties by reason of rejecting the amorous advances of the daughter of a Dutch general. Entering the Dutch army he fought bravely in the colonial wars until he became so outraged by the arrogance of the Dutch that he raised an insurrection against them. Eventually he founded his own kingdom in East Java in rivalry to the Susuhunan.

The story of the Balinese trade in slaves and opium was punctuated with romantic episodes such as those associated with Senopati and others which are merely squalid. It is one with regard to which the records are far from numerous or detailed, but it warrants effort at explanation. The Balinese radjas enjoyed and exercised the traditional right to enslave and to sell as slaves all such persons as would constitute an encumbrance or an embarrassment to the state. This general category included criminals, castaways, outcasts, orphans, drifters, debtors, and even the widows and children of men who died without leaving enough property for their support. It was regarded as both the right and the duty of the radjas to make sure that such persons did not impose a burden upon society but rather contributed to it, and when Western reformers later interfered with the system the Balinese neither understood nor approved. Balinese slaves, furthermore, were highly prized both in Bali and overseas. Balinese male slaves were famous for their manual skills and their courage, the females for their beauty and artistic attainments. The price of a healthy young slave was about 100–150 rijksdaalder at home and five to ten times that amount in overseas markets. The Dutch themselves wanted Balinese slaves both as recruits for their colonial army and as household servants in Batavia. But the biggest market of all was in French Mauritius, to which as many as 500 slaves would be sent by a single ship. The slavers often found it most convenient and profitable to make payment with opium, a commodity which found ready market among Balinese royalty and even more especially among Javanese, Bugis, and Chinese smugglers, who distributed it throughout the archipelago in defiance of Dutch attempts to enforce a monopoly. The island of Bali, of course, had more to sell than slaves and wanted to buy other goods as well as opium, especially arms; but the slave–opium link-up was extremely important to development of its commerce. The first commercial center was the northern port of Buleleng. Here the radjas recognized the advantages of foreign contact and a small resident community of Chinese, Arab, and Bugis merchants facilitated it.

The intermittent presence in Bali of certain Batavian merchants and the reports they brought back with regard to the wealth and power of the radjas several times stirred the V.O.C. to make overtures of alliance. In the year 1633 the Governor-General, Hendrick Brouwer, heard from the Batavian free burgher Jeuriaen Courten that the Dewa Agung was preparing a great military expedition against the Mataram Empire in Java, with which the Dutch themselves were at war. Brouwer determined to provide the Balinese with assistance in the expectation of so weakening Mataram's power that the Dutch forces could win an easy victory. He therefore dispatched a special ambassador, Van Oosterwijk, to offer the Dewa Agung provisions for his troops and ships to transport them to East Java. The mission was accompanied by Justus Heurnius, a missionary on his way to Ambon, who later reported briefly, favorably, and quite inaccurately about the readiness of the Balinese to accept Christianity—a report that was filed away in church and state archives and forgotten, which was just as well. Van Oosterwijk, who remained in Bali only briefly, and Captain Jochem Roloffszoon van Deutecom, who was sent as his replacement, both failed to achieve their purpose. Certain of the Dutch in Batavia intimated that the Governor-General had been impulsive and gullible and his emissaries clumsy. In fact the visitors arrived at a most inauspicious time, just when the Dewa Agung and his court were altogether preoccupied with preparations for the cremation of a favorite wife and two royal princes. The emissaries had brought a fine Persian horse as a gift for the ruler and they hinted that a gift elephant might be delivered later, but nothing availed to gain them an audience. They had to content themselves with a bit of trading by which they acquired, among other things, 2,000 skeins of cotton, 460 pieces of woven textiles, and 1,200 measures of rice.

In 1639, when Mataram suddenly invaded Bali, the Dewa Agung appealed to Batavia for assistance; for reasons now unknown, the Dutch withheld their aid, but the Balinese themselves succeeded in re-pelling the enemy forces. In 1651, when the Dutch were momentarily at peace with Mataram, they sent another ambassador, Jacob Bachar-ach, with instructions to negotiate an alliance with the Dewa Agung just in case of future need. Again nothing came of the mission.

In the course of the next century there were frequent outbreaks of hostilities between the Dewa Agung and the Susuhunan, and both Bali and Mataram applied repeatedly for Dutch assistance. The Dutch never obliged—at least not openly. But in the years 1717–18, when Balinese troops were roaming East Java and Madura, causing great destruction and dismay throughout the region, the Dutch themselves launched little clean-up operations which helped to chase the in-truders back home. If the Dutch refrained from intervening in the Balinese–Javanese wars, the English did not, or at least the Dutch believed that the English did not and that they were providing the radjas with arms. They were also selling opium and buying slaves; the northern Balinese port of Buleleng, according to vigilant infor-mants of the Dutch, was becoming a hotbed of British–Balinese an-ti-Dutch intrigue.

The persistent intrusions of the English into Balinese waters caused the Dutch the most excruciating seizures of political and financial agony. The English, they were convinced, were seeking to colonize and would seize any opportunity which they themselves might over-look to establish some British monopoly of their own in competition with those of the V.O.C. The Dutch were forced therefore to live with the awful suspicion that the predatory English were about to pounce upon some new island, large or small, among the thousand islands known or unknown, which they themselves regarded as the indisputable patrimony of the Netherlands. They entertained the recurrent premonition that the choice would probably fall upon Bali, a rich and strategic little island which they had never yet really explored even though it lay only one nautical mile off the tip of their stronghold of Java. Dutch and English rivalry over Bali was indeed to play a part, even though a very minor part, in the great new English–Dutch conflict which preceded the actual opening of the island to massive Western impact. But that was an eventuality which somehow managed to postpone itself from the early seventeenth to the early nineteenth century. During that interval, except for a few episodes such as those mentioned above, Bali enjoyed the priceless benefits of European neglect.

CHAPTER 3

Recruitment, Trade, and Travel (1800–1830)

Distant Effects of Napoleonic Wars

At the beginning of the nineteenth century Bali remained relatively unaffected by the Western influences which were already transforming much of the Indonesian archipelago. Bali's sixteenth century Hindu civilization was still inviolate to any serious religious, commercial, or political infiltration either by Muslims or by Christians. In the early decades of the century, however, there came intimations of what by mid-century amounted to the breaching of all the island's defenses. What happened in Bali was a remote, tragic, and elsewhere almost unnoticed side-effect of the Napoleonic Wars.

The early triumphs of Napoleon occasioned the fall of the Netherlands, the extension of French influence not only into Holland itself but also into the Dutch possessions overseas, and a challenge to English power everywhere in the world. The English determined to protect themselves in India by seizing Java, thinking to foil Napoleon's design of converting the Dutch colony into a base of Asian military operations of his own. This Java enterprise, in which the English succeeded brilliantly, several times focused incidental English and Dutch attention upon Bali. It served ever so slightly but significantly to illuminate and therefore to diminish the obscurity by which the island had previously been sheltered. Coming events were foreshadowed when the French–Dutch defenders of Java and the English challengers began to compete for Balinese allies in the forthcoming battle. The subsequent loss of Java to the English (1811) was a critical set-back to French interests in Asia and a far from unimportant episode in the defeat of Napoleon's ambition to dominate the world. The eventual restoration of Java to the Dutch (1816) revived their own determination to dominate the whole of the Indies, inclusive of Bali, where their failure as yet to establish themselves very securely exposed them to the possibility of being forestalled by their presumed English ally. It is doubtful whether Napoleon himself had ever heard of Bali and the Balinese never identified him as their antipodal demon, but it may still be said, without doing grave damage to histori-city, that Bali's relatively serene isolation from the much troubled international scene was one of the casualties of Napoleon's campaigns.

Daendels' Design for Recruitment; van der Wahl's Visit

Napoleon quite clearly signaled his own intentions with regard to Java by sending out French civilian and military personnel who quickly infiltrated the colonial administration. Napoleon himself picked a new Dutch Governor-General, Marshal Willem Daendels, appropriately known as the "Iron Marshal" and almost equally hated by the Dutch and the Indonesians. On behalf of the French, Daendels undertook enormously costly defense works which resulted in the swift completion of a military highway stretching the length of Java, the strengthening of many military garrisons, and the deaths of thousands of Javanese conscripted for corvée. Napoleon sent French troops under French commanders to reinforce the long neglected and badly demoralized Dutch garrisons which were stationed in all the important settlements. Daendels himself devised a scheme to import Balinese manpower to support the European troops. He commissioned a certain Captain van der Wahl of the Dragoons as his special agent to negotiate with the Balinese radjas.

Captain van der Wahl arrived in Bali in 1808 with instructions, it seems, merely to arrange with the radjas for recruitment (presumably by purchase) of Balinese soldiers and workers (i.e. slaves) for service with the joint Dutch–French forces. The doughty captain brilliantly over-fulfilled his mission. He succeeded in negotiating a very curious treaty of friendship and alliance with the Radja of Badung, who, as will be noted later, was always the most susceptible of all the radjas of the time to European blandishments. In return for the promise of military aid against his enemies, both domestic and foreign, and in return also for recognition as Susuhunan (Emperor) of Bali—a dignity which attached traditionally to the Dewa Agung, the Radja of Klungkung—the Radja of Badung placed himself and his realm under the personal protection of Marshal Daendels and the personal direction of Captain van der Wahl. At the same time the Radja designated van der Wahl as his private representative for dealing with foreigners, handling commerce, and working administrative reforms. The terms of the treaty reward word-by-word reading as an exercise of self-projection into the psychology of early Western negotiations with Balinese royalty:

> Treaty of Friendship between Sri Paducca Goesti Moerah Made Pamatjoetan, Radja of Bali Badong and Captain of the Dragoons van der Wahl, Commissioner of Willem Daendels, Marshal of Holland, Privy Counselor of the Foreign Service, Holder of the Great Cross of the Order of the Dutch Kingdom, High Officer of the Legion of Honor of the French Kingdom, Governor-General of the Indies and Commander-in-Chief of the King's Army and Navy therein.

> (1.) Sri Paducca Goesti Moerah Made Pamatjoetan, Radja of Bali Badong in consideration of the trust and fatherly concern which the Dutch Government has constantly manifested in him as a friend and associate, and also in consideration of the high qualities and honorable sentiments of His Excellency Herman Willem Daendels, Marshal of Holland and concurrently Governor-General of the Indies, joins himself and his entire kingdom with the Dutch Government, seeking not only that he himself be taken under His Excellency's personal protection but also his children, in life and death to be regarded as friends and kinsmen of His Excellency the Marshal and Governor-General, who accepts him and his into his most estimable fatherly protection.

> (2.) Captain of the Dragoons van der Wahl undertakes that in half a month after the signing of this treaty Sri Paducca G.M.M. Pamatjoetan, Radja Bali Badong shall be proclaimed

One of the radjas or rulers of Bali, from Thomas Stamford Raffles, *The History of Java*, London, 1817.

as Susuhunan of all Bali, the act to be signed by His Excellency the Marshal and Governor-General over the Great Seal.

(3.) Sri Paducca G.M.M.P., Radja of Bali Badong authorizes Captain of the Dragoons van der Wahl to build houses, forts, and batteries, to land cannons and troops of such kind and number as His Excellency the Marshal and Governor-General may see fit.

(4.) Sri Paducca G.M.M.P., Radja of Bali Badong, as of now places under Captain of the Dragoons van der Wahl all Chinese and other foreign residents with the power of administering them for their own well-being.

(5.) Sri Paducca G.M.M.P. shall receive from the Captain of the Dragoons van der Wahl all that he has need of from Bata-

A Balinese girl wearing ear-rings made from rolled lontar leaves, from Thomas Stamford Raffles, *The History of Java*, London, 1817.

via and Semarang, paying for it the price set by the aforesaid Captain.

(6.) Sri Paducca G.M.M.P. requests the aforesaid Captain to assume responsibility for the increase of the kingdom's revenues and the improvement of its internal policy.

(7.) Captain of the Dragoons van der Wahl undertakes in the name of His Excellency the Marshal and Governor-General to protect Sri Paducca G.M.M.P., Radja of Bali Badong against his foreign and domestic enemies.

(Translated from the Dutch text as published in Annex C of Dr. E. Utrecht's *Sedjarah Hukum*, etc., pp. 306–307.)

Had this quite outrageous agreement ever been implemented, the Island of Bali would have been converted into a fiefdom of the Iron Marshal with the dubious Captain of the Dragoons as regent. But Daendels was recalled and replaced shortly thereafter, the Captain vanished, the English conquered and ruled the Indies, and it served everyone's purposes to forget this improbable arrangement. Nor did the Dutch choose to revive it when Napoleon was overthrown and the English handed back their empire in order to bolster the post-Napoleonic Dutch-English alliance, in which the Dutch, without the Indies, would have been a crippled and crippling partner.

English Occupation; Raffles and Crawfurd

Whether or not he was aware of Daendels' overtures to the Balinese, and in all probability he was, Sir Stamford Raffles, the mastermind of the English invasion and the Lieutenant Governor-General of the occupation (1811–1816), entered into preliminary personal correspondence with certain of the Balinese radjas to entice them to favor the English side in the coming conflict. The radjas were at first disposed to be receptive to English advances. They sent a certain Njoman Bagus of Buleleng to meet with Raffles in Malacca, where he was induced to accept the rank of major in the invasion forces. After dispatching and perhaps forgetting Njoman Bagus, who never reappears in the records, the radjas remained aloof from the campaign and from the occupation. Bali itself fell just outside the sphere of English administration and the far-reaching changes which Raffles introduced affected it only indirectly. But one of Raffles' most important reforms, the abolition of slavery and hence of the traffic in slaves between Bali and Java, threatened to deprive the radjas of an important source of revenue. The Radjas of Buleleng and Karangasem, motivated apparently by indignation at the loss of a slave market, in February, 1814, mounted one of their periodic little military expeditions against Blambangan, where they clashed with British Sepoys. Small bands of armed Balinese in fact roved into other parts of East Java, occasioning no little consternation. In May, therefore, Raffles sent Major General Nightingale to Bali with a small contingent of troops to make a show of force and to receive prompt assurances, which nobody took very seriously, of Balinese "submission." The

English stationed no garrison in Bali, however, and made no further attempt to impose their control.

In early 1815 Raffles himself paid a visit of a few days' duration and exhibited his usual energy in collecting data for his historical and cultural studies. His administrative subordinate and literary rival, John Crawfurd, had visited the island somewhat earlier and had engaged in similar activities. In their published works, which included sections on Bali, neither Crawfurd nor Raffles, unfortunately, attained his usual standard of accuracy and perceptiveness. Both restricted themselves mainly to comment on Hinduism on the basis of observations made, apparently, not in Bali but in India.

Dutch Demarches of 1817, 1824, 1826; Kuta Post

In 1817, over Raffles' vigorous protest and obstruction, the Dutch regained control of the Indies. One of their first moves was to dispatch a mission to Bali to establish formal relations with the radjas. Their most immediate and compelling consideration was the well-founded suspicion that Raffles was casting about for some new island to colonize. Raffles eventually chose Singapore; but by then the Dutch had already made what they regarded as a successful preemptive move to reserve Bali for themselves. They had drawn up certain "contract concepts" which they interpreted to signify sweeping concessions on the part of the radjas, who had merely discussed but had not accepted the Dutch proposals.

The contract concepts of 1817 were the work primarily of H. A. van der Broek, a revenue officer who was named special commissioner. Van der Broek arrived in Bali in mid-1817, accompanied by Heer Roos as his aide and by Lt. Lotze heading a party of twenty well-armed soldiers. He had been provided with impressive credentials authorizing him to negotiate formal agreements with the radjas.

The van der Broek visitation was not altogether unsolicited. Gusti Gde Karangasem, Radja of Buleleng, had himself sent a mission to Batavia seeking aid for relief of famine and intimating interest also in arms. The shortage of food and weapons in Buleleng was occasioned, it seems, by British interference with the slave trade, from which much of the Radja's income was derived, and the Radja had been experiencing certain economic and political difficulties in consequence. The Dutch, happy for once to repair an English oversight, shipped off a modest quantity of rice, receiving in return the gift of three slave girls, whom they generously freed. They then decided that the time was appropriate for an official mission.

The van der Broek visit was not a success. He arrived in Bali just as war broke out between Buleleng and Karangasem, a war in which Klungkung and Mengwi supported the latter and the other southern states the former. He found the radjas unresponsive to his suggestion of political alliance and most of them unwilling even to receive him in audience. He attributed their hostility not to any recent experience with Daendels' Captain of the Dragoons or his own evasiveness about military aid but rather to defamatory reports which, he believed, the English had spread and were in fact still inspiring. Eventually van der Broek prevailed upon the Radja of Badung to intercede with his peers in Mengwi and Gianjar to join him in hearing what the Dutch wished to propose. In 1818 the southern radjas themselves sent a mission to Batavia, under escort of Heer Roos, to confer with the Governor-General. Van der Broek remained in Bali, where his stay was made most uncomfortable by reason of various petty annoyances, one of them the interception of supply shipments meant for himself and Lt. Lotze's soldiers. The atmosphere, in fact, was distinctly unfriendly. Nevertheless, as a result of various obscure maneuvers both in Batavia and in Bali, the Dutch drew up two somewhat different but very formalistic sets of contract concepts. They assumed that selected paragraphs would be incorporated, with, or preferably without alteration, into the series of treaties which they envisioned with the individual states.

The treaties did not materialize, for the radjas reverted to their non-cooperative stance. Nevertheless, the rejected contract concepts achieved a sort of quasi-validity in the minds of their Dutch authors. Nothing much resulted from this diplomatic exercise other than the demonstration that Western and Eastern concepts of appropriate treaty provisions were all but irreconcilable and that Western concepts would probably prevail. The radjas were interested in occasional military aid against Lombok, Mataram, and one another; the Dutch wanted to assert sovereignty and to assure themselves that Balinese political and commercial contacts with the outside world would remain in all perpetuity under their own exclusive control. Neither side quite understood what the other was driving at save that it was altogether unacceptable.

A few years later, in 1824, the Governor-General tried again. This time he chose as his agent not a Dutch official but an Arab merchant from Surabaya, a far-roving trader named Pangeran Said Hassan al Habeschi, who knew from long experience how to deal with Asian royalty from Bengal to the Molukkas. Habeschi visited the Balinese radjas and reported back to his principals that, save only in Badung, not even the promise of great profit would elicit any interest in a treaty. If Pangeran Hassan failed to achieve his major purpose, he returned good value for the Dutch outlay upon his rather expensive travel arrangements by bringing back important intelligence relating to a second subject in which they were very much interested: the size and strength and hideouts of the pirate bands which then infested the waters of East Java, Bali, and Lombok. Hassan reported that he had counted ninety pirate *perahu* manned by conglomerate crews of ruffians from Celebes, Borneo, and the Sulus, who found aid and comfort in Balinese port towns to which they retreated when Dutch marine pursuit became too hot. He suggested that the Dutch could deal definitively with these vicious sea rovers only by asserting effective control over the whole of Bali and Lombok. For the time being the Dutch contented themselves with sending warships to harass the pirate fleet, also to reconnoiter and map the Bali coast—first the frigate *Komet* in 1825, than the schooner *Iris* in 1827. They succeeded so well that in 1828 some 300 pirates abandoned Bali to reestablish themselves in the little archipelago of Pulau Laut about halfway between Singapore and Borneo, where they became the concern primarily of the British.

In 1826 Batavia sent yet another Dutch agent, a Captain J. S. Wetters, who managed that year to negotiate a simple agreement whereby the Radja of Badung permitted the recruitment of soldiers, at a royalty of five guilders per head, and the opening of trade. Wetters himself settled briefly at Badung's leading port town of Kuta, not far from the palace of the Radja. Thus began the modern Dutch presence in the island and the emergence of Kuta to compete in trade with the northern port of Buleleng.

The Kuta post did not prosper. Its main purpose was the recruitment of a proposed total of 1,000 Balinese on five-year contracts to serve in the colonial army. Most, if not all of the recruits, it is to be presumed, would be purchased as slaves and would earn their freedom after five years of military service. At just this time, however, the Dutch wound up their long but intermittent war against the Mataram Empire and decided that they no longer required so many more Balinese. The Kuta post, which therefore purchased few slaves, seems also to have sold little merchandise. For these and other reasons, relations between the Dutch and the Balinese were strained by mutual suspicion and at times overt animosity. Wetters' successor, Pierre Dubois, who managed the post from 1827 to 1831 with one Dutch sergeant and a few soldiers as his companions and guards, reported despondently that Kuta attracted few European traders (a total of exactly three during the entire period) and kept petitioning the government to close it down. To support his case he reported incident after incident of actual or threatened robbery, arson, murder, and plunder, and almost daily scenes of amok. Dubois regarded the local ruler, Gusti Ngurah Ktut, the nephew of the Radja of Badung, with a combination of apprehension and contempt. He charged him with all manner of villainy, of which, by report other than that of Dubois, he seems in fact to have been guilty. The local population, according to Dubois, consisted mainly of criminals and ruffians. It seemed to be a matter mainly of chance, however, whether the incautious visitor would be done in by violence or by pestilence, for the location was as insalubrious as its inhabitants were unsavory. Before he conclusively established his point that European survival was unlikely, Pierre Dubois himself was transferred. In 1831 Batavia notified the Radja that it was closing its Kuta station, requesting that its properties be reserved for discretionary Dutch use thereafter, a request which seems to have been ignored.

Visit of Dr. Medhurst and His Report

Despite early Dutch failures it was now apparent that Bali could not much longer expect to remain isolated from Western impact. Dutchmen and other Westerners were visiting the island in ever increasing numbers and reports were beginning to circulate in the outside world. One report in particular attracted much attention and realerted the nervous Dutch to the danger that if they themselves did not soon take Bali the British could be expected to do so. It was a study prepared by Dr. Medhurst, a much traveled English medical missionary from Malacca, who spent three months (late 1829 to early 1830) in Bali in company with a Reverend Tomlin studying the northern regions, especially the radjadom of Buleleng, which, as noted above, was the traditional center of foreign contact and trade.

Dr. Medhurst's report was published originally in certain English missionary journals and then reprinted (anonymously) in Singapore, first in the *Singapore Chronicle* (June 1830), later in J. H. Moor's famous compilation, *Notices of the Indian Archipelago* (1837). It was also translated into Dutch and republished in the Netherlands. Dr. Medhurst attempted, within the brief scope of his essay and the limits of available information, to do for Bali what Raffles had recently done for Java and other English writers were occasionally doing for other little-known lands. He adopted the classical approach of the generalist, dealing with matters of geographical, historical, ethnographical, and commercial interest and introducing such particulars as he had been able to assemble from local sources. His historical sketch focused mainly upon the family of the ruling Radja of Buleleng, in whom all Western visitors, naturally, were very much interested. Dr. Medhurst portrays this young gentleman, the twenty-year old Gedemgoorah Ratna Ningrat, as a princeling so sunken in torpor and licentiousness as to seem little better than an imbecile. Unattractive as he was, he seems to have been preferable as a ruler to various of his uncles and cousins who were his immediate predecessors. One uncle, Gusti Moorah Gde Karang (the ruler who asserted Karangasem hegemony), had been murdered twelve years earlier by his own rebellious subjects, who found his conduct too distasteful even to recall. One cousin, Dewa Pahang, had occupied himself principally in quarreling and battling with another uncle, Gusti Moorah Lanang, the Radja of Karangasem.

Royal Family of Buleleng; Its Blood Feuds
Dr. Medhurst's report is perhaps a bit over-ornamented with picturesque detail obligingly furnished by fanciful Balinese informants. But

if it does not reveal exactly what it was that had happened quite recently in northern Bali, it does show what perceptive foreign visitors were quite prepared to believe had happened. The blood feud between Dewa Pahang and Gusti Moorah Lanang, according to Dr. Medhurst, lasted for years and resulted in widespread disorders which had seriously affected the entire northern region. Dewa Pahang, a high-spirited youth of vulgar tastes, became so enraged that he took a great oath to drain and drink his uncle's blood, reserving a small part of it for his beautiful young sister to employ, more delicately, for washing her lovely hair. Gusti Moorah Lanang, not to be up-staged, vowed to cut off his nephew's head, slice his body into small pieces, send these morsels as admonitory gifts to neighboring royalty, then to build a temple of thanksgiving to be ornamented with the bones and skins of his nephew's retainers.

The fortunes of war first favored Dewa Pahang until, in dalliance between battles, he committed incest with his sister; the balance then shifted toward Moorah Lanang. In the course of a particularly audacious campaign, Moorah Lanang captured his unfilial nephew and proceeded, while professing grief at having to fulfill so impetuous a vow, to detach the head and to mince up the body to provide mementos for friends and relations. He then set out to accumulate the bones and skins necessary for his memorial monument. But Gusti Moorah Lanang's soldiers began to fear for their own hides and bones and many of them deserted. With his still loyal companions, Moorah Lanang retired into a nearby forest, where he made a sacrificial offering to the gods of fifteen plump infants upon whose roasted remains he and his party banqueted. This gruesome ceremony was so repugnant to others of his countrymen that the Radja found it advisable to flee to Lombok. He did not actively object when his nephew, Anak Agung Madi, was elevated to the throne of Buleleng or when the new radja was deposed by his unhappy subjects and replaced by his nearly catatonic brother, the above-mentioned Gedemgoorah Ratna Ningrat. Such was the gist of Dr. Medhurst's gory account, which the present writer has made no effort to reconcile, in the spelling of proper names, for instance, or other more significant detail, with less excruciating chronicles.

Two *brahmana* wearing products of Bali: hand-loomed *songket sarongs; kris* tucked into the back of the sarongs; and hand-woven mat pouches.

From earliest times, cockfighting has been a favorite pastime of Balinese men, including royalty. These photos were taken in the 1920s.

Dr. Medhurst did not acquire, or he did not choose to report any such intimate details with regard to the other royal courts. But he did mention, for instance, that the little radjadom of Gianjar (population about 10,000) was at war with Klungkung (population about 50,000) and that travel into and through the south, which he would have liked to visit, was therefore cut off. He was able, nevertheless, to accumulate a remarkable amount of information concerning geography, agriculture, and trade, and he gave genuine insight into manners and customs. He reported, for instance, on the large mountain lakes, the ingenious system of irrigation, the network of roads and trails, the bountiful produce of the land, the imports and exports, and the system of administration and taxation. The revenues of the Radja of Buleleng, he said, included the following items: annual customs duties equivalent in value to 4,000 Indian rupees; a tax of two rupees per acre on rice lands; a fine of one rupee to 200 rupees levied upon bridegrooms for engaging in the traditional practice of kidnapping their brides (usually with the bride's consent and collusion); the proceeds of the sale of personal property, including female members of the family, of subjects who died without male heirs; and the proceeds from sale as slaves of all indigent persons.

Bali's important products, according to Dr. Medhurst, were rice, cotton, corn, tobacco, salt, cattle, pigs, fowl, fruits, and vegetables, all of which were abundantly available for export. The island conducted a flourishing trade with Java, Sumatra, Ambon, and other islands. Most of the traders were transient or resident Buginese, Arabs, and Chinese, but Europeans also participated occasionally. The major items of export were cattle, beef, salt, cotton, cotton thread, and goods imported from the east for re-export. The imports were textiles, porcelain, iron, and opium, of which Buleleng took 20 chests annually from Singapore. Bali's most noteworthy manufactures were hand loomed textiles, *kris* blades of superior style and quality, and gun barrels skillfully bored by hand. In the local market one could purchase rice at the equivalent of one rupee per pikul (132 pounds), fine fat cattle for four rupees each, sturdy little ponies for 15–20 rupees, and coconuts at the rate of one rupee per hundred. The actual currency of the market was not rupees but Chinese "cash," the rate of exchange being one to six hundred. A man could live very, very comfortably in Bali, Dr. Medhurst said, on an income of fifteen rupees per month.

In his account of the Balinese people and their customs, Dr. Medhurst made special mention of the male's predilection for cockfighting, drinking, and gambling, while allowing women to perform the manual labor. He described the improvidence and extravagance of the islanders as contrasted with the prudent accumulation of wealth by the Chinese and Arabs, who generally found it wise to resettle elsewhere when their properties attracted very great interest on the part of the rulers. He deplored the arrogance and ofttimes, he said, the rudeness of the Balinese, at least of the northerners, in dealing with foreigners, and the swiftness of their being moved to passion or violence. He gave some description of the Balinese costume—generally scanty and coarse, he said—and of the homes, palaces, and temples, all of which he deemed dilapidated and in none of which did he appear to observe any evidence of sophisticated art or architecture. He reported on the elaborate cremation ceremonies which the islanders were given to staging for the radjas, and the spectacular more or less voluntary practice of suttee on the part of the radjas' widows. But his account of the Balinese religion was so inadequate as to indicate that he was virtually unaware of the major role of religious ceremonial in daily life. Or perhaps he was merely indisposed to discourage his missionary associates by reporting the degree of commitment of the Balinese to their Hindu practices. His report led in fact to the assignment of an English missionary, a Rev. Ennis, who arrived in Buleleng in 1838 but remained only a very short time and apparently exerted no influence.

The major shortcoming of Dr. Medhurst's admirable pioneering study is his failure to describe or apparently to appreciate the peculiar beauty and vitality of the Balinese culture and the special charm of the Balinese way of life. He depicts Bali as an island of great plenty, suffering occasionally from earthquake or volcanic eruption but not from famine or pestilence, experiencing misrule but not repression, offering opportunity to Western enterprise, including, by implication but not by explicit reference, that of Christian missionaries. But he misses the magic. In pointing out this omission it must be reiterated that Dr. Medhurst was unable to visit the southern part of the island, where the splendors of the Balinese civilization are almost everywhere manifest, as is the marvelous accommodation of man to nature and to art. But the one place in the south where this phenomenon was least visible, the port town of Kuta, was the one spot which Dr. Medhurst particularly wished to visit. He would have liked to observe the activities of the Dutch agent whom he presumed to be no better than

a slaver. It was Kuta that other Western visitors were already beginning to visit and describe. The very fact that early reports on Bali related mainly to the less attractive spots—Buleleng and Kuta—which
the presence of foreigners did not necessarily enhance, may help to
explain how Bali as a whole continued in the first few decades of the
nineteenth century to enjoy its relatively serene detachment.

CHAPTER 4

Monopoly and Sovereignty, Plunder and Salvage (1830–1845)

Dutch Alarm Regarding Western Interlopers

Dr. Medhurst's illuminating report on conditions in Bali in the year 1830 commanded a remarkably widespread audience for an article published originally in obscure ecclesiastical journals which one might expect to be read only by village clergymen. Bali was already becoming known, however, to the international world of traders and travelers, among them the ships' companies of English and American whalers which were beginning to frequent waters adjacent to Bali and sometimes sent parties ashore to purchase provisions in the port towns or to hunt deer and *banteng* (wild cattle) in the mountains. The recently established English colony of Singapore, which most of these voyagers eventually visited and from which no few of them came, was especially curious about its not so distant neighbor, hence the quick Singapore reprints of the Medhurst report.

Enterprising individuals from Singapore were making tentative efforts to establish themselves elsewhere in the Indonesian archipelago than just Batavia and Surabaya, where certain English merchants had managed to stay in business even after Raffles handed Java back to the Dutch. The Singapore concern of Dalmeida and Company, of which the proprietors were Portuguese by origin, was especially active; it sent its ships frequently to Bali and may have had a resident European or Eurasian agent for a time in nearby Lombok. The Batavia- and Surabaya-based firm of Morgan, King and Company, the enterprise of a pair of not very reputable English traders from Bengal, also seems to have traded extensively throughout the eastern islands. George Peacock King, one of the partners, did regular business both in Bali and in Lombok and may have established his own trading post in Bali as early as 1831. There were others as well, but one of the most aggressive of all Western traders in Asian waters at the time was a Scottish sea captain, John Burd, who affiliated himself with the Danish East India Company to trade under the Danish flag in Singapore, Macao, Canton, Batavia and wherever else profit offered.

John Burd and Mads Lange in Lombok

Captain John Burd recruited an especially energetic and promising young Dane, Mads Lange (b. 1807–d. 1856) of Rudkobing as one of his ship's officers and presently made him a business partner. Lange sailed with or for Burd on several voyages to the East and persuaded his three younger brothers, Hans, Karl Emilius, and Hans Henrick, to join him. In late 1833 Captain Burd set out on the heavily armed 800-ton merchant vessel *de Zuid* on a voyage to China and the Indies with Mads Lange as First Officer and the three other Lange brothers as members of the ship's company. In early 1834 *de Zuid* visited Lombok, and probably also Bali. It was decided that Mads Lange would establish a permanent trading post ashore in Lombok as the focus for region-wide commerce which John Burd would develop. The pair would build up a shipping fleet of their own, captained by themselves, the three younger brothers, and other willing adventurers.

The enterprise was an instant success. Lombok was a happy choice as a commercial center. It was strategically located on the direct sea route between Singapore and Australia which was beginning to carry a very heavy traffic. It was rich in rice and other local produce for which there was great regional demand. It was also a convenient provisioning and servicing center for the many ships' captains who preferred, if possible, to avoid the heavy charges and suspicious scrutiny of the Dutch in such ports as Batavia and Surabaya. Mads Lange established cordial relations with the Radja, accepted service as his *sjahbandar* (harbor master) for the port town of Ampenan, built a factory (trading post), set up a shipyard, and very soon became a man of such wealth and influence that he inevitably became known as "the White Radja of Ampenan."

Pak Djembrok's Espionage Report

The Dutch, naturally, were far from pleased with this development. A Javanese spy named Pak Djembrok, who was then in the employ of Rollin Coùquerque, the Resident of Besuki, East Java, in 1836 brought in a detailed and disturbing report. Between May 20 and December 27, 1835, Pak Djembrok had observed the arrival in Ampenan of fifteen European vessels—nine three-masters, three brigs, and three schooners—of which three flew the French flag and the others the English or the Dutch, some of those which flew the Dutch flag being English-owned vessels from Singapore. These ships brought in large cargoes, inclusive, said Pak Djembrok, of arms, ammunition, and opium. At Tandjung Karang, a point in Ampenan Bay where Lange had built his shipyard, Pak Djembrok noted two more ships, a schooner and a brig, the latter under the command of Captain George King. Pak Djembrok further reported that when he visited the island of Bali shortly thereafter he encountered the same Captain King in the market places in Badung with sixteen casks full of Singapore-minted coins (superior, he said, to the "cash" from China), with which he was buying up quantities of goods for export.

Pak Djembrok's upsetting report almost stirred the Dutch to immediate action to forestall any more foreign interlopers. But they procrastinated long enough that Mads Lange had time to acquire invaluable experience and contacts. By the time they took action, Lange was a seasoned and toughened operator—not in Lombok from which he had had to flee in the course of civil wars, but in Bali, where he settled himself at almost exactly the same place and time as did the Dutch themselves, that is, at Kuta in mid-1839.

Dutch Policy of Economic-Political Penetration

The Dutch in The Hague, Amsterdam, and Batavia, having engaged in a prolonged exchange of government and company papers formulating various policy alternatives with regard to Bali, concluded this rigorous intellectual exercise by taking a somewhat clouded decision. It was in effect that they would first infiltrate traders and presently assert sovereignty. The exact line of demarcation between commerce and politics was left so vague that a few years later the N.H.M. (Nederlandsche Handel-Maatschappij, the successor to the trading interests of the long since bankrupt and defunct V.O.C.), claimed but only after prolonged and acrimonious negotiations collected the sum of fl. 172,194.39 for losses sustained in Bali in pursuit more of governmental than of company interests.

Governor-General Merkus first considered proposals such as one for designating Banjumas, East Java, as a free trade entrepôt to enable the Dutch rather than the Singapore English to realize the profits of exporting opium, arms, and coins to Bali and Lombok in exchange for the islands' cheap and plentiful rice. He half rejected the idea on moral and pragmatic grounds, but half accepted it for commercial and political reasons. He authorized—in fact he prompted—the N.H.M. to establish its own factory in Bali in the expectation that it would be permitted to trade openly in opium, arms, and coins. The company was later to claim that the nonfulfillment of this expectation was one important reason for its losses; another was the necessity for housing, entertaining, sponsoring, and otherwise providing logistic support for the political missions whose activities it in part cloaked and in part promoted. It was mainly for the sake of these visitors that it had to place a special vessel at the disposal of the factory, build fine residential quarters protected by a high stone wall, and dispense expensive gifts and favors to the local rulers.

For this two-pronged colonial offensive against Bali (also neighboring and closely related Lombok), the Dutch could and did allege other motives, in particular humanitarianism. They proposed, they said, to impose peace and order for the benefit most of all of the local population, pointing to the serious disturbances in Lombok and Bali's continuing involvement in them as evidence of the need. They also mentioned four highly laudable specific aims to which no one except, perhaps, the people of Bali and Lombok could take exception. They were resolutely determined, they said, to wipe out opium smuggling and arms running, Bali and Lombok being the transshipment points for opium and arms from Singapore which found their way to Java and other Dutch-held islands in which the Dutch opium and arms monopoly presumably protected the public from many abuses. They were as resolutely determined to wipe out the two associated evils of plunder and slavery, pursuits in which the opium smugglers and arms runners also vigorously engaged, in diversification of their sources of income.

The special circumstances in Bali with regard to slavery and plunder have already been referred to in earlier context. The Balinese radjas routinely enslaved and sold indigent or unwanted persons. The Dutch themselves had been among their most importunate clients, for Balinese slaves, male and female, made excellent household servants and the males made splendid recruits for the colonial army. But Raffles had caused the colonial Dutch uneasy twinges of conscience, to which they paid special attention when their worrisome wars with the Mataram Empire ended and they no longer had much need for Balinese slave-soldiers.

With regard to plunder, from the Dutch point of view the material and metaphysical considerations were equally clear. The Balinese radjas entertained a traditional concept of ship salvage which seemed to the Dutch to combine the worst features of slavery, piracy, plunder, and lese majesty. In accordance with their principle of *tawan karang*, honoring Batara Baruna, the sea deity, the radjas accepted as a gift of the gods whatever ship came to grief on the treacherous reefs which ringed their island. They took the ship, the cargo, the crew, and the passengers as their personal properties, sharing, naturally, with those who actually performed the act of salvage or rescue but entertaining no doubts at all regarding the sanctity of the deed. From the Dutch point of view it was bad enough if the Balinese exercised their so-called reef rights (Dutch: *kliprecht)* upon a Chinese, an Arab, a Bugis, or a Javanese craft, many of which sailed under the Dutch flag and expected Dutch protection. It was quite intolerable if the ship in question was Dutch owned and operated. And it was acutely embarrassing even if it flew the English flag. The British then promptly and sternly protested. They were even so tactless as to intimate that if the Dutch presumed to sovereignty over the Indies, they were obliged to provide security and to suppress slavery and piracy, unless, that is, they preferred the English to do so for them.

At the end of the 1830s all circumstances combined to prompt the Dutch to address themselves quite earnestly to discussion with the Balinese radjas of the delicate subjects of trade and politics, slavery and plunder, and to try to blanket these various topics with treaties of friendship and commerce, in fact, recognition of Dutch sovereignty and monopoly. Batavia therefore dispatched three separate missions, first a small probing expedition headed by Captain J. S. Wetters (former recruiting agent at Kuta), then a commercial mission under G. A. Granpré Molière, the N.H.M. Agent in Surabaya, finally a political mission under H. J. van Huskus Koopman, a specially designated Commissioner for Bali and Lombok. Captain Wetters, who visited both Lombok and northern Bali between July 5 and September 3, 1838, reported that the time was at hand for some decisions. Molière and Koopman followed in due course.

Granpré Molière's Mission and Company Trade

Molière arrived in Bali on December 6, 1838. He traveled on the brig *Ondernemer*, chartered to the N.H.M. for fl. 2,500 per month, but he had decided to spare the expense of the war schooner *Zwaluw*, which was originally assigned to him as escort. On shore he practiced no economies, for he traveled with four to six horses and thirty to sixty porters, carrying with him everything needful for his comfort and dignity. Between December 6 and January I he made the rounds of the royal palaces of Badung, Karangasem, and Klungkung, but he failed to get an audience in which to present the impressive credentials with which the Governor-General had provided him.

Molière was not an inexperienced trader, so he resorted to well-tested devices for opening Asian palace doors. He poured out samples of ginever, demonstrated a music box, and he distributed a few firearms as keepsakes. The Dewa Agung and the Radja of Badung became friendly; both received him in audience; they even began to manifest a healthy spirit of rivalry in representing the respective merits of Kusumba, Klungkung, and Kuta, Badung, as the site of the factory which, Molière hinted, would be well stocked with other trinkets. It developed that what the Dewa Agung had in mind was no trinket. The Dewa Agung craved a rhinoceros, a creature which did not exist in Bali but was necessary nevertheless for an especially solemn state ceremony which he was hoping to conduct. Even apart from its ritualistic significance, a rhinoceros would be a sensation among all Balinese connoisseurs of curiosities, and the Dewa Agung's badly frayed prestige would be immensely enhanced if he, and only he, possessed one. Molière, disguising his dismay, promised to deliver one live rhinoceros.

The Radja of Badung, an earthier type than the Dewa Agung, yearned for one hundred pikuls of lead. He intended, he said, to cast it into balls for use with the bronze cannon which, it seemed, Wetters had promised but neglected to deliver. Wetters' oversight accounted for the coolness of his original attitude toward Molière, who seems to have convinced him, however, that the promise still held good. A daughter of Radja Pamat-jutan (a minor ruler of Badung) wanted quantities of linen and offered advance payment of three pikuls of tobacco, adding, as an afterthought to clinch the deal, three slaves. In view of the government's disapproval of slavery, Molière might have passed up this first trading opportunity except that the slaves insisted upon attaching themselves to him.

All in all, Molière judged his visit a success. On the basis of his own experiences he anticipated certain unpredictable difficulties, but he thought that a factory in Bali might flourish and he so reported to the N.H.M. and the Governor-General. He kept a meticulous record of his expenses, for which the N.H.M. was later to claim compensation. Inclusive of gin, guns, and incidental items like payment of ship charter, but not allowing for the rhinoceros (later procured and delivered at cost of fl. 839.25), the trip cost exactly fl. 9,738.58.

Schuurman, the Rhinoceros, and the N.H.M. Factory

After Molière's visit, the N.H.M. moved fast to establish a factory at Kuta, where the Radja of Badung had promised to prepare quarters for its representative. The company designated one of its brightest young men, D. Boelen Schuurman, as its Kuta factor at a salary of fl. 500 per month, placed an order for a factory trading ship, the *Merkurius*, to be completed and delivered at an early date, and meanwhile chartered the bark *Blora* at fl. 1,800 per month to get men, goods, and equipment moving Baliwards. On July 30, 1839, the *Blora* appeared off Kuta, carrying Heer Schuurman, his assistant, G. W. Veenman

Bouman, trade goods to the value of fl. 42,000 (inclusive of the linens for the princess), construction materials for a company warehouse, and one healthy young rhinoceros for the Dewa Agung.

Heer Schuurman hustled hopefully ashore only to discover that the Radja had made no provision whatever for his reception. He made his way wearily on foot to Kuta, then by horse to the *puri*, where the Radja allowed him to wait at the gate, much to the diversion of the public, while deciding whether to receive him. The Radja, whose intelligence in matters of commerce was better than his memory of his own promises, seems already to have been informed that although the ship's manifest listed one gift rhinoceros, it showed no lead and no cannon.

Schuurman, who may have deemed a rhinoceros token enough of company esteem not just for the Dewa Agung but for all the lesser rulers as well, spent a few frustrating days trying to interest the Radja in his factory and his residence. It finally occurred to him to make a present of a fine sword and to renew assurances of the N.H.M. intentions with regard to the lead and the cannon. The cannon was in fact to be delivered two years later. It cost the company fl. 1,007.95, and it had been cunningly miscast so that the Dutch need never fear looking this gift gun in the mouth. The Radja himself seems never to have tested it out. He made it the nucleus of what was to become rather an extensive palace armory, to which, in 1849, in appreciation of his good behavior during the Dutch–Balinese wars, the government added a mate. The second cannon probably was not miscast; it seems to have come out of current military stock with which the Dutch themselves had just subdued the island.

Heer Schuurman underwent many harrowing experiences highly educational to a young trader in the course of his first few months in Badung. He spent the early weeks as a not especially welcome and certainly an uncomfortable guest in rather a dingy pavilion inside the Radja's *puri*. Eventually he persuaded the Radja to assign him a scrap of property in Kuta—a run-down compound with one fairly habitable clay hut. But when he started building his factory, he had to rely upon the crew of the *Blora* and later that of the *Merkurius* for skilled labor which the Balinese themselves could not or would not provide. His precious rhinoceros had proved enormously difficult and costly to offload, and the people of Badung seemed more interested in obstructing than assisting. The eventual delivery to Klungkung, fortunately, was a great success. On his way back from Klungkung, however, Schuurman decided impulsively to drop in on the Radja of Gianjar. The Radja, no doubt apprised of the massive tribute to his near but undear neighbor, allowed the perplexed merchant to wait for an hour at the palace gate and then to go away unreceived and unenlightened. Schuurman's subsequent commerce in Kuta did not flourish and he was no happier than Pierre Dubois had been before him. The Balinese, the Chinese, and the Bugis visited his factory in droves, impelled, however, by curiosity rather than by desire to purchase. They took their trade to the Danish factory which Mads Lange was opening up just next door.

Schuurman could not complain that his life was either inactive or uneventful, and being young, vigorous, and ambitious, he labored mightily during the first year or two to make his factory a success. He had to adjust to the fact that his assistants were usually less rugged than himself. The first of them, Veenman Bouman, fell seriously ill almost immediately upon arrival and had to return to Java. The second, J. A. Santbergen, was his mainstay and remained in Bali until the end of the period of N.H.M. operations, well after Schuurman himself had been transferred. The third, Andries Beetz, died shortly after arrival and was buried at Kuta. Intermittently, there were others, and always there was an armed guard, but only Santbergen was of much comfort or assistance.

The factory itself gradually expanded, although its business did not. It became rather too overawing and fortress-like to create a very favorable impression upon the Balinese or upon certain later and highly critical Dutch visitors. At enormous expense, with materials and labor imported from Java, Schuurman built a high stone wall and behind it placed a big stone warehouse, providing also residential quarters for the staff and for visitors. From the very first the factory catered more to visitors than to customers, much better serving Dutch political than commercial purposes.

The first important guests were the officers of the government steamship *Phoenix*, who arrived on October 29 on a visit of inspection and wished to pay courtesy calls upon the radjas. It was an exercise which cost Schuurman much effort and many gifts and yielded no discernable results. Next, in early April 1840, came Navy Lieutenant Van Oostervijk accompanied by the important Pangeran (Prince) Hamid of Pontianak, Borneo, who also wanted to meet the radjas. In between these visits Schuurman took delivery on his own factory ship, the *Merkurius*, and sailed off on a trading cruise of all of Bali and Lombok, hoping to stir up more business than at Kuta, but with equally meager results. Then, on April 27, 1840, there arrived in Kuta, traveling presumably on the *Merkurius*, the soon to be famous political agent, Heer H. J. van Huskus Koopman. Schuurman and the N.H.M. factory played thereafter the support role in the evolving drama of Dutch colonial penetration.

Huskus Koopman, the Contract-Maker

H. J. van Huskus Koopman, famous in Dutch colonial history as the *"contractsluiter"* (contract-maker), had received his appointment on December 10, 1839, as special commissioner for Bali and Lombok, at salary of fl. 700 per month, plus fl. 300 for expenses, with instructions to perform what seemed at first rather a vague and innocuous mission. He was "to bring the radjas ... into such a relationship with the government [of the Netherlands Indies] that they will be removed from foreign influence." The foreign influence from which they were to be removed and isolated was mainly that of the English. The relationship into which they were to be brought and held was that of colonial subjects. These Dutch objectives, which were to become precise and categorical as time went on, were formulated into various sets of highly legalistic "contract concepts" which Huskus Koopman was charged with explaining to the radjas in order to elicit their concurrence. The preliminary contract concepts were to be converted into perpetually binding treaties just as soon as there was an agreed-upon text which both the Governor-General and the radjas had ratified.

Huskus Koopman's job was essentially that of the traveling salesman. It was the Governor-General's expectation that the Dutch-drafted texts would be endorsed with little if any necessity for modification. These Western documents, however alien they might at first appear to the Balinese mentality, would form the basis for an enduring new commercial and political relationship agreeable both to the Dutch and the Balinese without occasioning anything so distasteful to both as a military campaign. As it turned out, the radjas gave their preliminary concurrence, the Governor-General ratified, the radjas refused to ratify, the Dutch–Balinese wars followed, and Dutch might prevailed. But by then Huskus Koopman, who had been awarded the Order of the Netherlands Lion for his services, was already in his grave; so was Governor-General Merkus, so too were numerous of the offending Balinese princes, and a great deal of history had happened.

Impasse of 1840; Treaties of 1841; Afterthoughts of 1842

Huskus Koopman's first visit to Bali (April 27–late December 1840) was almost a complete failure. With Schuurman to guide and introduce him, he made the rounds of the courts, starting with the Dewa Agung who not only refused to receive him but dispatched a letter to the other radjas instructing, or perhaps merely advising them to do likewise. In November he voyaged to Buleleng, where the Radja also denied him an audience but did send a message (as did the Radja of Karangasem) saying that he would permit trade. The Commissioner meanwhile had picked up the clue which enabled him to dangle before the eyes of the radjas the political equivalent of Molière's rhinoceros. It was the intimation that the radjas might induce the Dutch to provide them with military aid for an adventure which they were eagerly anticipating—the reconquest of Lombok, where the recent civil wars had gone against Balinese interest.

The Radja of Karangasem dispatched a mission of his own to Batavia to inform the Governor-General that he was already raising troops to invade Lombok and to invite the Dutch to participate. When Huskus Koopman himself returned to Batavia to report the futility of offering political without military alliance, the Governor-General ordered him back to Bali to exploit what seemed like a favorable opportunity. Neither the Governor-General nor Huskus Koopman seems ever to have made any explicit commitment about military aid. But on his return trip Koopman did not actually discourage the Balinese from awaiting favorable response to their request for Dutch ships, arms, and men to help re-subdue their former dependency; later on, in Lombok, he did not encourage the Radja to think that the Dutch would decline to underwrite exactly such an enterprise.

Since Bali–Lombok animosities dovetailed very neatly with Dutch designs, on his second visit to Bali (May 1–December 15, 1841), Huskus Koopman achieved what seemed for a time like almost total success. His fortunes were further enhanced, it seemed, by an otherwise woeful event—the wreck of the Dutch frigate *Overijssel* on the Kuta reef (in fact, an islet named Serangan) and the plunder of some of its cargo. Koopman promptly demanded fl. 3,000 in compensation from the Radja of Badung, who paid no money but did rather suddenly concede (July 26) that he might accept the contract concepts which Koopman had just been rather laboriously and as yet unproductively explaining to him. With Badung all but signed up, Huskus Koopman journeyed to Klungkung. The Dewa Agung too was amenable, at least up to the point of giving his approval (July 30) to the Badung negotiation. With this prestigious backing Koopman next treated successfully with the Radja of Karangasem (November 11) and the Radja of Buleleng (November 26), both of whom were impatient to get on with the scheduled invasion which they expected soon to follow.

Having accomplished his purpose in Buleleng and Karangasem, Koopman traveled yet once again to Klungkung. There, on December 6, he persuaded the Dewa Agung himself to enter into the same preliminary arrangement and to state that whatever contract he might eventually sign would be binding also upon those of his vassal states which had not entered into similar agreements of their own. To the three original clauses of the contract concept, Huskus Koopman added three more which, with the approval of the Dewa Agung, automatically became part of the agreement with any of the other states. These contract concepts, to which the Dewa Agung and the radjas gave preliminary and tentative but by no means final approval, were later to be converted unilaterally and arbitrarily by the Governor-General into binding agreements which provided a pretext for subsequent demands.

The full text (inclusive of Article 7, which applied, of course, only to Klungkung) read as follows:

The following are the terms of a treaty between Hendrick Jacob Huskus Koopman, duly constituted Komisaris of the Government of Netherlands India, and Sri Paduka Ratu Dewa Agung Putera, Emperor of the Islands of Bali and Lombok ruling with full powers in the state of Klungkung:

1. We, the Emperor of the Islands of Bali and Lombok acknowledge our domain to be that also of the Netherlands India Government.

2. Therefore when any ship or boat enters any harbor of this domain the Dutch flag will be raised.

3. In accordance with this agreement, we, the Emperor, will never surrender to any other white people whomsoever or enter into any agreement with them.

4. We promise never to accept any other flag over our lands except that of Holland.

5. The Dutch merchants who are now in Kuta with our consent we shall always assiduously protect.

6. Should the Government of Netherlands India encounter difficulties in warfare the radjas of Bali are obliged to assist them to the best of their abilities.

7. Finally, we approve the provisions of the treaties which have already been made by Komisaris Huskus Koopman with the radjas of Buleleng and Karang Asem and Badung.

Thus transpired in the palace of Klungkung on Isnin, the 21st day of the month of Sjawal in the year 1257 (i.e., 6 December 1841).

Ratu Dewa Agung Putra

Witnesses:
Tjokorde Dewa Agung Putra
Ratu Dewa Agung Gde
Anak Agung Ktut Rai
Padanda Wayahan Pidada
Ide Wayahan Sidaman

Translated from the original Malay of the treaty text found in the National Archives in Djakarta and published as Annex G (pp. 321–323) to Dr. E. Utrecht's *Sedjarah Hukum Internasional di Bali dan Lombok*, Bandung, 1962.

Huskus Koopman returned to Batavia in early 1842 in full expectation of receiving the warmest congratulations of the government and of being honorably discharged from his arduous mission. But the Governor-General refused just then to ratify, and Koopman found himself formally accused of negligence. It was all because of the unfortunate *Overijssel* incident, which had aroused the greatest of indignation and outrage in the Netherlands and in Batavia. The Governor-General himself was therefore under strong pressure to get categorical assurance from the radjas that they renounced reef rights and would refrain from plunder. The question of reef rights having been deemed of secondary priority, the Governor-General had not dealt with it in the original contract concepts. And even though Huskus Koopman had seized upon the *Overijssel* incident as pretext for pressuring the radjas into accepting his contracts, he had not considered it advisable to insert a special clause to deal with a problem which, once Dutch sovereignty were exercised, might be expected to resolve itself. But the furor over the *Overijssel* had caused the Governor-General to draw up a very lengthy and detailed set of new contract concepts which amounted virtually to a codified law of salvage, with stipulation of rules of conduct and scales of payment, and he was determined to make these a part of the original package. He therefore ordered Huskus Koopman to return to Bali to renegotiate with the radjas, those of Lombok as well as Bali, for he put no faith at all in his Commissioner's assurances that the Dewa Agung could speak for all of his presumed vassals and he was determined to leave no loopholes.

On July 31, 1842, Huskus Koopman wearily embarked on his third voyage. Once he arrived in Bali he very quickly persuaded the radjas to approve if not actually to read and study his rules of ship salvage. In October he traveled onward to Lombok. There he got the radja's consent to renunciation of reef rights but failed to convince him to forgo sovereignty as well. That required a fourth voyage (January 1843) and the rather thinly veiled threat of force. Then, to his great dismay, it was necessary to make yet a fifth trip (September 1843) to get acceptance of a clause which had been inadvertently omitted from the Lombok copies. This time all was complete. The Governor-General wearily approved and hastily ratified, Huskus Koopman got his Netherlands Lion and soon died—and the Balinese radjas repudiated the whole *"Bali-bundel,"* as some of the more irreverent Dutch were already beginning to refer to the documentary coups of their highly skilled *contractsluiter* and *traktaatsluiter,* who could so artfully transform concepts into irrevocable commitments.

Once they had a chance to reflect, the radjas decided that they had been hustled, threatened, tricked, cajoled, deceived, and betrayed in making commitments which they never intended. What upset them most was the mysterious and sinister matter of sovereignty, which remained both ill-understood and ill-explained. They had acknowledged their own domain to be the domain also of the Netherlands. They had been offered Huskus Koopman's standard explanation: "You say your realm is your friend's realm, and so it is with sovereignty." But as a clarification of the concept of sovereignty, the remark seemed on careful consideration to be singularly specious. The Dutch word for domain, as used in the treaty texts, was *eigendom* (property) and the Malay word was *negeri* (country), but it made as little sense in Dutch as in Malay to say that the radja's *eigendom* or *negeri* was also the Dutch *eigendom* or *negeri* without adding further mystification such as only a constitutional lawyer could have provided. There was no attempt to render the text into Balinese, in which the mystical significance of this imprecisely shared sovereignty over domain might at least have been endowed with symbolical validity.

What the radjas began to realize and indeed also to assert was that they had never intended to raise the Dutch flag over their ports and palaces (they themselves flew not flags but banners), or to elevate the Dutch crown over the many-tiered royal umbrellas (tiers signified rank but a crown was a suspicious alien device suggestive of black magic), or to seat a Dutch official on a golden chair as ornate as that of the radja, let alone one even more ornate and placed on a higher level. And it was one thing to say that their realm was their friend's realm but quite another for the friend to move in to stay. It was to take three Dutch military expeditions to persuade them to think or at least to act more like the loyal and tractable protégés of the Dutch Crown which they were already destined to become.

The *eigendom–negeri* conundrum was illuminated for them by the *tawan karang* (reef rights) episode of the *Overijssel*, which the radjas deplored as deeply as did the Dutch but for different reasons. It had demonstrated to their own subjects that they were powerless to prevent the Dutch from intervening in affairs either more or less innocent than the ancient practice of taking possession of a stranded ship. The *Overijssel* had yielded them little in plunder but had cost dearly in prestige.

Shipwreck and Plunder of the *Overijssel*, Kuta Scene

The sad tale of the *Overijssel* began on July 19, 1841, when the vessel, on the hundredth day of its maiden voyage from Plymouth to Surabaya with a valuable cargo of machinery for a sugar factory in Java, hit the Kuta reef and was promptly plundered. Subsequent Dutch outrage served in part to cloak their humiliation that a large and heavily armed frigate was wrecked by reason of an egregious navigational error, the captain having mistaken the coast of Bali for that of Java, and that the ship was looted notwithstanding the presumed vigilance of the ship's company against exactly that contingency. The captain, Govert Blom, was soon to publish a highly controversial and quite incoherent "impartial" account of his experience. He blamed poor visibility, poor charts, and poor judgment. It was not his own poor judgment, as others alleged, but that of Heer Huskus Koopman, who failed to control the radjas; of the N.H.M. factory personnel, who neglected to save the cargo and salvage the ship; of the Dutch naval Captain Willinck, who delayed in responding to call. Captain Blom had good words only for Mads Lange, who provided good advice and good company and eventually purchased the wreck to cannibalize it for repairs to other vessels.

For a period of a week the *Overijssel* incident much enlivened life in Kuta. Lange and Santbergen both showed up on the beach to welcome the castaways, to warn them against Gusti Ngurah Ktut's gang of ruffians, and to offer them the shelter and the hospitality of their respective factories. The Balinese plunderers went to work on the wreck just as soon as did the company salvagers, the one crew apparently working by day and the other by night but to equally little advantage. The main cargo of heavy iron machinery and boilers was not salvageable by any Kuta methods and much of the rest of the cargo and ship's fittings were lost on the dangerous reef.

The Radja of Badung caused much excitement by sending an order commanding the Europeans, on pain of death, to desist from their efforts to remove property which now belonged to him; he rescinded the order on receipt of strong protest from Santbergen and Huskus Koopman; he revalidated it the next day under pressure from the Kuta looters. The dispute over salvage soon became academic; both ship and cargo were beyond hope of recovery. The N.H.M. factory bought up for fl. 197.50 what little salvage was offered for sale, and Lange, as mentioned, bought the wreckage. As Huskus Koopman pointed out in his own self-defense, the goods were very heavily insured (for fl. 170,000).

The *Overijssel* incident offered social as well as commercial, political, and economic diversion to the minute European community in Kuta, which suddenly found itself entertaining a total of 57 passengers and crew, among the former the large and important family of Colonel Lucassen—husband, pregnant wife, five children, and nursemaid, the Colonel being the owner of the cargo. Captain Blom and most of the ship's company remained in Bali until July 25, when they left for Surabaya on the factory schooner *Merkurius*. Captain Blom was to return briefly later on to try to repair his ship and his reputation.

The family Lucassen remained until August 9, when they departed for Surabaya on board a government vessel, the *Sylph*. Vrouw Lucassen, meanwhile, had given birth to her child—the first European child to be born in Bali—and the event had been celebrated by a champagne dinner attended by 24 Europeans. These familial and festive events, which, according to one account, occurred in the N.H.M. factory, and according to another in Lange's establishment, no doubt greatly enlivened Kuta and comforted the castaways. But they did nothing to appease the wrath of the Governor-General, at least not until Huskus Koopman brought off the second series of what seemed at the time to be major coups of diplomacy.

More Complications; More Treaties

The Governor-General had scarcely even promulgated the still un-ratified contract concepts and terminated his long correspondence with The Hague over the *Overijssel* incident when the Balinese rad-jas quite deliberately defied him by reverting to vigorous exercise of reef rights. In 1844, therefore, the year in which the radjas were scheduled by the Dutch to send a mission of homage to Batavia, there arrived instead in Bali a newly appointed Dutch Commissioner, J. Ravia de Lignij, the Assistant Resident of Banjuwangi. His mission was to protest the most recent outrages and to demand the ratification and observance, without further delay or discussion, of the Huskus Koopman contracts. Commissioner de Lignij made his call at Buleleng, where the latest reef incidents had occurred, meeting there with the Radja and his council of state. It was at this meeting that the great modern hero of Bali identified himself. He was Gusti Ktut Djilantik, a dramatic, dynamic young prince, the younger brother of the Radjas of Buleleng and Karangasem, who defied the Dutch Commissioner in the following, perhaps apocryphal words:

> "Never while I live shall the state recognize the sovereignty of the Netherlands in the sense in which you interpret it. After my death the Radja may do as he chooses. Not by a mere scrap of paper shall any man become the master of another's lands. Rather let the *kris* decide."

CHAPTER 5

Balinese and Europeans in Turbulent Lombok (1824–1843)

Balinese Conquest and Rule of Lombok

The island of Lombok (or Seleparang) is the disadvantaged counterpart of the island of Bali; it is remarkably similar in natural and
cultural features but it lacks Bali's great wealth of scenic and artistic
endowment. In the late sixteenth century Lombok was conquered
and colonized by the Balinese, and for the next hundred years it was
subjected to very strong Balinese cultural influences. But in Lombok
the Hindu Balinese, a 5–10 per cent element in the population, col-
lided with the Muslim Bugis from Makassar, seafaring traders who
were aggressively exporting their own manners, customs, and religion. The Sassak tribespeople were converted to Islam and the island
slipped almost altogether from Balinese control into that of Makassar and Sumbawa. At the turn of the nineteenth century Lombok
was reconquered by Balinese armies and again subjected to massive
Balinese infiltration. Radja Gusti Gde Ngurah Karangasem, Radja of
Karangasem-Bali, who made himself the paramount ruler of northern, eastern, and western Bali, made himself also the paramount
ruler of Lombok. As Radja of Karangasem-Lombok he installed other
Balinese princes as rulers of the numerous little states into which
the island was divided and named his own daughter, known as the
Tjokorda (a title, not a name), as regent.

Shortly after it reemerged as a Balinese dependency, Lombok
emerged also as a regional center of trade. The island was strategi-

cally placed on the heavily trafficked Europe–Asia and Singapore–Australia shipping routes, and its chief port of Ampenan, located in the big, sheltered Ampenan Bay, began to attract regional and international visitors. In the early 1830s several Westerners settled in the island as resident merchants. The most important of these were the Englishman, George King, and the Dane, Mads Lange, each of whom also introduced more or less permanent associates. Lange and King became bitter commercial rivals and attached themselves to the leading but rival local rulers. Civil wars were already inevitable, and the advent of the Europeans signified that they would come sooner, last longer, and prove more costly. Civil wars and Western traders' involvement in them meant, furthermore, that the colonial Dutch in nearby Java would interest themselves and therefore intervene in Lombok's affairs. Lombok, like neighboring Bali, was therefore destined sooner rather than later to become a Dutch colonial possession.

The domestic situation in Lombok in the 1830s was far from tranquil and equally far from transparent. The presence of the Western merchants enormously complicated the already involuted island politics, which is to say, the intrigues of the feuding members of the Balinese royal house of Karangasem who ruled the various principalities, for, with, and against whom conspired also various of the princes of Bali itself. The house of Karangasem, unhappily, was especially vulnerable to violent animosities because it was not only arrogant and aggressive but also degenerate, being given to that most heinous of moral offenses, the crime of incest. Whoever would start a war had only to allege incest to condemn his enemy and thus justify himself. Conspiracy, commerce, and incest, then, were the prime factors in the Lombok Wars of 1838 and 1839 which led directly to Dutch colonialism. These bizarre circumstances require an attempt at summation, even at risk of oversimplifying without actually clarifying.

Hostile Radjas and Rival Merchants

Gusti Gde Ngurah Karangasem, the founder of the modern ruling house of Karangasem, died in 1806, bequeathing to his numerous and mainly dissolute progeny an apparently endless series of quarrels over his domains both in Bali and Lombok. One of his sons, Gusti Gde Ngurah Lanang Karangasem, who made himself briefly and bloodily the ruler of Karangasem-Bali, committed such hideous crimes (allegedly both incest and cannibalism) that in 1824 he had to abandon his throne in Bali and seek shelter in Lombok. There he found himself almost equally unwelcome, but he did manage to assert his authority over a small state on Ampenan Bay. He made repeated and more or less polite requests to his sister, the Tjokorda, to terminate her regency and yield him the throne of Karangasem-Lombok, then later to join him in the reconquest of Karangasem-Bali. Instead, she invited their own half-brother, Ratu Ngurah Pandji, to join her as royal consort, and when this particular paramour died (1835), she chose his son, Ratu Gusti Ngurah Pandji, as his replacement. Ratu Gusti Ngurah Pandji himself compounded the incest by taking his own sister also into his harem. The outraged Radja Lanang appealed urgently and regularly to Anak Agung Ktut Karangasem, the Radja of Mataram, the second most important state of the island, to assist him in deposing his abominable sister and her abandoned consort and in establishing his own claim. The Radja of Mataram declined to undertake the military action which would certainly have been necessary for any such dynastic rearrangement.

Radja Lanang died in 1837, bequeathing his claim and little else to his son, Ida Ratu, who continued to press the reluctant Radja of Mataram to overthrow the wicked Tjokorda. Mads Lange, the Danish merchant, meanwhile, had built up his commercial enterprises under the patronage of Radja Lanang and his son with the apparent consent of the Tjokorda and her paramours. George King had attached his fortunes to those of the young, vigorous, and apparently much more admirable Radja of Mataram. This ambitious young ruler proved far from unresponsive to King's suggestions that the time had come to overthrow the Tjokorda and to establish Mataram's political—and King's commercial—hegemony over the island. It took only a minor crisis to spark a war—a routine quarrel over boundaries and water rights. In early 1838 the affair escalated into widespread conflict both by land and by sea, with King becoming the Commander-in-Chief and Admiral of the Fleet for the Radja of Mataram, and Lange, after a critical interval of hesitation, playing the same role for the Tjokorda.

Wars of 1838; Tjokorda's Defeat; Lange's Decline

The course of hostilities proved only slightly less mystifying than had been the preliminaries. Karangasem, with twenty times the population of Mataram, could and did raise about 10,000 troops; but the royal house of Karangasem was widely detested and its fighting men could easily be induced to defect. Mataram seemed an almost harmless challenger until King suddenly began importing soldiers from Bali, to an eventual grand total of about 10,000. Along with the troops, King imported also Gusti Bagus Karang, recently and briefly Radja of Karangasem-Bali, who, having been deprived of his throne, was willing to join Mataram in the fight against Karangasem-Lombok. King also imported Nachoda (Captain) Ismaila, a Bugis merchant, pirate, and slaver, who brought with him a gang of 200 Bugis ruffians to serve as a special task force. For payment of fl. 125 per day he chartered his private bark, *Pleyades*, as flagship of a small fleet of European and Asian vessels, some of whose captains were only with difficulty induced or impressed into service, which were used to transport troops from Bali and arms from Singapore. Lange and his partner, John Burd, meanwhile deployed their heavily armed merchant vessels, *Falcon* and *de Zuid*, to blockade the Lombok coast. King, in riposte, set up powerful shore batteries in Ampenan Bay to keep them out. Presently Burd sailed off to Batavia to appeal to the Dutch to come to the aid of the beleaguered Tjokorda.

The Dutch had already heard disquieting rumors of what was happening in Lombok, but they had contented themselves with sending a mission to investigate. They had had a report, for instance, from the Dutch captain of the *Monkey*, on an English owned ship from Semarang. The captain had engaged, more or less voluntarily, on behalf of the Mataram-King faction, in transport of troops from Bali. But certain events had convinced him that he had best confess all, and perhaps more than all, to presumably vigilant Dutch colonial authorities. His fourth voyage had ended in a bloody shipboard uprising when the Balinese troops began to suspect, perhaps with reason, that they were being kidnapped to be sold as slaves. The captain's rather extravagantly embroidered and self-exculpatory report was not much more fanciful than what was actually happening in Lombok; but the

War of 1838 was over before the Dutch investigators even arrived to check the various reports.

The decisive battle occurred in early June 1838 when the Tjokorda mounted a badly timed and ill-coordinated offensive by land and sea, relying upon hundreds of soldiers and scores of *perahus*, most of which never turned up, Nachoda Ismaila's task force having surprised them on their way to the rendezvous. Mataram thus won the war, but the Radja, who was shot in the head in the course of a minor skirmish, did not live to profit from his victory. Nor did the Tjokorda survive defeat. When her capital was invested, she set fire to the *puri*, plunged her *kris* into the heart of her consort, then turned it upon herself, inspiring some 300 members of the court to emulation in the traditional rite of the *puputan*—the self-destruction of a royal household when other disaster seems certain.

The Radja of Mataram was succeeded by his son, Gusti Ngurah Ktut Karangasem, who selflessly placed the former pretender, Ida Ratu, on the throne just vacated by the Tjokorda, but rather less selflessly made it quite clear to him that the overlord–vassal relationship had been reversed: Mataram was now the paramount state and Karangasem was the subordinate. There also occurred a beginning of reversal in the respective positions of Lange and King. King, the ally of the winner, was not about to let the commercial rewards of victory fall to Lange—and Western shipping had begun to seek out Ampenan Bay again in even greater numbers just as soon as King silenced the shore batteries and Lange lifted the blockade. But King was unable to persuade the young Radja to expel Lange, or at least not just yet. The Radja, who knew the Dutch fixation about English penetration, feared the Dutch reaction to any move which would seem to favor an English trader. He was already having difficulty enough with tiresome Dutch investigators.

The first Dutch mission to Lombok was headed by Army Captain J. S. Wetters, who was already familiar with the region, having negotiated the agreement of 1826 with the Radja of Badung for recruitment of Balinese soldiers. Captain Wetters arrived in Lombok on July 5, 1838, on the schooner *Kameleon*, impressively escorted by the corvette *Hippomenes*, the iron steamships *Etna* and *Hekla*, and the adventuresome *Monkey*. After visiting the ruins of the Tjokorda's capital and *puri*, Wetters proceeded to Ampenan. There King received him, shadowed him and monitored his very unilluminating conversations with the Radja. Wetters' trip to Lombok was productive of nothing except a side excursion to Bali, where he reconnoitered the situation in Buleleng and Karangasem in advance of Granpré Molière's visit.

The second Dutch mission to Lombok (December 1838) was headed by Navy Captain A. C. Edeling, who was sent with the corvette *Triton* and the schooner *Castor* to make stern representations in the case of the murder of a Chinese sea captain, Kouw Si An, and the looting of his vessel, the *Fatal Berakat*, which flew the Dutch flag. The incident had occurred in Ampenan on October 10, 1838. According to the report made by members of the crew when the ship reached Surabaya, the murderer was one of Nachoda Ismaila's Bugis ruffians; he had been relieved of his loot (opium and money), given shelter, and presently enabled to escape by George King. But the Dutch investigators in Ampenan were quite unable to pin down the facts. The Radja and King both professed themselves eager to see Dutch justice done but declared themselves unable to produce the alleged murderer, who had fled, they said, to Bali. The investigators were unconvinced; nor were they overly impressed with the fact that whereas Lange flew the Danish flag, King flew the Dutch. They had already been informed by reliable witnesses that during the recent war, when King had two shore batteries in Ampenan Bay, he flew both the Dutch and the English flags and trained the gunners, in the course of target practice, routinely and symbolically to shoot down the former. The Edeling mission was not a success, nor was that of Granpré Molière, who called at Lombok after his visit to Bali but was unable to travel to the capital to meet the Radja.

Wars of 1839; Fall of the House of Karangasem

The Lombok War of 1838 had not really resolved either political or commercial rivalries; it merely provoked the War of 1839. The Radja of Mataram, as paramount ruler, distrusted and detested the Radja of Karangasem, his ungrateful and therefore presumably rebellious subordinate; King distrusted and detested Lange; and everybody was suspicious of Gusti Bagus Karang, the ex-Radja of Karangasem-Bali who had helped the Radja of Mataram make the once forlorn pretender, young Ida Ratu, the now pretentious Radja of Karangasem.

Gusti Bagus Karang held that he had abandoned claims to his own throne in Bali to see justice done in Karangasem-Lombok, only to find himself later rejected and maligned. He made his resentment so unmistakable that both the Radja of Mataram and the Radja of Karangasem automatically assumed that he was conspiring to overthrow them in order to rule all of Lombok in his own right and perhaps Bali as well. The rulers of Karangasem-Bali and Buleleng-Bali, who had no reason to wish him well, decided to make his downfall a certainty. Justly or unjustly, they accused him of incest and secured the blessing of the Dewa Agung of Klungkung upon anyone who would depose him from the few scraps of Bali domain over which he ruled. The Radja of Mataram, after more or less scrupulous investigation of the incest charges, publicly pronounced him guilty. But Gusti Bagus Karang still had it within his capability to provoke certain local disorders which, in early 1839, developed into a small-scale civil war. A half dozen prominent princes of Bali and Lombok raised a much more powerful army than was really necessary and marched upon their lone adversary. It was a little ten-day war which climaxed in a *puputan*, with Gusti Bagus Karang ending his own life with greater dignity than he had lived it. The splendid *kris* with which he killed himself was sent, along with the rest of his regalia, back to Karangasem-Bali, from whence, it was hoped, no more troublesome refugees would come.

The ten-day war of February 1839 was followed by the four-day war of June. The Radja of Mataram decided that the time had come to depose the Radja of Karangasem, an enterprise in which he had the enthusiastic assistance of King, who had determined upon a definitive settlement with Lange. The Radja led one wing of his army and King led the other in an attack upon the *puri*. The Radja elected escape rather than the *puputan* and fled to the interior, where he was captured and imprisoned and six months later (December 1839) murdered. Lange, meanwhile, had been given exactly one hour in which to settle out his affairs in Ampenan and depart from Lombok forever. He made it within that deadline to his schooner, *Venus*, and sailed off to Bali. Or, according to a more heroic version of the story—his own—he fought his way through his enemies, leaped onto a fast horse, swam the horse out to sea, boarded his yacht, but still sailed off. Lange's partner, John Burd, tried to revisit Lombok later that year in order to collect debts and information, also perhaps to rescue the imprisoned Radja, but his vessel, *de Zuid*, was fired upon by King's *Pleyades*, and he thought it wise to withdraw.

George Peacock King and the New Dynasty

King remained in Lombok as *sjahbandar* to the Radja and as proprietor of the factory and shipyard which had once been Lange's, becoming, just as he had intended, the new merchant king and "White Radja" of Ampenan. He succeeded well enough in overcoming Dutch distrust that they did not put him out of business and actually at times engaged his services. He won Dutch confidence and gratitude mainly because he brought men and arms from Lombok to reinforce the Dutch armies in Bali in 1849. But he experienced increasing difficulty with his own patron, the Radja of Mataram, who showed evidence of being determined to be the master of his own kingdom. The Radja expelled King's friend, the arrogant and violent Nachoda Ismaila, together with his gang of Bugis, the Nachoda having in fact proved troublesome to King as well as to the Radja by reason of his attempts to share in the profits of the opium trade.

King apparently left Lombok in the mid-1850s, when he vanishes from the historical records. It seems probable that he sold out his commercial interests to another Englishman, named Cooper, who had been associated with him from time to time over the years. When Alfred Russel Wallace made his famous visit to Lombok (June–July 1856), he stayed with a certain Mr. Cooper, who was the proprietor of a commercial establishment. Wallace encountered three other Europeans: a second merchant whom he identified only as Mr. "S"; an unnamed "Dutch gentleman"; and Mr. Ross, an Englishman better known later on as "the King of the Cocos Islands," who had been engaged by the Dutch to settle the affairs of a bankrupt Dutch missionary. Evidently the European population of Lombok continued even after the time of Lange and King to include persons about whom one would wish to know much more. But Wallace was uncharacter-

istically reticent and other records are lacking. There were no European residents in the 1890s, when the Dutch returned in force to add
Lombok to their other colonial territories.

Dutch Investigations; Huskus Koopman's Contracts

After the visits of Wetters, Edeling, and Granpré Molière, the next
Dutch démarche upon Lombok was that of Huskus Koopman, the
accomplished *"contractsluiter,"* whose assignment it was to induce
the radjas of Bali and Lombok to acknowledge Dutch sovereignty
and thereafter, among many other concessions, to renounce the traditional practice of reef rights and to engage instead in more conventional ships salvage. Huskus Koopman made five separate voyages
(1839–1843) into the region before he fully accomplished his mission, but on the first two trips he visited only Bali and it was not until
October 1842 that he first traveled to Lombok. The Commissioner
had tried to convince both himself and the Governor-General that
contracts binding upon the Balinese radjas would be binding also
upon Lombok, the presumed dependency of the Radja of Karangasem, himself the presumed vassal of the Dewa Agung of Klungkung. Recent events had made it apparent, however, that all such
assumptions were ill-founded. Huskus Koopman had suggested to
the Governor-General that if Lombok objected to this reading of the
contracts, the Dutch might spare themselves much money and blood
by backstopping the Balinese invasion and reconquest of Lombok
which the Dewa Agung, the Radja of Buleleng, and the Radja of
Karangasem could, in fact, only with difficulty be restrained from
mounting. But Dutch official priorities, as established in The Hague
and Batavia, called for documentation first, conquest later, hence
Koopman's somewhat tardy visit.

Huskus Koopman arrived in Lombok in October 1842 on board
the corvette *Argo*, whose captain, Den Berger, faithfully followed his
detailed instructions about firing off salutes when the Commissioner landed, staging dress parades ashore, and otherwise making of
the visit a state occasion. Koopman negotiated not with the Radja of
Mataram himself, but with his vigorous and quite ambitious brother,
the Radja of Salaparang, who was already clearly self-elected as successor. The Radja acceded to the terms which Koopman proposed

with regard to reef rights. The same provisions obtained as for Bali: authorization of payment of 15–50 per cent of the value of the cargo to any legitimate salvager, the exact amount and all other relevant matters to be determined by a three-man arbitration board representing the Dutch, the Radja, and the owner. The surprising part of the agreement was Huskus Koopman's nominee as Dutch representative on any future salvage commission—the English merchant, George King, who, he reported, seemed to have mellowed. The young Radja, having amiably agreed to salvage, refused categorically to accept any suggestion with regard to sovereignty.

In 1843 Huskus Koopman was back in Lombok with a very carefully drafted letter from the Governor-General stating that he wished to clear away any misunderstanding. The contracts already negotiated with the Balinese radjas, he said, were assumed to be binding also upon Lombok, which had been a dependency of Bali; but in view of the fact that Lombok had separated itself from Bali, the Radja's own acknowledgment of the validity of the contracts was now necessary; otherwise the Dutch would "find themselves obliged in safeguarding their own rights to support those of the Balinese and to make them operative." The somewhat clouded implication, which Huskus Koopman was perhaps indelicate enough to clarify, was that the Dutch might unleash another Balinese invasion. On June 7 the Radja yielded and in July 1843 he sent a mission to Batavia bearing gifts of a kris and a lance as tokens of submission.

Huskus Koopman, who had now repeatedly persuaded the radjas to agree to whatever contract concepts the Governor-General contrived and longed to rest from his arduous travels, was delighted to hear himself warmly commended and to be proposed for award of the Order of the Netherlands Lion. He was shocked, however, to discover that his labors were not yet finished. Somehow it had escaped everyone's attention that the contract concepts drawn up for the Radja of Lombok did not contain a clause whereby the Radja undertook thereafter to cherish and protect Dutch traders. The necessary addenda were incorporated into the new contract concept, which the Governor-General signed and sealed in advance and confided to Huskus Koopman to deliver. In September 1843 the contract-maker was back in Lombok. The Radja promptly signed and sealed his copy (September 23). Perhaps by inadvertence, he attached it to the Governor-General's original and sent both of them back to Batavia, thus perhaps clearing his files of business which he preferred to forget. As it turned out, he was the only one of the radjas actually to ratify the contracts without the necessity for a military expedition. The Dutch conquest of Lombok could thus be postponed for almost exactly half a century.

Princes of Lombok in Power in Bali

The Radja of Salaparang, with whom Huskus Koopman negotiated, was the youngest of three brothers who became joint rulers of Lombok after the triumph of Mataram over Karangasem. The new Radja of Mataram seems to have preferred to share, dilute, and obscure the lines of power, and his brothers, especially the younger, were more than willing to oblige him. In 1870 Gusti Ngurah Gde Karangasem, the Radja of Salaparang, succeeded the eldest brother, the Radja of Mataram, as paramount ruler. Commonly known as the Radja of Lombok, he ruled until he was deposed and exiled by the Dutch at the end of the Lombok War of 1894. He was mainly responsible for the military assistance which Lombok provided the Dutch in the course of the Dutch–Balinese wars of 1846–1849. By helping to make certain that the Balinese were never again to be in a position to invade Lombok, he made it equally certain that the Dutch would eventually do so. The second brother, a dissolute but nevertheless engaging prince, wisely refrained from disputing the throne. He fathered two sons, however, who succeeded respectively to the thrones of Buleleng and Karangasem in Bali. His third son was Gusti Ktut Djilantik, the hero of the Dutch–Balinese wars. All three perished in 1849. A fourth son was executed for "desecration of caste" (incest?). A fifth was exiled to Negara, Bali, for attempting to usurp the throne of Karangasem.

CHAPTER 6

Punitive Expeditions (1846–1849)

Northern Princes' Defiance of the Dutch; Gusti Ktut Djilantik
Once the impetuous young Gusti Ktut Djilantik said "Let the *kris* decide," both the Dutch and the Balinese knew that war was not far off. Emboldened by Djilantik, the Radja of Buleleng persisted in his affronts. In 1845 J. T. T. Maijor, the Resident of Besuki, East Java, traveled to Buleleng to convey the Governor-General's protests and demands. He received no greater satisfaction than had his predecessor. The Dutch therefore began making ready an expeditionary force, which assembled at Besuki to sail to Bali on the east monsoon of the following year. Djilantik meanwhile began building fortifications, raising troops, and acquiring arms, relying, as the Dutch correctly surmised, upon certain enterprising Singapore merchants for large shipments of weapons. Balinese–Dutch relations were rapidly moving into a new and altogether tragic phase.

Balinese military preparations centered upon the northern radjadom of Buleleng. The ruler, Gusti Madya Karangasem, was the elder brother of Gusti Ngurah Made Karangasem, the Radja of Karangasem (not to be confused with Gusti Ngurah Ktut Karangasem, the Radja of Lombok, a close relative and bitter enemy). Buleleng and Karangasem, the two most powerful radjadoms of the island and longtime rivals, were now closely allied in opposing the political and military aims of the Dutch. They had the blessing of the Dewa Agung of Klungkung, who was in no position to provide much more than his blessing but at least did not with-hold it. The Radja of Badung in the south, who wished to preserve the profits of trade and was no friend of the turbulent northerners, sought to remain detached from the coming conflict and exercised his not inconsiderable influence upon his friendly neighbor, the Radja of Tabanan, to do likewise. The other states—Gianjar, Mengwi, and Bangli, in south-central Bali, and Djembrana in the west—were allied rather tenuously with Klungkung but were also attentive to Badung. They were not disposed to become involved and, unlike Buleleng and Karangasem, they had no military tradition to uphold. Bangli in particular was determined to remain neutral and did so until the end. With local lines of allegiance thus confused, it periodically served the purposes of the radjas themselves to claim that they could not act without the prior consent of the Dewa Agung. Similarly, it sometimes suited the Dutch to hold that the Dewa Agung, whom they knew to be all but impotent, ruled as Susuhunan (Emperor) over a united Bali. In fact, everyone acted on the basis of his own best estimate of his own best interests. Dutch self-interest, it was quite apparent, dictated a show of force. Once the Dutch set themselves to subdue Bali, the ultimate outcome was not in doubt. But it took three campaigns to shatter the Balinese defenses and morale, campaigns in which the Dutch did not always by any means achieve either victory or glory.

First Dutch Military Expedition (1846); Success and Stalemate
The First Dutch Military Expedition against Bali (1846) seemed a formidable enough force to cope with any native impudence. The invasion fleet was made up of two frigates with a total of 34 guns, four steamships, four schooner-brigs, twelve schooners, and 40 small craft. The sea force numbered 1,280 men and the land force 1,700, the latter inclusive of 400 Europeans equipped with 230 pieces of field artillery. As the Dutch fleet prepared to sail, the Danish trader, Mads Lange, arrived at Besuki from Kuta on his schooner *Venus* to volunteer his own good offices, bringing with him six blacksmiths from Bali to aid the warmakers and five interpreters from Banjuwangi to aid the peacemakers. The English trader, George King, also appeared, coming from Lombok with offers of aid from the Radja, who was eager not to be left out of any expedition against the Radja of Karangasem, his sworn enemy.

A view of the old palace of Buleleng, showing the pavilion-style buildings with thatched roofs. A wall encircles the entire compound.

The Dutch invasion force was under the joint command of General Rochussen and Rear Admiral E. B. van Bosch with J. T. T. Maijor, the Resident of Besuki and Commissioner for Bali and Lombok as civilian representative. The fleet arrived off the Buleleng coast on June 22, 1846.

Maijor immediately sent ashore an ultimatum denouncing the Radjas of Buleleng, Karangasem, and Klungkung for not observing the terms of the 1841–1843 agreements and demanding that they undertake to do so forthwith. He also required the Radjas to pay the costs of the expedition and admit a Dutch garrison both to collect the payments and to guarantee the peace. Heer Maijor entrusted his ultimatum to the Chinese trader-captain of a junk from Bangkok, who delivered it to the Chinese harbor-master, who dared not hand so rude a message directly to the Radja. The princes, nevertheless, were quickly apprised of the content.

The two Radjas, inspired by Gusti Djilantik, whom the Dutch conceded to be a man of military genius, had made unexpectedly systematic preparations for resistance. The town of Buleleng was ringed with barricades one to three meters thick and five to seven meters high, constructed of stone and clay packed between tree trunks, with sharpened bamboo stakes set in the sides and top, and some fifty cannons artfully placed and disguised. On both sides of the barricades had been dug deep pits and trenches, and all about were treacherous little traps of pointed slivers of bamboo. Djilantik had not only supervised the building of defense works but had raised and trained an army, a total of some 10,000 soldiers stationed in Buleleng itself and thousands more outside of the town. Many if not most of the recruits were mere youths armed with bamboo spears, but others were stout warriors equipped with European weapons.

Heer Maijor's ultimatum allowed the Balinese rulers "three times twenty-four hours" to comply with Dutch demands. The Radja sent the reply that he needed ten days to consult with his brother, the Radja of Karangasem, and also with the Dewa Agung. Maijor granted an extension of twenty-four hours. The Radja and Djilantik thereupon disappeared from the town, but the troops ostentatiously busied themselves strengthening the defenses. A Dutch officer was sent ashore to protest. When the Balinese shouted abuse and threats, the Dutch fired off an admonitory salvo which killed one soldier. The Balinese forces then withdrew from the water front, which the Dutch, fearing a ruse, refrained just yet from occupying.

At dawn on June 28, the time limit for compliance with the ultimatum having expired several days earlier, the Dutch frigates laid down a bombardment, and a few hours later the troops landed. They fought their way through fierce resistance into the town of Buleleng, which they captured, pillaged, and burned. The next day they subjected the adjacent royal capital of Singaradja to the same treatment. The greatly depleted Balinese forces withdrew inland to the strong defensive positions prepared by Djilantik at the town of Djagaraga, ten miles to the east and five miles from the coast.

The Dutch had won a swift victory at little cost to themselves (18 dead, 47 wounded); the Balinese suffered immense losses of life and property. The Dutch victory was empty, however, unless they could enforce their will upon the Radjas, who were firmly entrenched in the nearby hills. Not knowing the country and not having made provision for supply lines extending any distance from the coast, the Dutch were afraid to push inland.

Lange's Intermediation and the Peace Settlement

At this moment of apparent but deceptive victory and defeat, Mads Lange volunteered to mediate. He proposed to travel by horseback from Buleleng to Djagaraga to negotiate with the radjas, taking with him only his Balinese assistant and one servant. The Dutch accepted the offer, thinking it most unlikely that he could get through to Djagaraga, or, if he did, that he could return. Contrary to their expectations, Lange made the trip swiftly and safely and brought back the report that the Balinese were willing to participate in a peace conference. The Radja of Buleleng, he said, would not himself appear—he had told Lange, with a laugh, that he was much too ill; nor would Djilantik—he feigned a foot injury. Although neither was willing to entrust himself to the Dutch, it was agreed that the Radja's younger brother, the Radja of Karangasem, would represent them.

On July 5, the Radja of Karangasem appeared at Dutch headquarters to make submission; to the surprise and gratification of the Dutch he was followed shortly afterwards by the Radja of Buleleng. On July 9 both radjas formally accepted the Dutch terms. They undertook to abide by the 1841–1843 contracts; they would bear the costs of the expedition (fl. 225,000 from Buleleng, fl. 75,000 from Karangasem), the total to be paid within 10 years; they would dismantle their own fortifications and build no more; they would accept a Dutch garrison, build a fort for it and supply it with provisions; finally, they would accept a Dutch official as regular visitor or as resident representative. The Dutch were jubilant. The Governor-General and the First Admiral of the Fleet came from Batavia to stage a splendid banquet at which the two radjas and Djilantik were the guests of honor. The expeditionary force then sailed triumphantly back to Java, leaving behind a garrison of 150–200 men to maintain the Dutch presence and collect reparations. The garrison was installed in a newly built fortification on the coast at Pabejan.

Celebrations of peace and victory proved to be premature. The radjas failed to pay even the first installment on reparations; they refused to provision the Dutch garrison, which was in fact so boycotted and harassed that some of the soldiers deserted to join the Balinese, who gave them very cordial reception. The irrepressible Gusti Dji-lantik traveled throughout the island radiating defiance of the Dutch. He inspired the Dewa Agung to send protest after protest to Batavia regarding the Dutch interpretation of the peace terms. The various radjas resumed the practices which were certain to fetch the Dutch back again in force, not hesitating, for instance, to exercise reef rights in the case of an English flagship out of Singapore and a Dutch flag-ship out of Batavia, which were wrecked off the south coast.

Second Expedition (1848); Dutch Débacle at Djagaraga

The Second Dutch Military Expedition against Bali (1848) followed inevitably upon the first. It was by far the strongest military force as yet employed against any of the princes of the Indies. The command-er, Major General Jhr. C. van der Wijck, was one of the most distin-guished colonial soldiers. He demanded and got more ships, troops, and artillery than had been deemed necessary two years before. The invasion fleet was made up of four steam vessels, five schooners, eleven transports, and miscel-laneous small craft. It was manned by 740 sailors and provided with 72 cannon. The land force consisted of 2,400 men (including Madurese, Javanese, and one company of Africans) with a support corps of 500 coolies to maintain a supply line to points distant from the coast. Some 775 members of the land force, 109 of them officers, were Europeans; the cavalry was well rep-resented and it brought with it 156 horses.

Before fully committing themselves to this troublesome new expe-dition, the Dutch had magnanimously offered the radjas (Buleleng, Karangasem, and Klungkung) the opportunity to repent, to send a mission to Batavia to implore the forgiveness of the Governor-Gener-al, and to hand over Djilantik as a hostage. The radjas ignored the in-vitation. The force therefore rendezvoused on schedule in early June off the Buleleng coast. Lange was there again on the *Venus*. King was also among those present. The stage was set and the cast was reas-sembled for a repetition of the 1846 performance.

The operation began on May 7, when the frigates shelled the small port town of Sangsit; it continued the next day with the landing of troops, who succeeded very quickly in establishing a base on shore at the cost of only eight casualties. As a matter of fact, Sangsit itself had been sufficiently subdued a week earlier. The advance patrol craft *Argo* had discovered unexpectedly strong defenses and had virtually demolished the town with a midday rain of shells which caught everyone by surprise—men, women, and playing children. The demoralizing effect of the *Argo* bombardment was still further extended that same night, when a sudden and extraordinarily violent volcanic eruption in Java produced light and sound effects which the population mistook for another attack further down the coast.

General van der Wijck was much gratified by his early successes, even when he discovered that the Balinese defenders had again withdrawn to Djagaraga, where they had greatly strengthened their fortifications and had dug a wide, deep trench barring the approach to the town. On the morning of May 9 the Dutch began confidently to march upon the Balinese stronghold. At first it was an almost effortless advance over gradually rising, mostly arid and treeless terrain which the Balinese made almost no effort to defend. As it soon turned out, they had a better plan. They had laid traps and built road blocks further on, and they had as their ally the blazing tropical sun. The Dutch began to tire and to take casualties, but they pushed doggedly forward. They captured the first of the major Balinese redoubts without too much difficulty and advanced upon the second. But the Balinese, boldly and brilliantly led by Djilantik, had installed 25 cannon and mustered 16,000 men—1,500 equipped with firearms, the others with lances and spears which they used to advantage; they fought off three Dutch attacks and then began harassing the enemy from the sides and the rear, inflicting numerous casualties.

By midday the Dutch were in serious trouble. They had already expended most of the 100,000 rounds of ammunition which they had thought sufficient for any eventuality. They were stunned by the unexpected strength of the resistance and the size of their own losses. They were also wilted by the heat, parched with thirst, and madly tantalized by the sight of cool shade and shimmering water just beyond the Balinese lines. Their supply lines were also breaking down; the bearers were suffering almost as badly as the troops from heat and thirst. They sank in exhaustion when drafted to carry off soldiers who had collapsed with sunstroke. Led by Djilantik, the Balinese pushed their advantage by launching a strong counter-attack. General van Wijck had no choice but to call a retreat. It swiftly turned into a rout. The Dutch abandoned their equipment and supplies and made for their ships. The Balinese almost succeeded in cutting off their line of retreat and challenged all weary, footsore stragglers to hand-to-hand combat with spear against sword.

That day the Dutch counted 264 dead, including 14 officers. It was small comfort that they thought the Balinese had lost 2,000, including 200 chiefs. From safe sanctuary on shipboard the Dutch petitioned Batavia to send reinforcements, mentioning two battalions of infantry and 1,000 porters. Batavia, instead of complying, ordered the whole forlorn expedition back to Java. There, while conducting an acrimonious inquiry into the reasons for the failure of their second expedition, the Dutch began readying a third.

Bali enjoyed a brief respite which no one expected to last. Mads Lange, who had hoped again to serve as mediator but had found no occasion to do so, returned to Kuta. His business was suffering and he sought to safeguard himself against further losses. George King returned to Lombok. There he counseled the Radja to prepare to intervene in the new disorders which he knew would soon break out. Djilantik flung himself with furious energy into reminding the Balinese radjas and people of their exploits, reminding them also, however, that for being twice worsted, the Dutch were all the less likely to forget and forgo their claims to sovereignty.

Third Expedition (1849); Theatrics of Conciliation

As was now becoming habitual, the Third Dutch Military Expedition against Bali (1849) arrived off Buleleng with the east monsoon (late March). The commander, General A. Michiels, had prudently reconnoitered the whole of the northern coast in mid-November. The General was convinced it would be a quick and decisive campaign and he would soon be back in Java. His fleet had over 100 vessels—heavily armed frigates, steamships, schooners, and scores of large and small auxiliary craft manned in all by some 3,000 sailors. The land forces were made up of 5,000 Dutch and indigenous troops, the the former more numerous than the latter, under command of 187 European officers. There were some 400 pieces of field artillery and 273 horses for the cavalry. There was also a support force of 3,293 coolies.

On March 31, encountering almost no resistance, the Dutch landed 700 men at Sangsit and marched into Buleleng and Singaradja, where the General made his headquarters in the Radja's palace. Within the next several days the rest of the expedition disembarked, still meeting with no opposition. The Balinese had withdrawn to Djagaraga, where they had decided to take their decisive stand. From there they sent emissaries to sound out the Dutch intentions, professing themselves loyal to their pledges and dismayed by Dutch hostility. General Michiels received several messengers and several messages, then announced that he would treat only with the Radja and Djilantik in person. It was arranged, therefore, that the General and the princes should meet on April 4 in the Radja's palace and, said the General, in response to questioning, the princes could bring with them as many of their followers as they saw fit.

On the morning of April 4 the Dutch deployed their troops in full dress uniform in parade formation within and around the palace, on the main street of Singaradja, and out along the road to Djagaraga. At 1:00 p.m. there appeared a small but alert, well-armed party of Balinese, followed at 2:00 p.m. by a force of 3,000 picked warriors. At 3:00 p.m. came the main body of some 9,000 men followed by the Radja of Karangasem and Gusti Ktut Djilantik.

The Balinese troops were dressed in their most splendid costumes, as if prepared not for battle but for the *baris* (warrior dance). They carried themselves haughtily, struck theatrical stances, and fingered their weapons suggestively—many of these weapons obviously being those captured from the Dutch a year before. They eyed the Dutch with suspicion and hostility and were clearly ready on signal from their leaders to rush to attack.

The Radja and Djilantik were especially magnificent in brilliant red sarongs nattily gathered up to display short tight trousers, below and above which gleamed bare, bronze skin. Their waists were nipped in by golden girdles in which, at the back, each displayed a huge jeweled *kris*, the ornate handles extending above shoulder height for quick, dramatic draw. Their thick, flowing black hair was bound by white headcloths in which were inserted, in the case of the Radja, a green sprig, and in the case of Djilantik a crimson flower.

The Radja himself was a slim young man of thirty, aristocratic in face and figure, but not, it seemed to the Dutch observers, an especially decisive or dynamic person, being, in fact, almost without animation or expression. But Djilantik, a striking young man of the same age and build, they described as "a very handsome fellow," with fine oval face, straight, thin nose, piercing eyes, and highly mobile features, obviously a man of fierce passion and courage. One Dutch military historian, writing in French, paid him this tribute: "esprit fécond en ressources, caractère énergique, coeur ardent de patriotisme, un de ces adversaires qu'il est difficile mais glorieux de vaincre."

The princes were accompanied by other royalty and by the high priests, some almost as richly dressed and proud in carriage as were the two chief figures. The Radja of Buleleng was not one of the participants. This time his excuse was that he was much too old and frail to risk the exertion and the excitement. In fact, he deemed it certain misfortune to enter his own palace on sufferance of another.

The encounter, which started as a triumph of Dutch and Balinese showmanship, deteriorated into a miserable failure of statesmanship. The Dutch brusquely reiterated their familiar and expected demands except that this time there was no talk either of reparations or of hostages. The Balinese listened politely and seemed to concur but with no very visible display of conviction, the bare points of their spears signaling to those who knew Balinese custom, as the General and his staff did not, that they remained defiant. The General explained that he expected the Balinese to return to Djagaraga to dismantle their fortifications and prepare for peaceful takeover by the Dutch two days later. The Radja, the prince, and their numerous following staged an impressive processional exit and returned to Djagaraga to reconsolidate their position.

Djagaraga Defense and Dutch Seizure

The next ten days were filled with tentative little maneuvers on the side of both the Dutch and the Balinese. The Dutch were testing out the road to Djagaraga, which proved to be impassable without major effort to remove barriers and subdue forts. The Balinese were trying to determine exactly how willing the Dutch might be either to fight or to compromise. On August 13 there occurred yet another staged encounter between the princes and the intruders. The Balinese once more made a show both of splendor and power, this time with much clearer intimation than before that they were quite prepared to fight to the death. Again they talked of yielding Djagaraga peacefully, but they then retired to the hills not to remove the road blocks but to install more. At Djagaraga itself, as the Dutch had already been advised by informers, the barricades were even more imposing than those in Buleleng in 1846; other fortified positions radiated out from the town in all directions; and a wide flooded trench eight meters deep cut off the approach from the road.

General Michiels decided to attack without further delay. The Dutch troops marched on Djagaraga early in the morning of August 15, overcoming all resistance along the way until they arrived in front of the town itself and its impressive defenses. Within the town Djilantik had massed an army of some 15,000 men, of whom 2–3,000 were armed with rifles and the others with lances 15 to 20 feet in length. After making several costly probing attempts, the General decided not to risk a frontal attack. Instead, during the night, he dispatched a strong detachment of troops on a flanking maneuver. Early the next morning these troops succeeded in breaching the westernmost defense position and entering the town from the rear. At 11 a.m. on August 16 a salvo of 21 cannon shots signaled that the Dutch had seized control of Djagaraga and the Dutch flag was raised over the fortress. But Djilantik, the radjas, and most of the troops made their escape and withdrew in good order in the direction of Karangasem and Klungkung.

The Dutch casualties in the battle for Djagaraga totaled 33 dead and 148 wounded; the Balinese lost thousands. Among the victims, according to some reports, was the wife of Djilantik and a party of high born ladies whom she led in the rite of the *puputan*, advancing in a state of near trance directly into the line of Dutch fire in a deliberate act of self-destruction.

Once again the war had scarcely started before it was suddenly stalemated. The Dutch were neither ready nor willing to risk an overland advance beyond Djagaraga. General Michiels decided to leave garrison forces in Buleleng but to shift the main theater of operations to the south, where he could conduct a campaign against Karangasem and Klungkung in the coastal region without having to run the risk of maintaining long lines of communication from the ships. Direct action against the Dewa Agung, he thought, would result in quick Balinese capitulation. So he ordered the troops back to the transports and the fleet sailed off.

Transfer of Operations to the South; Lombok Intervention

Mads Lange, who had counseled against a wider war, went back to Kuta to prepare for the apparently inevitable spread of violence. The Radja of Badung was already engaged in a conflict with Mengwi, and Lange feared that an injection of Dutch troops into the already incendiary situation in the south could only mean widespread and long-continued disorders. George King returned to Lombok. From the Radja of Lombok the Dutch immediately received assurances that he would gladly provide troops to help the Dutch discipline Karangasem and any other Balinese principalities of their choice. Djilantik circulated from radjadom to radjadom, rallying, or attempting to rally, all Bali to repel the Dutch aggressors. The Radja of Karangasem returned to his palace to deal with long neglected affairs of state which suddenly became enormously complicated by reason of the agents of the Radja of Lombok, who were stirring up insurrection. The Dewa Agung merely waited while others came to his defense.

On May 12 the Dutch fleet reassembled in the bay of Labuan Amok and troops landed at Padang Bai to attack Klungkung and if necessary also Karangasem. Encountering fierce resistance, the Dutch pushed westward along the coast toward the especially strategic and sacred temple town of Kusamba; which, on May 24, they seized and virtually demolished. In this operation they had the very efficient aid of some 4,000 troops from Lombok, whose special function it was to infiltrate the countryside behind the battle lines and create disorders which contributed to the Lombok-inspired insurrection against Karangasem. The Radja himself, despairing at news of the insurrection and of the Kusamba battle, killed his children, his wives, and himself. The Radja of Buleleng and Gusti Ktut Djilantik prepared to

AUX INDES NÉERLANDAISES
Le Rajah de Boeleleng, dans l'île de Bali, se suicide avec quatre cents de ses sujets

A contemporary illustration from the French newspaper *Le Petit Journal* depicting the *puputan* of the Raja of Buleleng.

continue the war from the capital town of Klungkung, which the Dutch were determined to seize.

In Klungkung the Dewa Agung's protectors had assembled a force of some 33,000 men, but their arms were inferior, their defense works were rudimentary, and their chances of victory in any pitched battle were exceedingly dim. But then the Dutch, who seemed on the point of decisive victory, were yet once again betrayed by the tropics. This time it was an epidemic of dysentery which did them in, virtually all of the invaders being seized with the most excruciating cramps of the bowels. Before they had a chance to recover, the Dewa Agung's redoubtable sister, the Dewa Agung Isteri, with her ally, the Radja of Gianjar, staged a surprise nighttime raid on their camp at Kusamba. The Dutch suffered heavy casualties. General Michiels himself was critically wounded and died the next day. Lt. Col. van Swieten, who succeeded to the command, ordered the troops, along with the work coolies, to retreat to the ships. He also petitioned Batavia for reinforcements. What had looked like victory for the Dutch and defeat for the Balinese had suddenly turned into disaster for both. And then, just as suddenly, came mutual reprieve, but not without prior reversals.

The fluctuating fortunes of war were dramatically signaled by the commander of the Lombok forces, who visited Lt. Col. van Swieten on shipboard and displayed to him three especially valuable and significant prizes. The first was the *kris* of the Radja of Karangasem, signifying that the Radja was dead and the kingdom had fallen; the second was the *kris* of the Radja of Buleleng; the third that of Gusti Ktut Djilantik. The Radja of Buleleng and Djilantik had been ambushed by the wily troops from Lombok. The Radja had been killed on the spot; Djilantik, seeing no escape, had taken poison.

Victories, Disasters, and Reversals

With Djilantik and the two Radjas dead, with the Dewa Agung and his surviving protectors deeply grieved and dismayed, the Balinese resistance was in a state of complete disarray. The Dutch, decimated though they were by disease, could scarcely even have blundered into defeat. Lt. Col. van Swieten still hoped, however, to avoid the hazards of battle. On June 1 he was reassured to receive a message from Klungkung stating that the Dewa Agung was prepared to make peace. On June 2 he received similar messages from Mengwi and Gianjar, which had both come openly and vigorously to the defense of Klungkung, thus compensating somewhat for the disasters which had overtaken Buleleng and Karangasem. Then came subsequent messages indicating that the Dewa Agung was willing to make peace only on the unthinkable condition that the Dutch send a mission humbly to ask forgiveness for the desecration of Kusamba. If the Dutch failed to do so—and perhaps even if they did—the Dewa Agung, it seemed, planned not to surrender but to attack. Van Swieten gloomily decided to renew hostilities. On the morning of June 8 he gave the command and the badly depleted and demoralized Dutch forces began a weary march toward Klungkung.

Just when the climactic conflict seemed unavoidable, Mads Lange again emerged as the worker of miracles. Lange had prevailed upon his special friend, the Radja of Badung, who had been threatened with attack from Mengwi, an ally of Klungkung, to persuade the Radja of Tabanan to join him in a bold maneuver. The two Radjas raised a force of 16,000 men and marched into Klungkung. There they negotiated or intimidated or otherwise dissuaded the Dewa Agung and his surviving allies from offering any further resistance. Mads Lange himself had accompanied the Radjas by land. He had dispatched his assistant, L. V. Helms, to travel by sea to inform Colonel van Swieten, who thought Helms and Lange quite mad and disregarded the message. But just as his unwilling troops began their arduous march, van Swieten saw advancing toward them a small contingent of Balinese led by a European. It was Mads Lange and his bodyguard. They had come to report that the main body of the 16,000 Badung-Tabanan troops remained in Klungkung, where, in case of attack, they would fight a holy war in defense of the Dewa Agung, but that the Dewa Agung himself was now willing to make an honorable peace. The Dutch column turned back toward the ships and in due course it was agreed that Klungkung need not be taken.

The Dutch and the Balinese were almost equally happy that hostilities were at an end. Both were disposed to engage at once in the peace-making ceremonies which serve to dispel old animosities. In a grand gesture of reconciliation, the Dutch announced that they would bring in Hertog Bernard von Saksen Weimar Eisenach, the new German commander of the Dutch colonial army, who was in fact already on his way to Bali with the reinforcements which van Swieten had requested. The Dewa Agung and the other radjas were pleased to learn that they were to deal directly with genuine European nobility and the Dewa Agung ordered that the Hertog was to be received as befitted his station. The two sides had little difficulty in agreeing upon the venue of the preliminary peace negotiations. It would be Mads Lange's factory at Kuta. The final solemn formalities, which most of the surviving royalty of the island would attend, would be held, symbolically, at Kusamba.

Peace Conference and Celebration

The negotiations took place July 10–15, with Mads Lange playing the genial and lavish host. He entertained not only the Dutch and the Balinese dignitaries but virtually the whole of the Balinese army— some 20,000 men, according to the estimate of the Dutch, 40,000 according to Helms. This time the Dutch made no attempt to tot up a tradesman-like bill for the invasions. They insisted, to be sure, upon a treaty based upon their own reading of the 1841–1843 contracts with regard to such matters as sovereignty, slavery, and salvage; but they promised not to occupy the kingdoms and not to interfere in internal affairs. They insisted also upon the right to station permanent Dutch representatives in the island, and they dictated certain very significant arrangements with regard to redistribution of territories and reestablishment of royal families. They rewarded Lombok for its wartime collaboration by putting radja-less Karangasem under its rule. To Bangli they gave Buleleng, first detaching Djembrana, recently a Buleleng dependency, and making it a separate kingdom. They rewarded the Radja of Badung merely by giving him a bronze cannon to display in his palace alongside the one he had received from the N.H.M. as the price of his consent to the 1838 compact which led to all subsequent agreements and disagreements. The Dutch were destined to recover custody of both these weapons in 1906, when, as a prelude to the *puputan* in Den Pasar, they seized the Puri Kesiman nearby. In it they discovered two bronze cannons of which nobody, it seemed, knew the origin. One, ornamented with an elaborate Napoleonic N, especially puzzled them. In all probability it was the cannon, already an outmoded relic of the Daendels era, which they had off-loaded onto the Radja as a token of gratitude in 1849.

For the time being at least, the Balinese leaders seemed relatively little concerned about wearisome reformulation of old or new contract concepts which they obviously had no other choice than to accept. They devoted themselves with characteristic enthusiasm, however, to the preparations for the forthcoming ceremonies, which were scheduled for July 5. With the Hertog and many Dutch officers in attendance, also the Radjas of Badung, Bangli, and Gianjar, but not the Dewa Agung, who was quite old and also genuinely ill, the occasion proved almost as splendid and as festive as anyone could have wished. Two weeks earlier the main Dutch expeditionary force had already returned to Java. The Hertog and his entourage soon followed, leaving the Balinese to reorder their badly shaken kingdoms. It was a difficult task which involved the installation of no few new rulers, the redefinition of overlord–vassal relationships, and also, of course, a whole new Balinese–Dutch modus vivendi.

CHAPTER 7

Saga of a Danish Trader
(1834–1856)

Arrival in Lombok of Mads Lange and His Brothers

The Danish trader, Mads Lange, who lived in Kuta from 1839 until 1856 and made his appearance at critical times and places in Balinese history, was fortunate in having sympathetic witnesses and biographers. In the accounts left by these writers, Lange appears as the courageous and loyal friend of the Balinese radjas and people, deliberately cushioning the shock of their early encounters with the outside world. Had the record been less full and factual, Lange might have the reputation today of the betrayer of the Balinese radjas to the Dutch builders of empire.

The best known account of Lange's role in Bali, or, to be more precise, the least unknown, was written by L. V. Helms, a versatile Danish adventurer who served as one of Lange's assistants in the Kuta factory from early April 1847 until June 21, 1848 and made a nostalgic return visit not long after Lange's death in 1856. Helms went on to seek and to find his own later fortunes in Borneo with Rajah Brooke, in California and Australia with the gold miners, and in Lapland as a prospector and speculator in Arctic mineral deposits. He eventually found the leisure in which to write his memoirs, *Pioneering in the Far East* (London, 1882), in which he included several chapters on the life and times of Mads Lange as reflected, naturally, in his own engrossing experiences.

Lange emerges through Helms' reminiscences as a man of enormous energy and agreeable personality. This report is supported by the observations of certain distinguished visitors who enjoyed Lange's generous hospitality for more or less extended periods in his Kuta establishment. Among them were the German philologist R. H. Th. Friederich, the Swiss botanist Z. H. Zollinger, and the Dutch ethnographer Baron van Hoevell, who grouped themselves about Lange as though his factory were a Kuta salon. A popular Danish writer of the early twentieth century, Aage Karaup Nielson, searched out the more readily available records of Mads Lange, inclusive of comments by these guests, and wrote a lively biography, *Leven en Avonturen van een Oostinjevaader op Bali* (Amsterdam, 1828). Nielson's account, which was brought out both in Dutch and in Danish, reached an appreciative Dutch and Danish audience, but it has never, unfortunately, been published in English. Nor has it been published in Indonesian or in Balinese, although the graves of Mads Lange and his brother at Kuta lead people to ask questions which very few can answer.

Lange as *Sjahbandar* and Merchant in Ampenan

As noted in an earlier chapter, Mads Lange (1807–1856) began his South Seas adventures in 1834, when he established a factory (trading post) in Lombok in partnership with Captain John Burd, a Scottish seaman closely associated with the Danish East India Company. Lange's three younger brothers, Hans, Karl Emilius, and Hans Henrik, were junior members of the firm from the first; his nephew, Christian, later joined them. John Burd established business contacts in Singapore, Macao, Canton, Batavia, and later Hong Kong, and on his own ship, *de Zuid*, frequently visited Lombok and later Bali. The younger Lange brothers and the nephew captained some of the growing fleet of sailing vessels which the senior partners acquired. Mads Lange himself became *sjahbandar* (harbor-master, meaning also customs collector, a valuable post for which he paid an annual fee) to the Radja of Karangasem-Lombok; he built a shipyard adjacent to his factory at Tandjung Karang, close to Ampenan town on Ampenan Bay. Soon he became a man of great wealth and influence but vulnerable nevertheless to the whims of Asian rulers. In order to achieve his position he allied himself with Radja Ngurah Lanang, who had recently had to flee from Karangasem-Bali to Karangasem-Lombok to escape retribution for various atrocities, and also with the Radja's sister, the Tjokorda, who actually ruled the kingdom as regent together with an incestuous consort. He associated himself commercially from time to time with George King, an English trader who had recently skipped his debts in Surabaya to settle in Lombok. King aspired to displace and replace Lange as *sjahbandar*, and in order to do so he attached himself to a junior ruler, the Radja of Mataram, who, in turn, aimed to depose and succeed the Tjokorda.

The involuted dynastic rivalries of the Balinese princes of Lombok and the intrigues in which the princes of Bali itself were always eager to share, plus the commercial rivalries of Lange and King, both of whom had arms to sell, signaled certain trouble. War broke out in early 1838 between the radjadoms of Karangasem and Mataram, with King providing the latter with arms, men, and advice, and Lange coming to the aid of the former. The more vigorous new house of Mataram (also of Balinese origin) prevailed over the decadent old house of Karangasem, and King prevailed over Lange, who boarded his yacht *Venus* and sailed off to Bali.

Kuta Factory and Kuta Town in 1839

Arriving in Bali in mid-1839, after five years of exposure to the hazardous life of the trader in the Indies, Lange had just been despoiled of most of his personal property; he was in debt to Chinese merchants in Singapore and Canton for something like 30,000 silver dollars; he had little except his own quite extraordinary experiences and abilities to rely upon as his trading capital. He assumed personal command of a little trading post at Kuta, one which may have been opened by King as early as 1831 and seems for a time to have operated as a King–Lange joint enterprise under the occasional supervision of an Englishmen named Pace from Surabaya. The scale of operations of the Kuta post had formerly been quite minute, but under Lange's personal direction the enterprise suddenly flourished. Lange soon achieved even greater means and influence than before.

In settling at Kuta, Mads Lange gave new impetus both to Balinese trade in general and to the shift of the center of trade from the traditional market of Buleleng in the north to the radjadom of Badung in the south. Radja Kasiman, the ruler of Badung, was much better disposed than were the radjas elsewhere to the establishment of systematic contacts with the outside world. The Dutch themselves had already perceived the possibilities of Radja Kasiman's little port town of Kuta. They had established a factory there in 1826 but had built up no trade and had therefore allowed it to lapse in 1831. They returned in mid-1839, at just the time that Lange was starting up business. The new Dutch venture was as inauspicious as the former, and in 1844 the Dutch were to close it out and to write off a cumulative loss of fl. 172,194.39. By that time Mads Lange had made himself a fortune.

The town of Kuta, so profitless to the Dutch and so productive for the Dane, was (and is) located on an isthmus one to two miles wide and five miles long which connects the southern headlands of Bukit (Dutch Tafelhoek on the older maps) to the Bali mainland. With easy access to sandy beaches and sheltered anchorages both to the east and to the west, Kuta enjoyed a major advantage over the northern port of Buleleng in being accessible from one direction or the other no matter which way the monsoon might be blowing. Given ordinary skill and luck, ships' captains could find passage through the coral reefs and put in reasonably close to shore for loading and offloading. The town itself was built along a small stream, the Dawan, which flowed by 39 leisurely bends into the sea near Tuban and was navigable at high tide to small boats. On the edge of Kuta town and on the bank of the stream was located the original factory which Lange expanded into a large compound filled with storerooms and living quarters.

The Kuta site was favorable to trade but the town itself had an evil reputation. It was thought to be populated almost exclusively by scoundrels and ruffians and to be conducive not only to death by violence but to almost equally lethal chills and fevers. Whether guided by knowledge or instinct, Mads Lange chose a well-drained site for his factory and worked such far-reaching improvements that his frequent visitors never echoed the complaints of the early traders that the spot was all but uninhabitable. He also established cordial relations with the townspeople, who seem either to have been grossly maligned by earlier visitors or to have changed quite recently and rapidly for the better. Dutch restraints upon the traditional practices of piracy and slavery may have exerted a tranquilizing influence.

The nearby Bukit peninsula, just south of Kuta, with its high sea cliffs and its dangerous coral reefs, had played the natural role in times past of luring and wrecking incautious seafarers. The people of Kuta, acting upon the belief that whatever the seas cast up was for them to take possession of for themselves, their rulers, and the gods, had made a good thing of the frequent shipwrecks. The Kuta market, in which looted cargo and enslaved sailors were often put up for sale, was also the market in which the radjas themselves could conveniently and profitably dispose of such worrisome persons as criminals and paupers, who might make good slaves. The buyers were Chinese and Bugis dealers, who gladly paid fl. 100–150 per head, the handsome and accomplished Balinese being much in demand in overseas markets. Prospering as it did on looting and slavery, Kuta had become the home of various unamiable characters, the most infamous of whom was Gusti Ngurah Ktut, the ruling local prince. Gusti Ktut's personal 40-man gang terrorized local residents and visitors alike, but not quite to the extent of inhibiting the growth of the town. At the time that Mads Lange arrived, Kuta had a population of several thousand persons, including local fishermen (100 families), Chinese and Bugis dealers in slaves, opium, and other merchandise (30 families each), and assorted Balinese refugees and renegades who had found it expedient to vanish from other island kingdoms and resettle in Badung.

Radja Kasiman and the Badung Dynasty

The town and the district of Kuta, which the widely detested Gusti Ngurah Ktut ruled as local overlord, was part of the rich rice growing state of Badung, over which ruled Radja Kasiman. When Lange first encountered him in 1839, Radja Kasiman was already a venerable white-haired gentleman of fifty who had been ruler for the past ten years and was destined to remain on the throne until 1861. He was the son of Gusti Ngurah Made Pametjutan, the founder of the modern radjadom of Badung. Gusti Pametjutan had thrown off the overlordship of Mengwi, conquered Djembrana, and made himself the first radja of the south whom the more warlike Radjas of Buleleng and Karangasem respected and feared. His exploits in building his kingdom—and in building his family, which consisted of 500 wives who bore him 800 sons and uncounted daughters—were commonly attributed to his possession of a marvelously potent magical *kris*. His *kris* did not protect him from one of his own sons, to whom he forfeited the throne in 1810; nor did it preserve the successor, who died in 1813, or endow another of his sons, Radja Kasiman, with sexual prowess to match his politics. For all of his own 80 wives, Radja Kasiman, to his great grief, fathered only one child, and that not a son but a daughter.

Radja Kasiman, as Lange knew him, was a benign and jovial old autocrat, six feet tall and heavy set, who bore himself regally on state occasions but could relax happily over food, wine, music, and dancing, and was especially given to collecting firearms, not for battle but for display, or possibly as fetishes. But Radja Kasiman, who sometimes seemed a little simple-minded and in the late 1850s became childish, could be both crafty and cruel, as his earlier record quite plainly showed. Upon the death of his father, Radja Ngurah Made Pametjutan, who had greatly confused matters by fathering so many sons and assigning them small semi-autonomous regions to rule, the radjadom-proper passed to his eldest son, who died in 1813, leaving the kingdom to be disputed by many claimants, among whom Radja Kasiman eventually prevailed. Radja Ngurah's second successor was a young prince, Gusti Gde Pametjutan, who died in 1817 and was followed by his sister's son, Gusti Ngurah Pametjutan, a very weak and short-lived ruler. It was widely believed in Badung that the untimely demise of these two rulers was not unrelated to Kasiman's own aspirations to the throne and that he had quite certainly supplied the second with excessive quantities of opium. He had further strengthened his own position by marrying the widow of another of the princes, whose claim to the throne was stronger than his own and whose death occurred under suspicious circumstances. The widow, a strong-willed woman who preferred to enter Kasiman's harem rather than perform the rite of suttee, was eager to gain status as a radja's consort. When the next radja, the son of Gusti Ngurah Pametjutan, also conveniently died, Kasiman possessed himself of the sacred royal regalia, without which the heir apparent could not establish his legitimacy but with which Kasiman could and did successfully demand that the priests proclaim him radja. Nevertheless, Radja Kasiman ruled over only about 6,000 of the 10,000 households of the radjadom, the others remaining under the control of some 15 minor princes, one of them his nephew, the infamous Gusti Ngurah Ktut of Kuta. These quarrelsome princes came together occasionally in royal council, which, for some 30 years, Kasiman successfully steered.

This annotated royal genealogy goes to show that in resettling himself at Kuta, Lange required all of the acute political and commercial instinct which he had had an opportunity to develop in Lombok. He was to deal with the devious Radja of Badung as he had previously had to deal with the dubious Radja of Karangasem-Lombok, and at the same time he had to cope with the N.H.M., a business rival much more formidable than George King. The Radja and the Dane seem to have developed mutual affection and confidence, and the N.H.M., after competing with Lange, was soon to co-opt him as its own agent. The Radja, who may well have mellowed with years and profited—or suffered—from Lange's guidance, played a conciliatory rather than an inflammatory role in the Balinese–Dutch conflict which soon ensued after he granted trade and other privileges to the Westerners.

Kuta Factory as Home and Trading Post

At Kuta Lange built up his new factory as a commercial and residential complex placed in a spacious Balinese-style compound surrounded by high walls and approached through an ornamental stone gateway. Just inside the gate were installed brass cannon—not for protection, but for signaling ships. Several large *pendopo* (open pillared halls) provided public rooms and offices, and many little *bale* (closed pavilions) served as private quarters for the staff. The resident and transient population of the factory came to number at least one hundred persons. It included Lange himself, his brothers, visiting ships' captains, his English doctor, his wives (one Chinese, one Balinese), and his numerous retinue of servants and slaves. Much to the amazement and gratification of visitors, some of whom stayed for months as Lange's pampered guests, the establishment manifested some of the aspects of a gentlemen's club in the West. One of the *pendopo* served as a music room where staff and the visitors might be called upon in the evening to perform. Mads Lange himself played the violin, one of his brothers the flute, another the cello, and the third the piano. Resident talent was not lacking and musically inclined visitors received and earned an especially cordial welcome. Lange also had a billiards room and somewhere, above or below ground, a cellar well stocked with European wines and liquors as well as other drinks, among them the very agreeable Balinese *berum* and *arak*. Cooks trained in Balinese, Chinese, and European cuisine prepared a memorable table, for which fish, flesh, and fowl, fruits, vegetables, and spices were all abundantly available. A visit to Lange's factory was a revelation with regard to the degree of refinement and luxury to which a European in the East could then aspire.

The factory was as well arranged for efficient business as for gracious living. Certain of the *pendopo* served as market halls where imported goods and local produce could be displayed and sold. Beyond the *pendopo* were warehouses in which could be stored many hundreds of tons of rice and great quantities of other goods. Alongside the warehouses was an oil press, especially imported at great cost from Europe, for the extraction of coconut oil intended both for local sale and for export. Outside the compound were pens for cattle, pigs, and poultry. Beyond were rich farm lands, which Lange himself gradually acquired in order to produce rice and coconuts to augment his purchases. Stretching both eastward and westward from the compound to the seashore ran roadways, over which Lange traveled in style in a fine carriage. It was the only such vehicle on the island, and it was drawn by high-stepping Makassar horses which dwarfed the ponies of the Balinese. Inevitably Lange came to invite comparison with certain other White Radjas—naturally, with George King, the new White Radja of Lombok, but also with the great Rajah Brooke of Sarawak. Their impact upon the East, like the impact of the East upon them, served in still not especially well-understood ways to illustrate the Victorian concept of the white man's burden.

Riches from Rice, Gambier, *Kopeng,* and Ships Servicing

Lange's business was built originally on rice. The Balinese produced high quality rice in such superabundance that the grain sold on the local market for no more than one half of what it would fetch in Java, Singapore, or China. Lange exported rice in 1,000 ton quantities and on the quick, easy profits of rice he built up a commercial fleet of a dozen or more schooners, brigs, and barks which the brothers and various other Westerners captained. To pay for the rice he imported whole shiploads of commodities for which the Balinese demand seemed insatiable, especially gambier from Singapore and Chinese coins.

The gambier was intended for use with betel nut. In Lange's day and much later, Balinese men, women, and older children were almost universally addicted to betel chewing, a practice which did nothing to enhance their physical appearance or the general surroundings. The plug of betel, which was chewed with lime and gambier to soften the nut and bring out the flavor, distorted the lips and jaw and stained the teeth. The red spittle dyed the ground around about all the homes and market places. Betel nut, which possesses mild narcotic qualities, was no doubt less harmful and expensive than the opium which the wealthy Balinese also fancied. A case can be made for betel as somewhat preferable to marijuana, which was also known and used. But the practice of betel chewing, which never had much to recommend it, did not begin to die out until long after Lange's time.

The Chinese coins which Lange imported along with gambier served purposes which were at once utilitarian and aesthetic. Stamped with Chinese characters, perforated with a square hole which permitted them to be strung into convenient loops of several hundred each, these brass coins—then and now widely known as *kopeng* or "cash"—constituted Bali's basic currency. Commodity prices might be quoted in the market place in Indian rupees, Dutch rijksdaalder, or Singapore dollars, but cash transactions were generally in "cash" and it was sometimes a matter of nearly equivalent weights of coins and purchases. According to Helms, Lange bought "cash" in China at the rate of 1,400 to the Singapore dollar and sold them in Bali at the rate of 700 to 1, thus realizing a neat 100 per cent net on the transaction. Greatly increasing quantities of these "cash" were absorbed by the Balinese market, which was just then moving out of the long sustained barter phase. Because of their intrinsic and ornamental value, the coins were also used in preparation of many of the offerings which were taken on all festive occasions to the palaces and the temples. *Kopeng* therefore became an important element in certain Balinese arts and crafts. In constituting himself the principal supplier, Lange made himself in effect both the national banker and a leading patron of the arts.

Mads Lange's specialization in rice, gambier, and *kopeng* did not deter him from dealing in any other commodity in which he might make a profit, and in Bali the opportunities were dazzling. Lange imported English and Indian textiles; Western firearms of all descriptions and the bullets, lead, and powder to keep them functioning; porcelains—particularly celadons—and silks from China. It must be mentioned also that he brought in opium from Calcutta and Singapore, some of it for local consumption, much of it to be smuggled over to Java in contravention of the Dutch monopoly. On behalf of the radjas, always his best local customers, Lange held himself ready to undertake special commissions. These included the acquisition of precious stones, Chinese and Western medicines, and various novelties and curiosities such as European clocks and chandeliers, engravings and paintings.

Lange's purchases in Bali for his own account or on behalf of the captains of trading and whaling vessels, for whom he served as comprador, included the full range of local products. He acquired large quantities of cattle, pigs, dried meat, hides, ducks, chickens, coffee, tea, sugar, coconuts, tobacco, fruits, and vegetables, much of which went to provision ships' crews and the rest to be sold on the Singapore market. He bought these commodities from Balinese traders, mainly from certain extremely enterprising females. These ladies, some of them from the royal families, handled most of the market goods, the men deigning to deal only in rice or cattle. On signal from Lange that he needed supplies for a whaler or a trading ship, the women would converge upon Kuta with processions of ox carts and pack trains of ponies, fetching him—all neatly done up in wicker baskets—live pigs and fowls, fresh fruits and vegetables, and whatever else they might wish to offer for sale. Lange would often buy much more than he actually needed at the moment, for he was reluctant to disappoint these cheerful tradeswomen. He knew that he had only to wait a few days for another ship's captain to call for cargo and provisions.

At the peak of his career in the mid-1840s, Lange's factory at Kuta was doing a million guilders' worth of business per year with Java

alone. The trade with Singapore and China must have been even greater. Lange's own fleet of ships, some in the 800–1,500 ton range, came
to number between 10 and 15, all very profitably employed. His favorite craft, the *Venus*, served him as a yacht for his frequent trips to
East Java and various coastal towns of Bali where he maintained
warehouses.

N.H.M. Competition and Concession of Defeat

During his early days at Kuta, while his operations were still tentative, Lange was kept under close scrutiny by the Dutch, who also
provided him with what might have seemed like almost prohibitive
competition. Heer Schuurman, the agent for N.H.M., together with
one or two Dutch assistants, set out to monopolize the Bali trade; but
the radjas preferred always to deal with Lange, as did the common
people. The Balinese preference was so unanimous that the Dutch
were convinced at first that Lange was using his influence with his
special friend, the Radja of Badung, to effect a boycott of their interests. But then, after an interval of regarding him as a dangerous
and unscrupulous competitor, they decided that he might better be
treated as a useful partner. Schuurman began to make regular recom-
mendation to Batavia that rather than compete with Lange at Kuta,
the N.H.M. would be better advised to appoint him as its own commercial agent.

Schuurman's own mode of life and manner of doing business
sharply pointed up the contrast between the Dane and the Dutch.
Lange chose to build in the Balinese manner and to make his factory
and himself easily accessible. Schuurman put up a solid Dutch-style
building surrounded by forbiddingly thick, high walls on which he
mounted a row of cannon so conspicuous that the Balinese found it
difficult to believe he intended to use them, as Lange did his, merely
for signaling. Schuurman and his assistants deported themselves as
though they anticipated siege rather than trade and for months at a
time lived lonely, morose lives, isolated from Bali and the Balinese.
Just how much Schuurman's personal distaste for Bali influenced his
views regarding prospects for Dutch trade and the reliability of his
Danish competitor as potential colleague it is impossible to determine. But his recommendations carried weight with Batavia. In 1844

the N.H.M. wrote off its heavy losses (for which it was to be compensated by the government), closed down its Kuta factory (which Lange bought for the bargain price of fl. 3,095.83), ordered the staff back to Java, and appointed Lange to represent it. Already in 1843, for services performed or anticipated, the Batavia government had granted him *burger rechts* (right of residence). In 1849 The Hague conferred the Order of the Netherlands Lion upon him in appreciation for his services during the Dutch–Balinese wars of 1846, 1848, and 1849.

Lange's Political Role; His Later Years and Death

The decade of 1839–1849, in the course of which Lange built up his business success at Kuta and his reputation as a peacemaker acceptable to both sides in the Dutch–Balinese wars, was the period of his greatest prosperity and influence. After 1849 his career went into gradual decline, a circumstance which reflected deteriorating conditions in Bali itself and the uncertain and unhappy state of his friends, the radjas. After the war and the peace of 1849 Bali did not enjoy the prosperity and progress which the beginnings of the process of modernization might have been assumed to bring. Distressing new trends were readily discernible in the market place, and Lange was one of the first to feel the effects.

Lange had expected that the end of the wars and the lifting of the partial Dutch blockade would result in the quick revival of agricultural production and commercial activity. His expectations were swiftly and bitterly disappointed. Bali experienced a series of droughts and bad harvests—sure omens of divine displeasure. Produce was far from plentiful, and people murmured that worse was yet to come. Rather than exporting rice in the same huge quantities as before, Lange found it necessary at times to import from Lombok in order to satisfy Bali's own requirements. He took less profit or pleasure in such a trade. The royal courts, furthermore, were not soon again in a position to make lavish outlay on ceremonies and on the luxury goods which royal pomp required. It was clear that the day of the independent or semi-independent Western trader was passing. With the appearance of the steamship, the big Batavian concerns became even more aggressively monopolistic than before, and only the Chinese, with their clan loyalty and organization, were really able to compete.

Even Lange's ship provisioning service very sharply declined. The whalers, which had come to be his best customers, were now following the whales into other and distant waters. And even though he was only in his early forties, Lange was beginning to show the strains of an extremely eventful life.

The true spirit of Mads Lange, just as his powers passed their peak, comes through best in the affectionate description by Helms:

> The protracted blockade which [the Dutch] had maintained during their languid operations against the Balinese had destroyed the trade of the island, and caused him losses which he never recovered. He could not adapt himself to the altered circumstances in which the Dutch expeditions had left him; and he was not the man to retrieve his position by long continued thrift and prudence. There was more of the bold Viking than the prudent trader in his nature. He delighted in tossing about in a gale in his little yacht, the "Venus," which he loved as though it were a living thing. He knew every rope and spar in his considerable fleet, and no laggard captain would return from a needlessly protracted voyage with impunity. He delighted in overcoming all difficulties save those of commercial life. He was not a skillful rider, yet so bold a one, that I have seen him break in obstinate and vicious horses by sheer force of will. He was a power in the country, and the Balinese feared, yet liked and admired him, and, in truth, though severe, he was generous even to a fault, and loyal to his trust, without thinking of the consequences to himself.

In the early 1850s, Lange toyed with the idea of revisiting Denmark. He had not seen his native country since 1833, but he had relatives and friends with whom he had kept occasionally in touch, including a childhood sweetheart whom he may all along have intended eventually to marry. With thoughts of return in mind he built and outfitted a new brig, planning to load it with local produce and to captain it himself on the voyage to Europe. But he delayed too long. On May 13,1856, he died. He had just written but not yet dispatched a farewell letter to his longtime friend, the Radja of Tabanan.

This letter, inscribed on *lontar* (strips of palm leaf) in the Malay language in Balinese script, was carried to Denmark by one of his ship captains and turned up eventually in the National Museum along with various specimens of Balinese arts and artifacts which also came directly or indirectly from Lange. It is a touching document:

> In several days I shall undertake the journey to my homeland. Since I do not feel well, I cannot take my farewell in person but rather in this manner. I find it difficult to speak of all that my eyes have seen but there is no one in Bali to whom my feelings are as well known as to the King. Of my return I cannot speak. The King shall have news of me from the other side of the earth. As the King will be so good as to have his royal name engraved upon a goblet and send it to me. As I have always in all that I have done been my brother's friend, so shall I always live.

Subsequent Fortunes of Factory and Family

Lange's sudden death, at age 49, gave rise to reports, as was inevitable given the time and the place, that he had been poisoned and that good fortune had deserted his heretofore remarkably lucky establishment. The latter part of the report was confirmed by immediately subsequent events. The factory passed to his brother, Hans, who was not especially gifted in commerce and survived him by only a year or two. On Hans' death it passed to the nephew, Christian, who quarreled with the Balinese rulers and had little knack for dealing with ships' captains. The property began to look badly run down, the oil mill was abandoned, and trading activities languished. Christian had brought out a bride from Denmark just about a year before Mads Lange's death; there had been much celebration when she bore him a child; and Mads Lange had dreamed of establishing a family concern which would last for generations. But two of his brothers had preceded him in death—one in a distant shipwreck, the other drowned in the surf before his eyes on return to Bali after a long voyage. Now both Mads and Hans were buried in adjoining graves in a coconut grove not far distant from the factory. Christian decided to abandon the enterprise, including the lands and buildings, to which he could convey no clear title. He sold what goods he could, loaded all other portable belongings, his wife, and his child onto his one remaining ship, and sailed off to Denmark, where, in 1872, he died.

Several of the local princes and some of the Kuta Chinese competed to acquire possession of the factory, the rice fields, and the coconut groves which Mads Lange had built or acquired. Theoretically, any abandoned property fell to the radja; but a crafty Chinese, Lauw Ho Sen, persuaded Radja Kasiman's successor that the Lange property would bring him bad luck and he himself assumed the proprietorship. Gradually the property was divided and passed into other hands. But the graves of Mads and Hans were faithfully maintained by another Chinese, Ong Po Hien, who seems to have been a business associate of Lange's and also—to introduce the long delayed element of romance—a relative of Lange's Chinese wife.

In the course of his 17 years in Bali, Mads Lange took two wives, one Balinese, one Chinese, but very little is known about either. By the Balinese wife, who may have been the first and certainly preceded Lange in death, he had two sons. The first, William Peter, died as a child in Singapore, where he had evidently been sent to school. The second, Andreas Emil (later known as Henrik) was also sent to study in Singapore at Raffles Institution; he remained abroad after his father's death save for one quick trip back to Bali in 1906 in an unsuccessful effort to claim his father's property. By his Chinese wife, Teh Sang Nio, who survived him and inherited a comfortable home in Banjuwangi, Java, Lange had a daughter, Cecilia Catherina. Cecilia was educated in a Singapore convent and remained abroad after her father's death, making one trip back to Bali in 1859 to visit his grave. Lange attempted to make long-term financial provision for his children, leaving each of them fl. 10,000 by an early will (fl. 7,000 in a later one), but his will was never honored. Christian neglected to share the proceeds with his cousins when he sold off the remaining possessions in Bali and set out for Europe.

Andreas Emil (or Henrik) was somehow able to complete his education in Singapore, and he found employment (perhaps through L. V. Helms) which was at once most implausible and most appropriate. He went to Borneo to work with Rajah Brooke of Sarawak. In Sarawak he married a local girl, who eventually bore him nine children.

The family presently backtracked from Sarawak to Singapore, where descendants still live, but never, save for the one disappointing trip of the father, did any of the family return to the island of Bali. If Andreas Emil's destiny was dramatically fitting, Cecilia's was sensational: she became the Sultana of the important Malay state of Johore.

After her father's death, Cecilia was befriended by an English family, who took her to live for a time in India, then to England and France, and later brought her back to the East. On her return to Singapore, where she attended school in a convent, she met Abu Bakar, the Sultan of Johore, who fell in love with her and after an impetuous courtship made her his Sultana. Since Sultan Abu Bakar, unlike his peers, remained officially monogamous, the Sultana Cecilia enjoyed an especially honored position in his court. She eventually bore him two children: a daughter, who was to become the first wife of the Sultan of Pahang; and a son who was to succeed his father (d. 1895) and rule in Johore as Sultan Ibrahim.

A man of most extraordinary vitality, Sultan Ibrahim constantly amazed and shocked the conservative colonial British by behavior which they deemed outrageous. He gave almost equally grave affront, for instance, by denying the colonial officials the use of the palace golf links and by taking many wives and mistresses, European women among them in both categories, including a certain British woman in Singapore and his official Sultana, a Hungarian. Sultan Ibrahim was an avid sportsman, an indefatigable hunter of tigers, leopards, and elephants. He was also a shrewd businessman who built up a vast fortune in rubber plantations and other enterprises. Despite British disapproval of what would now be termed his life style, which caused them to put a 6:00 p.m. curfew on his visits to Singapore, Sultan Ibrahim was an Anglophile. He presented the British Royal Family with valuable gifts and the Royal Navy with warships to help, naturally, in the defense of his own prosperous little state, which was overrun nevertheless by the Japanese. He even forgave such affronts as the postwar occupation of his favorite palaces in Singapore and Johore by the British High Commissioner—from his point of view, a squatter on royal domain.

Sultan Ibrahim, in short, was a feudal aristocrat in the grand tradition, a ruler who seemed in many respects closely akin to the Balinese radjas of his grandfather's day, yet a progressive cosmopolitan. When he died in London in 1959 he was genuinely mourned both by his Malay subjects and his British associates. His European, Chinese, and Malay heritage combined to make him one of the commanding figures of early twentieth century Southeast Asian history.

The dowager Sultana, née Cecilia Catherina Lange, lived on in a secluded palace in Johore until about the year 1930, rarely appearing in public but occasionally receiving a European visitor. On one occasion, she was called upon by her father's Danish biographer, Mr. Nielson. The Sultana, said Nielson, was an animated little lady with white hair, blue eyes, and aristocratic features, who reminisced happily about her father and her childhood in Bali. She remembered a little Danish and sang for him several of the songs which the brothers Lange had sung in Kuta. She had already had his book about her father translated into English for her personal pleasure and she supplied certain supplementary information regarding, for instance, the shabby treatment she had received from her cousin Christian.

The visitor to Bali today can still find the Lange graves and the site of the Lange factory at the edge of the town of Kuta. The villagers who live in the neighborhood respond at once to the mention of the name of Tuan Lange, and guide any inquirer to the deserted spot on the river bank where the factory once stood. Until a few years ago the rusting skeleton of Lange's coconut oil press still remained intact, but recently it has been cut up and sold as scrap. On the adjacent property is a small lime kiln, and just in front of it stands a Chinese temple. The larger and more elaborate of the two Chinese temples of the island—the other is at Singaradja—it is a reminder that Kuta is still an important center of Bali's Chinese community. Kuta also serves as the home of a few score international hippies, who have imported their ugly life style to the splendid sandy crescent of Kuta Beach. That these wan apostles of latter day savagery should have selected the same point of penetration as did the early merchants need not signify equally lasting impact. Fortunately they are not drivers but drifters.

CHAPTER 8

Evolution of the Colonial Empire (1849–1900)

Resident and Controleurs; Regent and *Punggawa*

As a result of the military expeditions of 1846, 1848, and 1849, and of certain subsequent disorders, in 1854 the Dutch began to exercise a rapidly increasing degree of direct control over northern Bali and to interfere more and more frequently and vigorously in Balinese domestic affairs. In the 1849 peace settlement, they placed big Buleleng under the rule of little Bangli and isolated Djembrana under a new radja whose claim to the throne was obscure. These arrangements could not and did not last. In 1854 Buleleng rebelled against Bangli, whose radja appealed to Batavia for help. The Dutch assumed direct control and Buleleng became the first of the Balinese principalities to fall under overt Dutch administration. In 1855 the Radja of Djembrana, finding himself quite unable to assert his presumed authority, relinquished that kingdom also to the Dutch. In the case of both Buleleng and Djembrana the Dutch adopted the administrative device which they had found to be effective in Java. They appointed a member of the royal family as regent and assigned him a Dutch Controleur who, as the title clearly implied, controlled both the regent and the kingdom. Thus, as of the mid-1850s, the Dutch found themselves in the position of actually beginning to exercise the sovereign power which they had long claimed, or at least they were openly exercising it over northern and western Bali. Half a century later they ruled the entire island.

Patterns of Dutch Rule and Its Extension

The transfer of authority from the traditional rulers to the colonial officials was gradual but conclusive. The ceremonial investiture of a new regent or of a radja as regent, accompanied by his formal re-affirmation of existing treaty terms and perhaps acceptance of new ones, made it unmistakably clear that he ruled thereafter as much by Dutch sanction as by destiny. To assist each regent, or, more precise-ly, to guide and direct him, there was always the Controleur, a man of many departmental trades who was sometimes amazingly accom-plished and effective. Presently there were assistants to the Resident and the Controleurs, who also exercised de facto authority over the indigenous *punggawa*, or district heads, technically the subordinates of the regents. Thus there developed an interlocking Dutch–Balinese administrative bureaucracy which eventually worked out remarkably well. Resident and Controleur, Radja-Regent and *punggawa* made up the composite constellation of dignitaries by whom and about whom Balinese affairs were ordered.

The colonial administration in Bali remained centered in the port town of Buleleng and the adjoining royal capital of Singaradja, with Sub-Regency offices after 1906 in Den Pasar in the south. The first resident Dutch official was Heer P. L. van Bloemen Waanders, who, like certain of his successors, was to become a serious and sympathet-ic student of Balinese life and customs. Bloemen Waanders settled in Buleleng in 1855 with the rank of Controleur as the administra-tive subordinate of the Resident of Banjuwangi under whose juris-diction fell both Bali and Lombok. His counterpart for Djembrana, Controleur Schalk, arrived in 1856. In 1860 Bloemen Waanders was promoted to rank of Assistant Resident (still assigned technically to Banjuwangi), provided with one assistant as Controleur, and given responsibility not only for administering Buleleng and overseeing Djembrana but also for observing and reporting developments in all other parts of the island. In 1882, Bali, together with Lombok, was constituted a separate Residency with headquarters in Buleleng and varying degrees of control over the various radjadoms.

The expansion of the Dutch colonial service and the definition and extension of its functions proceeded by logical stages. In 1861–62 Batavia drew up an elaborate set of regulations to guide all routine administrative practices; in 1875 it announced new regency procedures (the same as those to be applied thereafter to all other Dutch-ruled areas). In 1894 Karangasem (and all of Lombok) was added to the list of kingdoms under overt but indirect Dutch rule; in 1900, Gianjar; in 1906, Badung and Tabanan; and in 1908, Bangli and Klungkung. The Dutch official presence remained inconspicuous throughout this entire period, never totaling more than a score of persons. But peripatetic officials from Buleleng made regular rounds of observation and inspection throughout the island and wrote regular reports to the Resident. Even though they had no official function within a state until it had been formally constituted a Regency within the Residency, they nevertheless offered advice which the radjas generally found it prudent to accept.

Western Studies of Balinese Institutions

After the difficulties of the first few years had been overcome and the Dutch and the Balinese had made certain basic accommodations to each other, for the northern states of Buleleng and Djembrana the latter part of the nineteenth century was a period of reasonably peaceful and satisfactory development. In assuming control of a land and a people about whom they had as yet very little knowledge, the Dutch themselves were gravely handicapped. Fortunately, however, the early officials were men of wide ranging interest and inquiring intelligence and some became serious scholars. They were able to rely for guidance on the work of R. Friederich, a German Sanskrit scholar who had been sent out in the 1840s to make a study of Bali on behalf of the Batavia Society of Arts and Sciences. Friederich's pioneering effort (published in 1849–50 in a learned journal) gave a remarkably detailed report on the radjas and the radjadoms, the religion and culture, the manners and customs of the people, serving in fact as a basic work of reference. To complement it Controleur Bloemen Waanders published a series of reports with regard to his own investigations of local administration, taxation, agriculture, trade and commerce, and his discerning observations in the course of his official travels throughout the island. Van Eck, the pioneer Christian missionary, gave up evangelism for social and cultural research, producing and publishing a series of sketches which illuminated both the more and the

Gusti Ktut Djilantik, Radja of Buleleng, north Bali, with his scribe, 1865.

less esoteric aspects of Balinese life. Controleur Liefrinck studied and explained the complex system of land rights and the historic circumstances of Dutch colonial penetration. H. Neubronner van der Tuuk produced a basic dictionary and translated important chronicles. There were perhaps half a dozen others of major importance, coming mainly later in the century, but these were the first great names of Balinese scholarship, which has not, in fact, been greatly supplemented since their time on the subjects on which they

Two state priests of Buleleng: Padanda Ida Gede Made Gunung and Padanda Ida Gede Wayan Buruan, 1865.

worked. Nor, unfortunately, have their works been collated, translated (except for Friederich's), or even very much remembered.

The first Dutch officials to live and work in Bali thus had much to learn from their own experiences and mistakes. One of the most difficult lessons they had to master was how to select and supervise the Balinese officials to whom they had to entrust most of the routine. In the early years they made a series of serious blunders. One regent after another had to be removed, exiled, and replaced. The Dutch

Gusti Ktut Djilantik, Radja of Buleleng, north Bali, with one of his daughters and a slave, 1873.

sometimes found it expedient therefore to designate a provisional regent, promising him eventual regent status as reward for good be-havior. Or they operated through a state council of whom the leader was given the less elevated rank of *Patih* (Chief Minister) and thus,

Two daughters of the Radja of Buleleng, north Bali, 1873. They are wearing traditional royal dress: hand-loomed textiles complemented by gold jewelry.

they hoped, less lofty pretensions. For a long period of years both Buleleng and Djembrana were both radjaless and regentless (Buleleng: 1872–1882; Djembrana: 1856–1882), the Dutch themselves assuming open responsibility for more and more state affairs. If regents and provisional regents and even *patih* were worrisome, so too were the *punggawa*, who quarreled with one another, conspired against the regent, and kept testing just how far they dared go in defiance even of the Dutch. It took two decades for a stable modus vivendi to work itself out. Meanwhile the population of Balinese royalty living in exile in Java assumed impressive proportions, and the Fourth and Fifth Military Expeditions had to be dispatched to put down two potentially serious little insurrections.

The troubles with the regents actually began, as already noted, with the failure of the Radja of Bangli to designate a suitable official who could or would rule Buleleng to the satisfaction of its people, the Dutch, or himself. The Dutch then designated Gusti Made Djilantik (1851), only to depose him a few years later and ban him from Bali for the numerous offenses of which his own people angrily accused him. They next tried a mere youth, Gusti Ktut Djilantik, appointing him as provisional regent with his own father, Gusti Putu Kbon, as his guardian-counselor. They delayed until 1861 in deciding which, if either, of the two to declare regent with the title also of radja. They then chose the younger man, only to have to depose and exile him in 1872 for his cruel and avaricious oppression of his subjects.

In Djembrana, meanwhile, Gusti Putu Ngurah, whom the Dutch had named regent in 1849, made himself so hated that in 1853 he had to flee to Buleleng. In 1855, to end his conspiracies to regain the throne, the Dutch forced him to abdicate and sent him off to join certain of his compatriots in exile. His son and successor, Gusti Made Pasekan, named merely as *patih* and not as regent, also had to take refuge in Buleleng; the next incumbent, Made Rahi, proved, according to the Dutch Controleur, to have more the mentality of a coolie than that of a radja. He was removed and exiled in 1866.

Njoman Gempol Insurrection; Fourth Military Expedition (1858)

It was the *punggawa* rather than the regents who actually gave the Dutch the most trouble, being farther removed from Dutch scrutiny, more secure in position as semi-hereditary chieftains with loyal village followers, and much disturbed by the changes which were being introduced, especially those which affected their own prestige and their revenues. In the mid-1850s one particular *punggawa*, Njoman Gempol, made himself especially objectionable by spreading reports, whether true or false, of ruthless Dutch exploitation in Java and urging his people to rebel while they still could. The Dutch rushed troops from Java, not even waiting for a military transport but chartering on emergency basis the merchant ship resoundingly and unforgettably named the *Jungheer Meester van der Waf van Puttershoek*. This Fourth Military Expedition (December 10–26, 1858), consisting of 12 officers and 707 infantrymen, swiftly accomplished its mission. It so systematically searched and ransacked the villages in which Gempol's adherents lived that the farmers soon handed over the fugitive *punggawa* in order to be free of the soldiers. He was sentenced, naturally, to exile in Java. Another *punggawa*, Ida Mahe Rai, was then also giving the Dutch too much trouble. He was banned to Java, from whence, in 1864, he returned without permission. Soon he was the leader of a new uprising.

Ida Mahe Rai Insurrection; Fifth Military Expedition (1868)

Ida Mahe Rai was a flamboyant character who made himself a folk hero of Buleleng despite the fact that he quite ruthlessly destroyed friends and foes alike. The hereditary *punggawa* of the prosperous and populous district of Bandjar, he gained early notoriety for his self-indulgence in opium, cockfighting, love-making, and theatrical performances, and later for his murder of a rival in love. When his uncle denounced him for the murder, Ida Mahe Rai charged the uncle with incest and contrived for him to be condemned to death by the great Kerta Court of the Radja-Regent. Ida Mahe Rai also feuded for years with a prominent neighbor, Ida Ktut Anon, his rival for the love of a beautiful young girl whom both sought to kidnap (this being the traditional sportive Balinese preliminary to marriage). His own well practiced techniques, which ensured success, and Anon's rather clumsy failure, served only further to inflame the feud.

The Dutch and the Radja, tiring of Ida Mahe Rai's escapades, exiled him to Java and appointed a new *punggawa* of Bandjar. When this incumbent died and was replaced by Ida Ktut Anon, Ida Mahe Rai returned from exile and devoted himself to stirring up trouble for the *punggawa*, the Radja, and the Dutch. He attracted such a large and powerful band of followers, including the chiefs of four villages and other highly placed persons, that the Assistant Resident and the Regent precipitately departed from Singaradja to solicit advice and assistance in Banjuwangi. During their absence Ida Mahe Rai's supporters attacked Singaradja and assassinated the *Patih*. The Resident himself hurried from Java to Bali and attempted, with no success, to reconcile the conflicting versions of events and the bitterly disputing parties. The case went to the Kerta Court, which found four of Rai's adherents guilty of crimes against the state and sentenced them to 12 years of hard labor. But Ida Mahe Rai himself remained free, ruling in fact in Bandjar like an independent radja. He had driven out Ida Ktut Anon; he had gained the support of the Radja of Bangli; and he had surrounded himself, according to common report, with an army of 2,000 well-armed men who were preparing to attack Singaradja with the intent of expelling both the Dutch and the Balinese authorities and declaring their own leader the new radja.

The Resident assembled and dispatched the Fifth Military Expedition (September 19–November 27,1868). It consisted of 800 men under a certain Major van Heemskerk, a poor second choice as leader, the original head of the expedition having died of cholera just as it was about to set out. Major Heemskerk and his men floundered about rather aimlessly for a full month, badly led and badly supplied. The Major was then replaced by a Colonel de Brabant, who brought with him some 700 reinforcements and made swift work of attacking and subduing the rebellious villages. Ida Mahe Rai and five of his chief associates tried unsuccessfully to find sanctuary in Djembrana and then fled to Mengwi, but not for long. The local population delivered them over to the Dutch who exiled them to Java. The campaign cost the Dutch the lives of two officers and ten soldiers, but there were no serious disorders thereafter in northern Bali.

Bloemen Waanders as Controleur and Observer

The first resident Dutch official in Bali, Heer van Bloemen Waanders, who arrived in Singaradja on August 12, 1855, settled himself rather uncomfortably into a dingy pavilion in a back court of the Radja's *puri*, hung out the Dutch flag, and began to cope as best he could with the problems of a strange land and people. Under Bloemen Waanders and his eventual associates and successors, the northern states of Buleleng and Djembrana began to experience changes of which some at least constituted notable improvements. One of the first official acts of the Dutch, for instance, was to introduce vaccine and vaccinators from Java, where the colonial government had pioneered in the prevention of epidemics. These measures proved so effective that in 1872, when smallpox next struck, Buleleng and Djembrana had few victims, whereas in the southern states the death toll was perhaps 15,000. The Dutch also took steps to stop the practice of suttee, which was formally banned in 1859, and to wipe out slavery. They exercised strict controls over the Kerta Court so that it could no longer hand down sentences of death without the Resident's review and approval; nor could it inflict barbarous punishments, such as maiming and burning alive. They established a Dutch-style court in which Europeans or Chinese would be brought for trial, also such Balinese as committed offenses against the government or its representatives.

Dutch Policy on Slavery, Opium, Land; Residency Finances

In dealing with the very delicate problem of slavery, the Dutch announced that all owners must register their slaves, that they could not thereafter claim ownership of anyone not so registered, that the sale of slaves would be prohibited, and that the slaves themselves had the right to buy their freedom They also undertook to persuade the owners voluntarily to free their slaves, the most effective method of persuasion proving to be for the government to pay compensation. In 1876 there were 60 slaves in Djembrana; in 1878, none. In Buleleng the total in 1876 was 800; by 1885 there remained only 500, whom the government then bought free.

The Dutch officials gave their attention from the very earliest days to the improvement of economic conditions, acting on the dual assumption that a more prosperous people would be a more tractable people and a more prosperous state would be a financial asset rather than a liability to the colonial government. They therefore encouraged the extension of the irrigation system for the improvement of

Slaves on Bali, including one from Papua (right) called "Brit," 1865.

the rice crop, the planting of coffee as a cash crop, and the construction of roads, bridges, and port facilities for the enhancement of trade, commerce, and communications in general, including, of course, official communications. By 1875 northern Bali was already a distinctly profitable colonial enterprise and by 1900 it was paying also for a good part of the administrative expenses of nearby Lombok.

Controleur Bloemen Waanders was largely responsible for putting the state on a paying basis. In an early attempt to analyze its actual and potential revenues, he made the following calculation of the income of the Radja-Regent of Buleleng for the year 1859.

Tax on rice lands	fl. 5,900
Tax on water (for irrigation)	1,500
Trade licenses	4,200
Special levies on imports and exports	20
Tax on coconut trees and gardens	40
Tax on salt making	10
Sale of postage stamps	100
Tax on gambling	430
Tax on cockfights	300
Share of court fines (2/3)	300
Proceeds from sale of property of persons dying without heirs	50
Proceeds from sale of indigent widows, orphans, and other persons impressed into slavery	200
Licenses for dancing girls	600

The Controleur quickly concluded that revenues could be very greatly increased, and in the course of the next few years he proved to be right. He noted the second largest item of revenue—the trade licenses which yielded fl. 4,200. This was the amount paid to the Radja each year by the Chinese *sjahbandar* (harbor-master) and *opiumpachter* (opium monopolist) of the seven port towns for the privilege of levying charges upon imports and exports, by far the most important single item of trade being opium. The annual import of opium into Buleleng came then to approximately 300 chests valued at a total of fl. 450,000, of which the Radja, it seemed, was getting less than one per cent. So the Dutch themselves assumed the responsibility for licensing and controlling the *opiumpachter* and by 1875 the trade was yielding them fl. 217,000. With such sure and sizeable profits from opium, it scarcely seemed necessary to encumber other trade with the assessment of duties. So the Dutch, breaking with their long tradition of monopolistic practices, declared Buleleng a free port. They kept it open even to their formidable rivals, the Singapore merchants, who accounted in fact for at least half of its trade, including almost all of its opium. It was one of the special anomalies of the situation in Buleleng that a good half of the opium which was legally imported under the approving eyes of the Dutch officials was promptly smuggled over to Java, where the Dutch monopoly maintained prices so high that smuggling was well worth the risk.

Bloemen Waanders noted that the largest item in the state revenues was the yield from the tax on rice lands, a tax paid either in cash or in kind on the basis of a certain percentage of each harvest. He began surveying the *sawah*, checking on yield, studying the complicated method whereby the taxes were collected and passed from level to level in the Radja's hierarchy. He decided that the Radja was receiving only a small proportion of the tax which was presumably being collected for him, that many fields were escaping the tax in whole or in part, and that merely by instituting a more efficient and honest method of collection he could greatly increase state revenues. He did, but he himself and his successors probably also increased the percentage to be claimed from the farmers. By the end of the century the Buleleng rice fields—by no means the most extensive or productive—were yielding fl. 150,000 annually in taxes.

Not content with sharply rising revenues from opium and rice, the Dutch instructed the *punggawa* and their agents to count and recount every coconut palm and coffee bush and to assess standardized taxes upon them. They also taxed cockfights and games of chance, making the fees much higher than they had been before, on the assumption, probably known to be fallacious, that this would discourage the frivolous Balinese from trifling away their time and substance when they might be productively laboring in the fields.

Bloemen Waanders calculated Buleleng's imports and exports in 1859 as follows (one picul being approximately 132 pounds):

Exports:

30,000	picul rice	fl. 100,000
700	picul tobacco	34,000
10,000	picul beans	30,000
3,000	picul cotton	19,500
300	picul coconut	7,500
1,500	picul coconut oil	22,500
200	kilograms coffee	36,000
100	cattle	18,000
150	horses	4,500
600	pigs	3,600
	TOTAL	275,600

Imports:

300	chests opium	450,000
700	picul gambier	7,350
420	picul iron	9,250
80	cases cotton goods	20,000
10	picul silk	7,500
Other (including gold)		10,000
	TOTAL	540,100

After 1859 Buleleng trade increased quite rapidly. Allowing for the fact that opium remained by far the single most important article of import, accounting generally for at least two-thirds of the total value, and that at least one-half of this opium was re-exported without being recorded in trade statistics, there remained a consistently large excess of exports over imports even as more and more luxury goods began to be brought in for the wealthy. By 1873 imports totaled fl. 3,414,000 in value (of which fl. 2,101,800 was in opium), and recorded exports fl. 2,034,000. Trading capital in Buleleng rose from fl. 800,000 in 1858 to fl. 11,000,000 in 1874. The government itself lent new impetus to trade by starting a monthly shipping service between Buleleng and Java by the officially subsidized *Indische Stoomvaart-Maatschappij*. In 1874 the Singapore Surabaya–Makassar Line began including Buleleng as a port of call, and in 1876 the *Stoom-vaart-reederij Banda* started regular service to the eastern islands. In the mid-1870s Buleleng was being visited by an average of about 125 European-style vessels each year and some 1,000 local craft.

Christian Missions; Vroom–Nicodemus Tragedy

The ever-increasing contact between Buleleng and the outside world resulted in attempts to introduce Christian missions. There ensued a protracted and highly charged debate over the appropriateness of such intervention in the area of custom and culture, which in the treaties of the 1840s the Dutch had formally undertaken to respect and protect. The debate had started in fact in about 1830; it continued for well over one hundred years with impassioned dispute whether the Balinese were or were not implacably hostile to conversion and whether the Dutch officials were or were not misguidedly paternalistic and indulgent in trying to shelter hedonistic pagans from missionary morality.

The first mission enterprise in Bali began and ended in early 1838, when as a consequence of Dr. Medhurst's report of 1830, a certain Englishman, Rev. Ennis, settled in Buleleng to preach the gospel only to leave forthwith for failure to gain a hearing. The second attempt was in 1865, when the Utrecht Missionary Society sent out Rev. van der Jagt, who experienced the same sense of futility, despaired and departed. In 1866 the Society tried again, this time sending Rev. R. van Eck, a man of many resources. Quickly determining that the exercise of proselytizing among the contentedly Hindu Balinese was likely to be unproductive, he converted himself instead into an authority on Balinese life and thought, diligently studying language, literature, religion, manners, and customs—everything which attracted his interest. But Rev. van Eck did score one soul—a certain Gusti Wajang Nurat Karangasem, to whom he taught the Ten Commandments and the Lord's Prayer and then arbitrarily pronounced him a Christian, conferring upon him the baptismal name of Nicodemus. Gusti Wajang seems in fact to have been a servant in van Eck's home whose curiosity about foreign rites and whose tractability to his master's wishes deterred him from protesting.

Rev. van Eck enthusiastically reported to his sponsors and supporters that he had converted a Balinese prince. If so, said van Eck's later critics, he was a prince unknown to his peers. He elaborated glowingly upon the opportunities for exporting salvation to an island which, like Houtman before him, he rapturously described as "Young Holland." Van Eck's subsequent reports to Utrecht were curiously empty of statistics on conversion but full of learned discourses on the beauty of the island and the wonders of its culture. The Utrecht congregation, much edified but perhaps equally mystified, decided to send two assistants to perform the ecclesiastical chores which, it was feared, this erudite agent might be somewhat neglecting. In due course there arrived a Rev. K. Wiggelendam and a Rev. J. de Vroom, who took up some of Rev. van Eck's duties in Buleleng and moved also into Mengwi. Rev. van Eck himself presently returned to Holland, where he assumed a professorial post in the Royal Military Academy in Breda, lecturing on the Netherlands East Indies and writing learned articles for Dutch journals.

The position of the inadvertent catechumen, Nicodemus, meanwhile, was becoming quite untenable. De Vroom and Wiggelendam, feeling impelled to demonstrate greater evangelical fervor than had their predecessor, but finding themselves unable to match even his modest record of a single convert, concentrated much of their attention upon Nicodemus himself. Nicodemus was caught between two spiritual fires. On the one hand, his new Dutch mentors were admonishing him that all the punishments of hell awaited him if, feeling himself saved, he failed to win other Balinese to the true faith. On the other hand, his own village priests and such relatives and friends as would associate with him at all—for any apostate from Hinduism was automatically rejected as un-Balinese and to all intents and purposes both physically and spiritually dead—were reminding him of the fate of those who ventured into the hereafter without benefit of Hindu rites. His family, they pointed out, would certainly not provide him with cremation, without which he would be reincarnated, if at all, as a serpent or demon. The pressures upon Nicodemus became so intolerable that he attempted to run away. But de Vroom pursued him and either persuaded or forced him to return.

Shortly thereafter Nicodemus once again disappeared, returning, it seems, to his original home in Mengwi.

In early June 1881, Rev. de Vroom was found dead, brutally murdered by unknown assailants. Two household servants—I Klana, a Balinese from Karangasem and Udin, a Javanese from Madura—were suspected of the crime and soon confessed. But the instigator, they said, was Nicodemus, who had paid them 35 pieces of silver and persuaded them to make away with the missionary. His motive, it seems, was to free himself from all ties to an alien faith. Nicodemus himself was apprehended in Mengwi and more or less freely confessed. He was sentenced to be encaged in a bamboo basket and exhibited throughout Buleleng and neighboring radjadoms as a criminal apostate, then to be executed. The shocking fate of the intense Rev. de Vroom and his unbalanced disciple Nicodemus moved the Resident to notify the Utrecht Missionary Society to recall Rev. Wiggelendam at once and to send no replacement.

The de Vroom–Nicodemus tragedy demonstrated to the Dutch administrators very early in the colonial history of Bali the danger inherent in tampering with a well-adjusted social system. This one experience was to a remarkable degree responsible for developing within the Dutch establishment in Buleleng the conviction that if changes were to be introduced they should be initiated only by the competent authorities. In the short term this signified an artificial limitation upon social contacts, corresponding to the economic and political monopoly which always weighed heavily in the Dutch colonial mentality. In the long term it meant the development of a policy of benevolent paternalism which, in the case of the Bali administration, became remarkably enlightened.

CHAPTER 9

Disintegration of the Dewa Agung's Empire (1843–1908)

Patterns of Conflict among States of the South

For the northern states of Bali the latter part of the nineteenth century was a period of not especially easy adjustment to Dutch rule, but on the other hand, except for the brief insurrections of Njoman Gempol and Ida Mahe Rai, one of relative calm. For the southern states it was an era of great turbulence induced by the disintegration of the long declining empire of the Dewa Agung, a process to which the Dutch military expeditions of 1846, 1848, and 1849 gave fatal impetus.

Dewa Agung Gde Putra was old and ill at the time of the wars and lacked either the inclination or the capacity to make more than feeble pretense to past glories. He died in 1849, leaving the throne to Dewa Agung Sakti, his son not by a noble but a commoner wife, the succession thus still further diminishing the much depleted authority of the royal line. Dewa Agung Sakti ruled for only about one year before he too died. Sakti was succeeded by a brother, Dewa Agung Gde Putra, who tried to enhance his position by marrying princesses of Bangli, Mengwi, and Badung. Putra succeeded in reviving the rather tenuous allegiance of Bangli and Mengwi and the tolerance of Badung, but in counting upon the very limited support which they were prepared to offer, he began to play power politics without reliable strength upon which to fall back.

Power, such as it was in Klungkung itself, had long since passed from the male ruler to the female members of the royal household. Dewa Agung Gde Putra's father had been completely dominated by one of his many wives, a formidable princess of Karangasem who had dared even to contrive the murder of a rival, a princess of Badung, and had then boldly defied all accusers, a set of circumstances which had done nothing, naturally, to improve the already badly frayed Klungkung–Badung relations. Dewa Agung Gde Putra's half-sister, the daughter of the infamous Karangasem princess, who had arrogated to herself the title Dewa Agung Istri (a distinction traditionally reserved for the first wife of the ruler) lorded it over the court of her own day. She gained fame as the heroine of one of the great Balinese exploits in the war of 1849, when she planned and led the surprise nighttime attack upon the Dutch camp at Kusamba, a Balinese victory which cost the Dutch many lives, including that of their commanding general. But momentary glory could not disguise the fact that Klungkung was now virtually a matriarchal monarchy, a sure sign to the Balinese that it was both decadent and decayed.

In the 1850s and later, despite his effort to revive dead loyalties by numerous marriages, the Dewa Agung was unable to command much respect, let alone obedience. He could put no more than about 10,000 soldiers into the field, as contrasted with the 25,000 which the neighboring and especially defiant state of Gianjar could at times muster.

Emergence of Gianjar; Quarrels with Its Neighbors

The Radja of Gianjar, whose usual title, that of Dewa Manggis, suggested that he aspired to achieve status comparable to that of the Dewa Agung, proved to be the most disruptive influence of the times in the southern region. The Dewa Manggis seemed almost always to be embroiled in conflict either with his peers of the other radjadoms or else with his own *punggawa*, of whom there were 35, each with aspirations and grievances and conspiracies of his own. The first Dewa Manggis had emerged as ruler of a distinct new state only in the latter part of the eighteenth century, the very fact that his was the newest of the royal houses signifying an abundance—his neighbors thought an excess—of energy and ambition. In his early years he had been the commander of a small 200-man garrison of the vil-

The Radja of Gianyar and his punggawa in the front courtyard of the palace at Gianyar, ca. 1900.

lage of Gianjar, then a mere sub-district under the *punggawa* of Sukawati, one of the most important district heads of the Dewa Agung. He was never much admired by his contemporaries or even by his progeny. According to the report of the German scholar, Dr. Friederich, who collected historical information in Bali (1845–46) from the royal families themselves:

> By deceit, violence, and poison he gained the mastery over those *punggawa*, and conquered from Mengwi to the country of Kramas. On account of his infamous deeds, his poisonings, etc., he is said to have changed after death into a serpent, which was kept for a long time in the palace at Gianjar, but disappeared in the last few years. His success in all his undertakings was probably owing to the fact that he began in a time when Klungkung was defeated by Karang-Assam, and deprived of all power. Gianjar, however, has submitted to the Dewa Agung as the supreme ruler, and sends him numerous presents, which cause him to forget that his nearest relatives are disgracefully oppressed—for the former *punggawa* are still living in Gianjar.

The late nineteenth century descendants of the Dewa Manggis were more amiable by far than their forebears, impressing Dutch visitors always with their cultivated manner and the relative enlightenment of their administration. They were usually preoccupied, nevertheless, with feuds against their neighbors, especially the Dewa Agung. Gianjar's relations with the nearby radjadoms, complicated as they were, provide the clearest thread of continuity in the chain of events in southern Bali between 1840 and 1900, events which were even then opaque to the outside observer and have since been embellished by Balinese fantasy.

Beginning in the 1840s, when south Bali waged several small conflicts of its own before, during, or in between the Dutch military campaigns, the countryside was never altogether at peace. For the most part these conflicts meant only occasional pitched battles involving a few score troops. But numerous little bands of mendicant soldiers constantly roved the landscape, burning, looting, and killing when they met with any opposition to their requisition of provisions, shelter, and valuables. The quarrels between and among the radjas, to whom these freebooters were more or less formally attached, were occasioned by disputes over land and water rights, or collection of tolls on roads and bridges, or runaway slaves, fugitive wives, and broken pledges. Gianjar being the newest of the states, and one created by seizure of land from the others, it became the focus of rancorous claims and counterclaims to legitimate control of its rich *subak*—rice-growing villages lying within a given irrigation system which might draw water from one district for land in another. Gianjar not infrequently found itself pitted simultaneously against all of its neighbors—Klungkung, Bangli, Mengwi, Tabanan, and Badung. It survived only because these states were in turn inimical to one another, Mengwi being generally hostile to Tabanan and Bangli to Badung, so that there emerged at times a rather fragile alliance between Gianjar and any one, two, or even three of its customary enemies.

War on Pajangan (1843); Gianjar Provocation

The chain of circumstances which led to the final upset of equilibrium among the southern states and their complete control by the Dutch began in 1843. The Dewa Manggis then allied himself with nearby Klungkung and Mengwi, also the large northern states of Karangasem and Buleleng, to make war upon Pajangan, a virtually autonomous district of Bangli which was often regarded as a separate radjadom. The ruler of Pajangan, taking advantage of his strategic position across the main route between the north and the south, had been conducting himself quite arrogantly and barbarously. At one point, for instance, he seized six men from Buleleng who had given him some offense, put out their eyes, and left them to fend for themselves in the forest. The Gianjar–Klungkung–Mengwi–Buleleng–Karangasem coalition forces, under command of Gusti Ktut Djilantik (who was to be the hero of the Balinese–Dutch wars of 1846–49), swiftly conquered the whole of Pajangan. The victors deposed and killed the troublesome *punggawa* and as a compromise measure with regard to the disposition of his land, they offered it to the Dewa Agung to distribute. The Dewa Agung assigned the major part of the conquered territory to the royal family of Bangli. The new ruler-apparent, knowing that the imposition of authority would not be easy, applied to Gianjar for support. Gianjar, instead, seized the greater part of the territory for its own. The Dewa Manggis thus so outraged the other radjas that they would no doubt have launched a concerted campaign against him had the wars of 1846–1849 not intervened. He himself died in 1847, to be succeeded by Dewa Pahang, who died in 1856 and was succeeded by Dewa Manggis VII, who found himself, not unsurprisingly, surrounded by enemies.

Dewa Manggis VII was almost immediately involved in open warfare with the Dewa Agung, who succeeded in 1860 in seizing and holding the region of Gunung Rata on the Gianjar side of the strategic ravine which presumably constituted the boundary between the two states. The Dewa Manggis consequently did not trouble himself to acknowledge, let alone to accept, an invitation, i.e. command, to attend upon the Dewa Agung in his wedding journey from Klungkung to Badung, where, in 1861, he was to be married to a daughter of the Radja. The Dewa Agung could not forgive such lese majesty, especially when the Dewa Manggis dared add ridicule to insult. He refused to chastise—perhaps because he had in fact inspired—two of his close friends who perpetrated an outrage which almost everyone conceded to have been in rather bad taste. A pair of commoner brothers, Made and Ktut Pasek, who consorted with royalty because they were prosperous dealers in opium and hence very influential citizens, had caused a ludicrous straw effigy of the Dewa Agung to be placed in the public square in front of the Gianjar *puri* and had invited passers-by to kick it and spit upon it.

Despite these several offenses, and in part because the Dutch Resident himself several times intervened to settle certain quarrels in the south, Gianjar enjoyed a period of relative calm during the 1870s and did not again find itself in really serious trouble until the early 1880s. Then, suddenly, everyone seemed to be fighting everyone else. Mengwi was fighting Tabanan, Badung, and Gianjar; Bangli was fighting Gianjar and Mengwi. The Dewa Manggis was even fighting some of his own *punggawa*, who had broken away to ally themselves with various of his enemies and were receiving as strong support from the Dewa Agung as he could then provide. The situation was further complicated by the fact that the Dewa Agung himself ruled, presumably, over four scattered enclaves within Tabanan and Gianjar, greater in total area than Klungkung proper, and these enclaves constituted cells of intrigue and villainy almost as vexatious to the Dewa Agung himself as to the neighboring radjas. Furthermore, Karangasem, the big eastern state, which normally held itself aloof from the south, was beginning to aspire to slices of southern territory. It was being incited by its own overlord, the Radja of Lombok, to help to dismember the empire of his long-time enemy, the Dewa Agung.

Feud with Klungkung; Seizure of Gianjar Royal Family

In 1882, in the interest of sheer self-preservation, seeking maximum insurance at minimum risk, the Dewa Manggis made certain rather unconvincing professions of renewal of allegiance to the Dewa Agung, even going so far as to imply willingness for Gianjar to merge with Klungkung. In 1885, as a measure of last resort when his many enemies were still pressing in upon him, the Dewa Manggis and all his family and his court journeyed to Klungkung to perform the ceremony of homage. They also sought the Dewa Agung's intervention with the two states still reasonably loyal to him, Mengwi and Bangli, which were Gianjar's two most dangerous enemies. The Dewa Agung, deftly matching treachery to expediency, caused the whole company to be seized and detained. He sentenced the Dewa Manggis and his sons to lifelong internment under vigilant guard in a nearby village. He then assigned the state of Gianjar to one of his own sons to rule as regent. When the son was forced to flee from his new subjects, who immediately rose up against him, the Dewa Agung partitioned the state between Klungkung and Bangli and called upon Bangli to make the arrangement work. The partition of Gianjar so outraged the Radja of Karangasem, who had certain rather dubious claims of his own to assert, that with the support of 500 soldiers shipped over to him by the Radja of Lombok, he prepared to launch an invasion.

The Dewa Agung called upon Mengwi to make itself master of Gianjar and thus to forestall Karangasem. But the Mengwi attack miscarried, and presently many armies were moving confusedly in many directions. Badung attacked Mengwi. So too did Tabanan. Badung captured the capital of Mengwi and killed the Radja but was unable to subdue the state as a whole. Karangasem tried to march through Klungkung to participate either in the reconstitution or the dismemberment of Mengwi, as might seem the more expedient, but encountered unexpectedly strong opposition from the Dewa Agung's own forces. Karangasem succeeded briefly in investing the Klungkung *puri* but suffered such heavy losses that it had to withdraw to the east. Klungkung, meanwhile, had called upon Bangli for aid, and Bangli again occupied most of Gianjar. Badung and Tabanan partitioned Mengwi, prudently allotting some of the remoter border area to Karangasem. A son of the late Radja of Mengwi escaped from exile in Badung to raise a Mengwi insurrection. Tabanan and Bangli allied themselves with Badung to put down the insurrection and repartition the state. There were other complications too numerous to recite.

Dewa Gde Raka and Gianjar's Revival; Regency Status (1900)
In the midst of all these alarms and excursions, two sons of the Dewa Manggis had made their escape from Klungkung (1889) and returned to Gianjar. The second of these sons, Dewa Gde Raka, succeeded in enlisting the aid of Tjokorda Sukawati, the powerful *punggawa* of Ubud, who rallied some of the other *punggawa*, raised a new army, and began a war for the reconstitution of the state. In 1892 Dewa Gde Raka gained recognition as Radja by most of the Gianjar

punggawa, but not from the other rulers. He then devoted himself to the delicate and dangerous task of impressing his personal authority over those other *punggawa* who still wavered and persuading all of them to share with him such revenues as they were still able to collect, the Radja himself being impoverished and the *puri*, the symbol of royal prestige, being only very shabbily restored as yet after having been sacked by the men of Klungkung a decade earlier. But his royal neighbors were still implacably hostile to him and his own state was still in disarray. With the support of Tjokorda Sukawati, Dewa Gde Raka convinced the other *punggawa* that there was only one way to preserve the radjadom—to place it under the protection of the Dutch.

In 1898 Dewa Gde Raka, the new Dewa Manggis, began negotiating with the Dutch Resident to accept the radjadom as a protectorate, a move which the Dutch were hesitant to make for fear of provoking the Dewa Agung and the other southern rulers. The Dewa Manggis solicited the good offices of the ruler of Karangasem, who enjoyed the special confidence of the Dutch; he also sent his most distinguished *punggawa*, Tjokorda Sukawati, to consult with the Resident personally in Buleleng. The Resident referred the decision to Batavia and on February 28, 1900, received the historic telegram from the Governor-General authorizing him to name the Dewa Manggis as Dutch-designated and protected *Stedehouder*, or Viceroy, a more elevated rank than that of Regent, which was conferred upon the rulers of the other states, except only Karangasem, where the Radja also was entitled *Stedehouder.* The Dutch thereby extended their overt control from northern into southern Bali.

On March 8, 1900, Radja Dewa Gde Raka was duly installed as *Stedehouder*, the occasion being celebrated in Puri Gianjar by eight days of feasting and entertainment with the Dutch Resident and all of the *punggawa* in attendance. The Dewa Agung immediately protested that Gianjar belonged to Klungkung and could not be alienated without his consent, a claim which Bangli, Badung, and Tabanan were easily persuaded to endorse. The Dutch replied at their leisure to the general effect that the new status quo in Gianjar was already a fait accompli. The newly appointed Dutch Controleur, Heer Schwarz, had already taken up his post, having occupied a pavilion within the *puri* itself in order to be close to the Radja. According to the Controleur's own account, the Radja sought him out eagerly by night as well as by day in order to elicit advice. With Schwarz's appearance, the Radja's position vis-à-vis the Dutch and his own *punggawa* was greatly strengthened and the turbulence which had beset the state for the better part of the last half century began rapidly to subside.

Controleur Schwarz and Modern Progress; *Sri Kumala* Incident (1904)

Thus, in 1900, the Dutch presence began to make itself clearly felt in south Bali just as it had almost half a century earlier in the north. With Controleur Schwarz at hand to guide the Radja, Gianjar went through much the same transformation as that which had occurred decades earlier in Buleleng under the influence of Controleur Bloemen Waanders. The administrative system was regularized; taxes were more efficiently collected and more wisely used; roads and bridges and irrigation systems were improved; other public works were built; health and educational services were introduced; the system of justice was reformed. The whole state experienced such unaccustomed security and tranquility that the Dutch hailed it as a model of colonial achievement in pacification and development. The model was not one which pleased its neighbors; as the Dutch tactlessly pointed out, Gianjar in the south, like Buleleng earlier in the north, became a sanctuary for refugees from the tyranny of the other radjadoms, such refugees including runaway slaves and persons falsely accused of crimes.

The Dewa Agung in particular could not be reconciled to the presence of a Dutch Controleur within only a few kilometers of the sacred Puri Klungkung. He determined to assert his customary authority and he strongly advised Bangli, Badung, and Tabanan to do likewise. In his defiance of the Dutch he elected Gianjar as the surrogate object of his attentions. He therefore tolerated if he did not actually instigate the practice of certain of the farmers in the Klungkung-Gianjar border area, who took to planting sharpened bamboo splints in their fields in order to impede the work of the surveyors attempting to determine exact state and property lines. He provided shelter for fugitive criminals and tolerated trade in stolen or smuggled merchandise and committed other minor nuisances far too numerous even for the meticulous Dutch to catalog. The Dutch attempted to deal with the Dewa Agung by sending officials to lodge formal protest and by deploying warships in maneuvers offshore as they did so, but he persisted in his intransigence. It was widely assumed, therefore, that there would soon occur some especially outrageous incident which would launch another Dutch expeditionary force.

The incident happened on May 27, 1904. The *Sri Kumala*, a Chinese-owned schooner out of Bandjarmasin, Borneo, struck the reef near Sanur close to the Badung-Gianjar border, and was allegedly plundered by the people with the approval of the radjas. The Chinese owner of the craft gave an altogether implausible account of his misfortune and demanded an altogether fanciful indemnity for the cargo, to the original itemization of which he added as a curious afterthought large quantities of silver and gold. The Dutch scaled down his claims to a mere fl. 7,500 ($2,500) and presented the bill to the Radja of Badung, who flatly refused to pay. The Dewa Agung backed him in his defiance and so too did the Radja of Tabanan, who happened also to be involved just then in a crisis over a recent ceremony of suttee which he had permitted despite Dutch protest. So in June of 1906 the Dutch blockaded the coasts of Badung and Tabanan while they drew up and presented certain ultimata and assembled a military expedition.

Sixth Military Expedition (1906); *Puputan* in Den Pasar

The Sixth Military Expedition, under the command of General Ross van Tonningen, consisted of three battalions of infantry and a detachment of cavalry, two batteries of artillery, and strong naval support. It arrived off the southern coast of Bali in early September. On September 12 the General sent a final ultimatum, which the Radja of Badung rejected. On September 14 the Dutch landed their troops on Sanur beach. In the course of the next few days, without meeting any significant resistance, the forces proceeded inland. On September 20, early in the morning, they moved into the town of Kesiman, the seat of a minor ruler, also titled Radja, who administered the district on behalf of the Radja of Badung. They discovered that the aged, half-crazed Radja had been killed by his own high priest for refusal

The Radja of Gianyar greeting Lt Schutsal of the Sixth Dutch Military Expedition, 1906.

to lead a resistance, that the *puri* was in flames and that the people had deserted both the *puri* and the town. Having little to detain them in Kesiman, they continued their march toward Den Pasar, expecting the action to be more of a dress parade than a pitched battle.

The Dutch troops, marching in orderly ranks along a long roadway, walled on either side, which led to the royal palace, were not surprised to find the town apparently deserted and flames and smoke rising over the *puri*, the most disquieting factor being the sound of the wild beating of drums within the palace walls. As they drew closer, they observed a strange, silent procession emerging from the main gate of the *puri*. It was led by the Radja himself, seated in his state palanquin carried by four bearers, dressed in white cremation garments but splendidly bejeweled and armed with a magnificent *kris*. The Radja was followed by the officials of his court, the armed guards, the priests, his wives, his children, and his retainers, likewise dressed in white, flowers in their hair, many of them almost as richly ornamented and as splendidly armed as the Radja himself.

One hundred paces from the startled Dutch, the Radja halted his bearers, stepped from his palanquin, gave the signal, and the ghastly ceremony began. A priest plunged his dagger into the Radja's breast, and others of the company began turning their daggers upon themselves or upon one another. The Dutch troops, startled into action by a stray gunshot and reacting to attack by lance and spear, directed rifle and even artillery fire into the surging crowd. Some of the women mockingly threw jewels and gold coins to the soldiers, and as more and more persons kept emerging from the palace gate, the mounds of corpses rose higher and higher. Soon to the scene of carnage was added the spectacle of looting as the soldiers stripped the valuables from the corpses and then set themselves to sacking the palace ruins. It was a slaughter and self-slaughter of the innocents and a plundering of the dead made all the more appalling by reason of its recurrence that same afternoon in nearby Pematjutan, a minor appendage of Badung. There the frail old Radja and his terrified court, having heard what had already happened in Den Pasar, elected the same fate. When the victorious Dutch troops marched from Den Pasar to Pematjutan, the Radja and his retainers were ready to enact yet once again the grisly rites of the *puputan*. This time the Dutch were prepared to refrain from participation if not from profit.

Wesatia (1904) and Suicide (1906) of Tabanan Royalty

Equally moving scenes occurred in adjacent Tabanan both shortly before and shortly after the Badung spectacle, first despite and later because of Dutch intervention. The venerable Radja Ngurah Agung, who had come to the throne in the year 1844 and was the last well known survivor of the stirring events of the mid-nineteenth century, died on March 3, 1903, and his cremation, scheduled to be held seven months later, was a signal for a reunion of royalty from all of the other radjadoms. It quickly became known throughout Bali—and in Batavia as well—that two of the Radja's aged widows intended to follow their husband in death by performing the rite of *wesatia*, or suttee. The Resident advised the old Radja's son and successor that he expected him to prevent this sacrifice. The new Radja replied that he knew of no clause in the famous contracts in which *wesatia* was even mentioned, let alone proscribed, and that the Dutch themselves had in fact undertaken not to interfere in internal affairs of the radjadom, especially those which related to *adat* (tradition). He added, in a more placatory tone, that this Tabanan ceremony would no doubt

A self-sacrifice ceremony (*westaria*), from Ludvig Verner Helms, *Pioneering in the Far East*, London, 1882.

be the last of its kind and that he himself could not and would not deny the wishes of the grieving widows. The Dutch sent two warships to cruise suggestively close off the Tabanan coast and assumed that this would suffice to dampen traditional ardor. But the Radja's pride and prestige were at stake, and on October 20 the ceremonies of cremation and suttee occurred exactly on schedule. The Dutch press, public, and administration in Batavia and The Hague debated for weeks what, if anything, should be done about this "barbarous" or "sacred" custom and Tabanan's defiance of civilized norms and Dutch wishes. The Resident of Bali finally drew up a contract (1904) in which suttee was explicitly prohibited and the Controleurs were instructed to make quite certain that no subsequent crises arose with obstinate radjas and determined widows, and none did.

Seventh Military Expedition (1908); *Puputan* in Klungkung

Very soon after the Tabanan suttee, men of Tabanan were implicated, along with those of Badung, in plundering the shipwrecked *Sri Kumala*. The Dutch expeditionary force which arrived subsequently, having dealt conclusively with Badung, marched next upon Tabanan. The new Radja and the Crown Prince, who rejected the advice of certain of their priests and courtiers that they had no choice but to resort to the *puputan*, fled from the *puri* together with some of their more timorous followers and sent emissaries to bargain with the rapidly advancing Dutch. They offered peacefully to accept regency status, which was about to be imposed upon Badung, but they sought some reassurance that they themselves would not be exiled, as seemed all too likely. They were required to present themselves in Den Pasar as humble petitioners, as they hastened to do, only to be detained, interrogated, and abruptly informed that exile to Madura or Lombok was indeed to be their well-deserved punishment. The Radja and the Prince preferred suicide in their Den Pasar prison. For lack of a *kris*, the Radja plunged a *sirih* knife into his throat, and the Crown Prince took poison. Their closest relatives were exiled to Lombok: their palace—the finest in all of Bali—was plundered and razed; and Tabanan followed Badung into the Dutch sphere, itself to be followed, in 1908, by Bangli and Klungkung.

As a side excursion to their invasion of Tabanan, the Dutch made a show of force in Klungkung. They hoped thereby either to prevent or perhaps to provoke a show of resistance by the Dewa Agung, for there were certain of the military who thought the time was opportune quite definitively to pacify and occupy the whole of southern Bali. But the Dewa Agung was either cowed or prudent. He resisted the urgings of the *Punggawa* of Gelgel, the one real firebrand in the state, and declined his offer to man and lead an attack. He even went so far as to command his own small palace guard to ring the *Punggawa's puri* to prevent him from taking any rash action on his own authority. The Dutch presently withdrew, some of them predicting that they would soon be back.

For the time being the Dutch contented themselves with presenting the Dewa Agung with a whole new set of agreements almost indistinguishable from ultimata, all of which he accepted virtually at sight. The Dewa Agung was required to dismantle all fortifications, to deliver all firearms, to renounce all levies upon imports and exports, and to cede to Gianjar and Tabanan certain remaining Klungkung-ruled enclaves within their territory. In compensation for his loss of revenues from customs, the Dutch granted him an apparently generous annual pension of fl. 7,117. But opium, by far the most important item of trade, was soon yielding the Dutch themselves much more than that amount under their new opium monopoly.

Everyone knew that the next move would be Dutch imposition upon Klungkung of the same sort of general administrative guidance which their Controleurs provided in other states and that any small incident would provoke it. Disorders duly broke out, especially in the town of Gelgel. Some of the *Punggawa's* men intimidated and attacked certain agents of the opium monopoly, the incident resulting in the death of the Gelgel shop manager and two of his assistants and the subsequent looting of the stock. The Dutch brought in warships and landed a small party of troops which marched into Gelgel to seek out and to punish the *Punggawa*. The *Punggawa* and his supporters offered resistance and a sharp engagement ensued in which 180 Balinese were killed and so many of the Dutch soldiers were injured that the detachment had to withdraw to the seacoast. The *Punggawa* sought shelter in Klungkung, where the Dewa Agung, correctly anticipating naval bombardment and land maneuvers, had already authorized certain measures of defense. The weak little Klungkung defense force reintensified its rather forlorn efforts to contrive shelters against shells, to buttress the *puri* walls, to dig protective pits and ditches, and to plant bamboo spikes and sharpened bamboo splints where they might do the expected attackers the greatest damage. The bombardment swiftly followed, virtually demolishing the guilty town of Gelgel and working great destruction upon innocent Klungkung. Then came the troops with their field pieces, which they deployed in the square in front of the *puri* at a distance of no more than 200 meters from the main gate and began firing admonitory salvos.

The Dewa Agung ordered the gongs to sound the call to the *puputan*. He himself led a procession of some two hundred persons who emerged from the *puri* to confront the Dutch soldiers. Clad all in white, he carried in one hand a ceremonial lance with a golden tip and in the other his ancestral *kris*, magically and mystically the most potent item of the royal regalia. Pausing about one hundred meters from the momentarily silent cannon, he bent over and with an imperious gesture thrust the *kris* blade into the ground. Thus, if the prophecy of his high priest came true, he would create a great chasm in which would be swallowed up all of his enemies. As he straightened, he received a gunshot in the knee, and before he could even crumple, he was killed outright by another. Six of his wives knelt around him and solemnly drove their *kris* blades into their own hearts. The whole company, men, women, and children alike, engaged in ritualistic self-immolation or sacrificed one another while murderous cannon and gun fire contributed to the mayhem.

There were very few royal or other survivors of the Klungkung *puputan*, but 19 of them were exiled to Lombok. The *puri* was razed, except for one gateway which led to a barracks and a prison. What little had remained of Klungkung's ancient glory had vanished, but the last bright blaze of martyrdom had burnt away many stains. Thus, on April 18, 1908, after 600 years of rule in Bali, the lineal descendants of the Modjapahit emperors were decimated, the ritualistic victims of relentless Western intrusion.

CHAPTER 10

Tragedy in Lombok
(1891–1894)

Origin in Bali and Lombok of Sassak Insurrections

The chain of events which culminated so disastrously in Bali proper with *the puputan* in Den Pasar (1906) and Klungkung (1908) had in fact already led in 1894 to a penultimate climax in Lombok which was in certain respects even more shocking and horrible. The Lombok tragedy of 1894 clearly signaled the fate of the Dewa Agung and those of his vassals who objected to the active exercise of the Dutch sovereignty which they had long since acknowledged but never fully accepted. This catastrophe on the nearby island was directly related to the late nineteenth century turbulence in Bali itself. In playing a minor role in the dissolution of the Dewa Agung's empire, the state of Karangasem, a dependency of the Balinese Radja of Lombok, triggered a crisis which destroyed the Lombok radjadom.

Lombok and Karangasem enjoyed almost half a century of peace and obscurity between the troubles of the earlier part of the century and those which broke out in the 1890s. At the end of the Balinese–Dutch War of 1849, the Dutch rewarded the Radja of Lombok, who provided the troops which conquered Karangasem, by recognizing his claim to the state and permitting him to rule it through his own regent. Neither Karangasem nor Lombok gave the Dutch any special trouble for decades thereafter. In 1870 Lombok came under the rule of Radja Ratu Agung Agung Gde Ngurah, who proved to be extraordinarily capable and durable. In Karangasem a Balinese prince of Lombok, Gusti Gde Putu, was Regent, but his half-brother, Gusti Gde Djilantik, had become the actual ruler.

Gusti Gde Djilantik; His Career in Bali and Lombok

Gusti Gde Djilantik, one of the most controversial figures in Balinese history, was a prince of the Balinese royal house of Karangasem who was born and brought up in Lombok and was treated by his uncle, the reigning Radja, as a prime favorite. In his early youth he fell in love with his uncle's daughter whose caste (Brahman) was higher than his own (Wesya). When the affair resulted in accusations of defilement of caste, an offense for which the death penalty was mandatory, Gusti Djilantik was suddenly forced to flee to Bali, doing so, it seems, with the connivance of his uncle and his half-brother.

In Bali, very soon after his arrival, he all but openly ruled Karangasem. His domination of the state was so complete that when the Regent's son committed the same offense of which he, Gusti Djilantik, had been guilty in Lombok, he prevailed upon the father to cause the son to be krissed. His influence over the Regent and his obvious intention to clear the way for his own succession aroused intense resentment among various members of the Karangasem court. But at just that time Karangasem was being pressured by Lombok to intervene in the wars in the southern Balinese states, and Gusti Djilantik was the obvious choice for command of the joint Karangasem-Lombok forces then assembling. His subsequent campaign in Klungkung ended in disaster, especially for the Lombok soldiers, who were poorly armed, clothed, and provisioned and suffered frightful losses. These Lombok troops were reluctant recruits drafted from the native Sassak population into the service of their Balinese rulers; their decimation in Klungkung combined with efforts to impress and send replacements precipitated outright Sassak rebellion at home. Gusti Djilantik, who had so recently been fighting a war for Lombok in Bali, was suddenly called upon to lead a Balinese expeditionary force of 1,500 men to go to the aid of the Radja of Lombok. Djilantik and his army crossed from Bali to Lombok on November 29, 1891, and there, for the next year, he himself was deeply involved in the tangled affairs of the Lombok rulers.

Royal Family of Lombok; the Radja; Gusti Made; Gusti Ktut

In 1891 Radja Ratu Agung Agung Gde Ngurah was already long since past his prime, frail, deaf, and at times childish. He was given to unpredictable displays of the alert intelligence for which he had been famous but also to studied or unstudied senility and stupidity. He had placed the affairs of the realm largely in the hands of his eldest son, Anak Agung Made, or Gusti Made, the son not of a noble wife but of a low caste concubine. According to conflicting accounts, Gusti Made was possessed of enormous capability and courage or of almost infinite craftiness and cruelty. As his heir apparent, the old Radja had designated his eldest son by a noble wife, Anak Agung Ktut, or Gusti Ktut, a youth who seemed to the Dutch to be moronic. Since the Radja had dozens of wives, scores of children, and hundreds of royal relatives holding high positions at court, the radjadom was riddled with intrigue. The three closely adjacent towns of Ampenan (the port), Mataram (the seat of the Crown Prince) four kilometers away, and Tjakranegara (the seat of the Radja) two kilometers further distant, were Balinese Hindu enclaves in an island where 95 per cent of the people were resentful and rebellious Sassak Muslims. The Sassak complained, and were able to cite convincing evidence, that the Balinese rulers, especially Gusti Made, oppressed, exploited, terrorized them, in fact brazenly robbed and murdered and might be planning a war of extermination of Muslims as a countermeasure to Sassak rebellion. Such was the stage setting for the reappearance of Gusti Djilantik together with his force of 1,500 Balinese warriors at the court of the old Radja, with whom he swiftly reestablished himself as favorite.

Sassak Petitions; Radja's Appeal to the Dutch and the English

Both the Radja and the Sassak rebels had addressed themselves frequently to the Dutch, the Radja seeking aid in putting down the rebellion, the Sassak requesting a Dutch punitive expedition against the Balinese leaders and promising to join it. The Dutch were cool to the Radja's advances, being much preoccupied at the time with a long and costly war in Atjeh, Sumatra, and indisposed to open a distant second front. They sententiously reminded the Radja of their recently redefined colonial policy of "abstinence," signifying non-intervention in local disputes. The Radja turned to Singapore, seeking to buy arms and charter ships and to invite the colonial British to intervene. He employed as his intermediary Said Abdullah, an Ampenan merchant who belonged to a wealthy and influential Singapore Armenian family and held the post of *sjahbandar* which had once been occupied by Mads Lange and George King. Said Abdullah and his sons were murdered not long afterwards, presumably because they served also as intermediaries for the Sassak, who turned to them as coreligionists and potential confederates.

The Radja, it might seem, could have caused no greater dismay to the Dutch than to appeal to their British rivals, but he managed to compound his offense in an objectionable manner and thus to destroy the possibility that they would espouse his cause. When Dutch agents journeyed to Lombok to investigate the Sassak complaints—first and several times later a Controleur, once the Resident himself—the Radja refused on one flimsy pretext or another to receive them. The Dutch dignitaries indignantly departed to report unanimously that they had confirmed the worst of the Sassak charges and to recommend firm measures against the insolent and cruel Balinese. They had laboriously drafted a letter which was not exactly an accusation or an ultimatum but included nicely calculated nuances of both; they were especially annoyed that they were never able to deliver it.

Ultimatum and Military Expedition of 1894

In June 1894, when the Atjeh war seemed to be won and troops could be released for other operations, the Governor-General drew up an ultimatum in which he made four demands, to which, later on, another three were appended. From the Radja he required: (1) sincere repentance for his disrespectful behavior; (2) solemn assurance of future compliance with Dutch wishes; (3) immediate banishment of the evil Gusti Made; (4) acceptance of Dutch mediation to restore peace between the Balinese and the Sassak; and later, (5) abdication in favor of the Crown Prince; (6) declaration of willingness to conclude new treaties; (7) payment of indemnity. The Radja rejected the ultimatum. The Dutch launched the Lombok Expedition.

The Lombok Expedition of 1894 was assembled in Batavia and Surabaya out of elements hastily withdrawn from Atjeh and was placed under the command of Major-Genera J. A. Vetter with Major-General P. P. H. van Ham as his Deputy. The designation of these two highly respected and experienced officers to joint command signified the importance which the Dutch attached to the new enterprise and the high regard in which they held Balinese warriors. The expeditionary fleet consisted of four warships and eleven transports. The land forces consisted of 107 Dutch officers, 1,320 European soldiers (including 175 cavalry), 948 indigenous troops (mainly Ambonese), 216 servants, 64 overseers, and 1,718 convict laborers.

The invasion fleet arrived off Lombok on July 5 and the Generals at once sent the Radja another ultimatum which would expire at sunrise the following morning. The Radja sent back a messenger requesting three days' delay; but the Dutch held to the original deadline and at 6:30 a.m. on July 6 they began landing their troops. They encountered no resistance whatever. The whole expedition was ashore by mid-afternoon and scouting parties were sent out into the countryside, where all seemed to be quiet. On July 8 a strong reconnoitering force set out in the direction of Mataram and Tjakranegara with Generals Vetter and van Ham in the lead and Controleur Liefrinck accompanying them as representative of the Resident of Bali and Lombok and expert adviser on matters of local psychology and politics. The party very soon encountered Gusti Djilantik who had come in fact to intercept it and report to it on conditions at court. Gusti Djilantik engaged in a long and friendly conversation with the Dutch officials and promised to meet them again the next day after first conferring with the Radja and Gusti Made. He kept his July 9 appointment and informed the Dutch that the Radja accepted virtually all of their conditions. His report was confirmed the following day by a letter from the Radja requesting modification only of the provision with regard to Gusti Made, suggesting that arbitrary banishment might incense the people; he would prefer that the Dutch first conduct an on-the-spot inquiry into his alleged offenses. The Commander replied that the prince must be surrendered to him at once or else the expedition would march upon Tjakranegara, as, on July 11, it did, no reply having yet been received.

The march on Tjakranegara had barely begun before messengers arrived with a letter saying that the Radja had given Gusti Made the choice between exile and suicide. A second messenger followed hard upon the first to announce that in fact the prince had committed suicide, and that his wife had joined him in death. The Dutch were skeptical but accepted the messenger's suggestion that they send someone actually to view the bodies. The assignment fell to Controleur Liefrinck, who was personally acquainted with the persons in question. Arriving in Tjakranegara without incident, Liefrinck was admitted at once to the *puri*, which seemed to be virtually deserted, but was then subjected to a long wait. Eventually he demanded to see Gusti Djilantik, who presently appeared, asked him to wait just a little longer, then vanished. After another long delay, Liefrinck again demanded to see Djilantik. The prince returned and escorted the Controleur into an interior courtyard in which lay two bodies clothed all in white. Liefrinck recognized one as that of Gusti Made, who just at that moment drew his last labored breath.

The Dutch never determined to their own satisfaction, and Gusti Djilantik never confided in them, exactly what had been the circumstances of the prince's death. He had plunged his *kris* into his own heart, just as the old Radja had said, was the official version of the incident. Most persons thought Gusti Djilantik had guided his hand. Others held that the old Radja had condemned him to death just then in expiation of the crime of incest and that the high priest had been the executioner. Whatever the true explanation, Gusti Made, whom the Dutch regarded as the evil genius behind the Lombok troubles, was undeniably and opportunely removed from the scene and there seemed to be no further obstacle to peaceful relations. The troops marched into Mataram and Tjakranegara that same day through what appeared to be a friendly countryside. Seemingly cheerful spectators lined the roadways; the town markets remained open with stall keepers and buyers alike apparently unconcerned about any danger. Everybody in fact seemed much diverted by the military parade and delighted with the martial music.

General Vetter, General van Ham, and Controleur Liefrinck took up residence in comfortable compounds requisitioned from the nobility; they adopted Gusti Djilantik as their confidant and intermediary in their relations with the local people. The troops settled themselves into bivouac areas on the outskirts of Tjakranegara, Mataram, and Ampenan, with the largest contingents in Tjakranegara, and prepared to enjoy an agreeable stretch of not very strenuous occupation duty. The old Radja abdicated; the Crown Prince succeeded him and exchanged ceremonial calls with the Generals and the Controleur. Negotiations began for fulfillment of Dutch conditions, most of which the young Radja seemed to accept with such compliance and indeed indifference that the Dutch suspected, and Gusti Djilantik confirmed, that he really did not comprehend except when it came to payment of indemnity. The Dutch demanded fl. 1,000,000 and the prince quickly paid over the first three installments—200,000, 250,000, and 250,000 in silver coins—but not without evidence of anguish. The only real trouble the Dutch encountered came not from the Balinese but from the Sassak. It was part of the Dutch mission to reconcile the Sassak to Balinese rule; but it was not until they promised to station permanent Dutch representatives in Lombok to look out for Sassak interests that the Sassak leaders became receptive to Dutch suggestions.

The Generals were elated by their bloodless victory; the Controleur was delighted with progress in treaty-making; the troops were so relaxed in their bivouac areas that they neglected to take the most elementary precautions against trouble. They drilled and paraded and staged concerts of band music for great crowds of admiring, respectful spectators, among whom were many Balinese soldiers. It seemed only mildly curious that Gusti Djilantik's own army of some 1,500 men from Bali proper still remained in Lombok, even though it had been several times scheduled to return home. Then in late August there were certain danger signals.

The Balinese soldiers became less respectful and in fact occasionally provocative, one of them, for instance, throwing a bottle at soldiers who were counting the coins in the latest installment of indemnity payment. One morning the market places were almost deserted and the population of both Mataram and Tjakranegara seemed strangely diminished. Then came an informer on August 24 to report that the Balinese were planning a surprise attack upon Tjakranegara for that same night. The Dutch sought to consult their trusted friend, Gusti Djilantik, and also the simple-minded young Radja. Both were much too ill, it seemed, to be visited. They sent a military doctor to diagnose Gusti Djilantik's sudden seizure; he pronounced it a stupor induced by opium. It was already much too late in the day to stage an orderly withdrawal from Tjakranegara, and to retreat in great haste, said Controleur Liefrinck, would only make the Dutch appear cowardly and ridiculous in the eyes of the bold, proud Balinese warriors. So they called a special alert and posted a heavy guard and the night passed without incident. They learned only much later that the Balinese had suddenly discovered that the horoscope readings were inauspicious for an August 24 attack. Next day the Dutch roused Djilantik from his torpor long enough to get him to swear that he had absolutely no knowledge of any conspiracy. That night, at 11:15, just as they were congratulating themselves that danger was quite certainly past, the attack came.

The camp in Tjakranegara was suddenly surrounded by hundreds, perhaps thousands, of Balinese warriors, firing off rifles with deadly aim, their battle cries as blood-curdling as their attack was furious, massacring Dutch soldiers who had no place to take shelter. The attack continued all night. At 7:00 a.m. on August 26 the Dutch withdrew in reasonably good order to a nearby temple in which they would have stone walls to protect them. But they were without food, water, or adequate ammunition, and the Balinese soon began boring holes through the walls and firing into the closely packed masses of troops in the restricted and sweltering compound. At 3:00 p.m. the Tjakranegara forces began to retreat toward Mataram.

General van Ham himself was fatally wounded just after he emerged from the temple gateway. The troops suffered frightful losses as they moved from Tjakranegara into and through the town of Mataram. The Balinese could and did take shelter behind thick stone walls in order to fire with quite devastating effect upon the confused Dutch ranks, especially at one point where the road made a right-angle turn. When the retreating troops reached the Mataram bivouac area, they discovered that the Mataram garrison had been subjected to equally strong attack and had already withdrawn toward the coast. The next day the Tjakranegara forces also retreated to the port town of Ampenan, suffering losses all along the way but not as severe as on August 25–26. By final official report, once all the scattered detachments were accounted for, including several which had been dispatched to the interior and one which was captured—and freed—by the Balinese, the Dutch casualties on August 25–27 totaled 98 dead and 272 injured. The dead were 60 Europeans (nine officers) and 38 members of the Ambonese and other indigenous auxiliary forces; the injured were 121 Europeans (17 officers) and 151 indigenous auxiliaries.

General Vetter's own telegraphic summation of the events of these dreadful days by which his career was irretrievably ruined warrants at least the following partial citation as a moving historical document:

> Tjakra attacked on the night of 25th. Firing continued all day. Losses in course of 26th are 14 killed and 85 wounded. No water, foraging impossible, losses increasing; at 3 p.m. retreated to Mataram. Baggage left behind so as to carry wounded in wagons. Heavy losses on the road. Situation Mataram worse. Camp deserted. Eight in the evening Bijlevelt's column from the interior arrived, also heavy losses. Provisions failed, could not reach bivouac, communication with Ampenan interrupted, hemmed in between Tjakra and Mataram; impossible to take offensive. Situation untenable on account of numbers wounded, on morning 27th retreated Ampenan in southerly direction, losses were comparatively small. Killed: four officers, 63 soldiers; Wounded: 12 officers, 153 soldiers; missing: six officers, 143 soldiers. Four field guns left behind at Mataram. Nothing known of Van Lawick's column in the interior.

"Treachery" of August 25–27; *Puputan* at Mataram and Sasari

The August 25–27 Battle of Tjakranegara and Mataram entered Dutch colonial history as "The Lombok Betrayal" or "The Lombok Treachery." When telegraphic word reached Batavia and the Netherlands, the wrath of the government and the people could only be assuaged by the immediate assembly and launching of a new expedition to reinforce the remnants of the old and to carry the battle back to its starting point. The reinforcements began arriving in Lombok in early September, eventually totaling at least another 1,000 officers and men, among them a higher percentage of Europeans than before; there were also large detachments of convict laborers—650 of them at first with more to follow.

The Dutch took every possible precaution against being surprised and advanced only very deliberately through the countryside in which every village proved to be strongly defended. Since each village was a maze of compounds with thick stone walls, the seizure of any one of them was no easy tactical maneuver. The Dutch resorted to virtual demolition, first laying down such heavy artillery fire that the walls began to crumble, and then, upon occupying a village, moving in the convict laborers to level the walls in order to preclude any possibility of reoccupation by the Balinese forces. Relentlessly they advanced upon Mataram, which they seized on September 29 and systematically razed, an enterprise which occupied them for the next several weeks. It was not until November 18 that they reached Tjakranegara and not until November 19 that they actually occupied the whole of the city, subjecting it afterwards to the same treatment as Mataram.

In Mataram the defenders took up their final stand in the *puri* of the young Radja, who seems to have roused himself from his habitual torpor to lead them in the final act of defiance, which was the performance of the rite of the *puputan*. The Dutch finally broke into the *puri* over mounds of bodies which piled up without and within as the defenders krissed one another and themselves. Among the corpses they discovered and with some difficulty identified that of the young Radja, so hideously mutilated that they later declined to show it to his grieving father. In Tjakranegara, after a day of hard fighting, the Dutch next morning captured a deserted *puri*. The old Radja and his court had fled during the night to the nearby town of Sasari.

On November 20 the Dutch marched upon Sasari and demanded immediate surrender. The old Radja delayed for two hours, then, dressed all in yellow, seated in a palanquin carried by four slaves, accompanied by escorts who carried two golden parasols—all that remained of royal splendor—he caused himself and a grandson to be carried to the Dutch lines. The Dutch refused him his last request, that he be carried by his own bearers to whatever destination they chose. They assigned him convict bearers, who carried him to Ampenan, where he was held until he could be sent to Batavia. But the rest of the court refused to yield. There was therefore enacted yet once again the appalling rite of the *puputan* as men, women, and children emerged as in a trance from the village and if they did not die by the *kris* rushed headlong into the fire of the troops. By Dutch count there perished that day at Sasari ten of the highest-ranking noblemen of the kingdom, and 50 of their wives and children. Even this was not the finale. More and more persons reported themselves to surrender, but others, including the next heir apparent, Anak Agung Nengah Karang, fled to a village still further distance, where, on November 26, occurred the last attack and *puputan*.

Before they razed the *puri* in Mataram and Tjakranegara the Dutch afforded both the native and the European troops opportunity to ransack and loot while officers sequestered the treasure which they found in the royal storerooms. In Mataram they found 1,000 pounds of gold and 6,996 pounds of silver, and that was only a part of the booty. In Tjakranegara they discovered to their amazement a room five meters square in which silver coins were heaped two meters high; other valuables such as *krises* and ceremonial vessels of sold and silver were piled upon the money. Together with fl. 450,000 of indemnity which the Dutch sent out from Tjakranegara before the surprise attack or else carried with them in their retreat, the proceeds of the Lombok War much more than offset the total expenditures, which, according to announcement in Parliament, came to exactly fl. 2,658,917.

Fate of the Radja, Lombok, and Gusti Djilantik

The Dutch thus swiftly and to their own satisfaction wound up the Lombok campaign. The deposed Radja was sent off to exile in Batavia, where his arrival and transit from the port of Tanjung Priok to the residence which the Dutch made available to him on Tanah Abang created a momentary public sensation. He died on May 20 of the following year, then all but forgotten and unattended, most of his own people having repudiated him for not having led the *puputan*.

As for Gusti Djilantik, who vanished from Lombok and reappeared in Bali well before the seizure of Mataram and Tjakranegara, the Dutch debated just how to reward or punish what had been, according to variant versions, his singular services or deceptions. They decided at last to make him Regent of Karangasem. Although he experienced grave difficulties at first with his own subjects and aroused profound misgivings on the part of the Controleurs, he proved in fact to be a loyal and effective ruler. In Lombok itself the Dutch established direct rule through an Assistant Resident and three Controleurs, dividing the state into 24 districts, 12 of them presided over by Balinese and 12 by Sassak chieftains. Lombok began almost immediately to prosper again and so too did Karangasem. Nevertheless, the events in Lombok in 1894 left deep scars upon the Balinese soul and the Dutch conscience.

CHAPTER 11

Turn of Century Tour
(1902)

Kol's Grand Tour and His Published Account

The first tourist in Bali was a member of the Dutch Parliament, Heer H. van Kol. He was a tourist, that is, in the sense that he visited the island on his own volition and at his own expense, not by reason of official assignment, and he traveled extensively while there as much for his own pleasure as for any other profit. He was atypical of the genre in that he briefed himself tirelessly before, during, and after his trip and visited also Sumatra, Java, and the eastern islands. He had the built-in advantage, furthermore, of previous acquaintance with the area, having served in the 1880s as a civil engineer in the colonial government. It did no damage that he entertained a certain ulterior motive for what proved to be his extremely arduous but also informative and enjoyable travels. As a member of the Second Chamber of the Dutch Estates General, he sought to inform himself, his colleagues, and his constituents about conditions in the Dutch East Indies and to influence colonial policy with regard to which he was disposed to be critical, especially in Java, but not, in 1902, in Bali. He also sought to bring back as a trophy, as he did, a travel book which would both inform and sell.

Notwithstanding such political and utilitarian objectives, Heer van Kol was first of all a discriminating traveler, as is evident from his serendipitist outlook upon all strange adventures and misadventures. He was secondarily a journalist, forgoing no opportunity to investigate recent events, to interview important personages, and to explore unknown regions. He made himself something of a scholar, reading Dutch official and unofficial reports, of which certain extensive collections could be discovered by the diligent searcher in some of the dustier archives. Undeniably, however, he was also a junketing parliamentary fact-finder, never hesitating to use official credentials and personal pressure to overcome Dutch bureaucratic obstruction and Balinese royal indifference. He traveled, all the same, in the already anachronistic manner of the underprivileged nineteenth-century politician. He made do without any staff assistants, although he did generally move about with a Controleur impressed into service as companion and guide, and with an explorer's retinue of servants and porters. He conducted his own inquiries, wrote up his own observations and experiences, and relied much more upon his own than upon any sifted, strained, and systematized official intelligence.

Heer van Kol's *Uit Onze Kolonien* (Out of Our Colonies), published in Leiden in 1902, is a massive 826-page travel account which includes 123 pages of closely packed information about Bali. It deserves to have been published in some other language than Dutch in order to have commanded a larger audience in its day than the very restricted Dutch reading public, and greater celebrity today than small-type listing in the catalogues of rare book dealers. The early twentieth-century panoramic view of the island of Bali which Heer van Kol so admirably presents would seem to be of some intrinsic interest to the more perceptive late twentieth-century visitor or would-be visitor, affording as it does, a multi-dimensional perspective. What follows, therefore, is a selective summation of Kol's report, with emphasis upon what is supplementary rather than duplicative of materials from other sources in the foregoing or the following pages, with resort, as seems appropriate, to direct quotes and bracketed editorial interpolation.

Reception in Karangasem; Impressions of Radja Djilantik

On the morning of July 4, 1902, traveling on the government steamer, *de Zwaluw*, Kol arrived in Labuan Bay on the southwest coast of Bali. He was met on shipboard by Heer Schwarz, the Dutch Controleur for Gianjar, who was assigned to him as escort and was by all odds the most knowledgable European with regard to the southern part of the island. Kol made the trip to shore, not in the ship's boat as he had expected, but in a little Balinese outrigger. It was an exhilarating transition from Dutch to Balinese ambiance, made on board a fragile and lovely craft skimming the high waves and the barely covered coral reefs into an enchanting bay. From the moment he set eyes on the seacoast and skyline of southern Bali and encountered the handsome and animated Balinese in their own milieu, Kol, like many a Dutchman and other Westerner before and since, fell, or rather prostrated himself under the spell of what was already becoming known as *l'île sans pareil*.

Controleur Schwarz, it immediately developed, was accustomed to asserting his dignity by riding a high-spirited horse decked out with saddle and bridle brightly ornamented with silver, preceded and followed by a procession of splendidly uniformed lance and banner bearers. The Controleur graciously provided Kol with a similar mount and together they went cantering off toward the royal capital of Karangasem, their dress parade attracting an excited crowd of children and being eyed with deferential admiration by all wayfarers. Thus they passed through bustling market towns, lush rice fields, and densely grown coconut groves, crossed precipitous ravines through which flowed rushing streams, with the blue-green sea sometimes within view and the majestic Mt. Agung rising above them. It was a romantic ride on a bright sunny day in a superbly scenic South Seas island. If Kol was not irrevocably spellbound when he set out, all resistance wilted when he arrived in Karangasem. There the Radja himself, Gusti Djilantik, regally dressed, met them ceremoniously at the *puri* gateway and made them welcome.

Radja Djilantik escorted his two visitors through grotesquely ornamented monumental gateways and then through courtyard after courtyard until he showed them into the most elaborate section of all—his own private quarters which he had vacated in order to make them available to his honored guests. The Radja then discreetly withdrew; and Kol explored his accommodations with growing amazement. It was a large walled pavilion opening off a deep gallery, all very serene save for the rather startling interior decor. The doors were intricately carved and brightly painted and gilded in the Balinese manner, as were the windows and beams, but the furnishings were exclusively European. In the center of the room stood a huge brass bedstead overhung by a richly worked canopy, provided with silken counterpane, cushions, and pillows. There were marble-top tables, carved and gilded chairs and mirrors, and hanging lamps with crystal pendants—all in purest rococo, including an especially fanciful music box. But there were also some dismaying omissions. On the toilet table there was no water basin but rather an ornate soup tureen. In the pitcher there was only a little water, which, upon being shaken up, became muddy. And there was no visible evidence whatever of any toilet facilities except for the garden. Close to his quarters Kol found a pond filled with fish (carp and gurame) which would come at the sound of a gong. [The fish pond probably was the toilet, such installations serving such purpose in rural Bali and other parts today.]

The entire furnishings, Kol discovered, had been the gift of the Dutch Queen in return for the Radja's own presentation of fl. 20,000 on the recent occasion of her birthday.

The Controleur and Kol were no sooner well settled than servants began arriving in relays. They fetched in great silver dishes loaded with fruits and other foodstuffs and great quantities of flowers, the gifts from the Radja and various of the princes, always duplicate gifts, one for Kol, another for the Controleur. Soon the Radja himself appeared again, accompanied by a large retinue of officials and servants, and the formal part of the visit, which was to include much speechmaking, feasting, and dramatic performances, began to get under way. Thus, in Puri Karangasem, Kol was initiated into the traditional life of a Balinese court, which was also, in many significant respects, the life of the people. He began to accumulate the detailed information which he later included in his travel account with regard to religion, art, agriculture, and many other aspects of Balinese life, not neglecting matters of such lasting concern to the Dutch and to others as slavery and suttee, cremation, taxation, and public administration.

Kol engaged in several long conversations with the Radja, one of the most important and controversial of the leading Balinese personages. The Radja often adroitly converted these conversations into occasions for extracting highly miscellaneous information from his guest, with regard, for instance, to the Dutch royal family, the cities of The Hague and Amsterdam, the uses of railways and telephones. The Radja also wanted to hear Kol's report on conditions in Lombok, but he was reluctant to speak of his own role in the events of the early 1890s.

In 1891 the Radja of Lombok had appealed for help from his Balinese vassals in suppressing Sassak rebellions. Gusti Djilantik recruited 1,500 well-armed warriors and sailed off to Lombok (1891) to join the infamous Gusti Made in attempting to pacify the island. In 1894, shortly after a Dutch expeditionary force suffered serious losses from a surprise attack in which his own soldiers probably participated, Gusti Djilantik and his 1,500 warriors sailed back to Bali, quietly to await the sequel. The Dutch conquered Lombok in due course and eliminated most of the royal family; they then found themselves in need of a Regent to preside over the Lombok dependency of Karangasem-Bali, where the last Regent, Gusti Djilantik's brother, Gusti Gde Putu, had recently died (1893). They chose Gusti Djilantik himself, the decision being immediately challenged both by Dutchmen and by Balinese, many of whom, albeit for quite different reasons, regarded him as a traitor. Certain of his own *punggawa* aroused the people to surround the *puri* and shout threats upon his life. He was saved by the guile of one of his followers, who challenged the crowds, if they were so bold, to storm the palace at once and get on with their wicked business, thus shaming them into disbanding. The Radja then retired to a sacred spot in the mountains, there to spend his time in prayer and meditation until he was visited by a delegation of *punggawa* inviting him to resume the throne. Since that time he had enjoyed the confidence of his own people and of the Dutch officials and had proven himself a shrewd ruler.

One evidence of the Radja's shrewdness—and of Dutch official blundering—was his way of handling his own investiture as Regent. Instead of making a great ceremony of it, as did the Radja of Gianjar later on, he received the Controleur in private audience, accepted the letter of confirmation of authority, then sped the Dutchman on his way again before his people knew what had happened. It was a change of status of which even yet very few of his subjects were more than faintly aware. Thus Gusti Djilantik maintained his own authority and made it more difficult for the Dutch to assert theirs.

Kol admitted that it was not easy to appraise the true character and capability of the Radja, but, after weighing all of the arguments, he came to the conclusion that his conduct in Lombok had been "correct" and that his rule in Karangasem was just. His conduct had been "correct" in that he had answered the call to come to the defense of his overlord; it had been no act of disloyalty to depart when the Radja of Lombok, under the evil influence of his Regent and advisors, broke his own pledged word to the Dutch. "More of him men could not ask," wrote Kol. "It was too much to require him and his army to range themselves on our side—he, who had no reason to trust us, quite the contrary, witness the lesson of history." His rule was both firm and beneficial, and his state was obviously prospering in spite of certain very serious shortcomings.

The radjadom of Karangasem, said Kol, was critically overpopulated. It could no longer grow sufficient rice to feed its people, and there was no possibility of developing new land or water resources. Great quantities of rice had to be imported from neighboring states. Other crops, such as coffee, which would grow in the high mountains, had recently been introduced and would help to pay for the rice, but coffee would not suffice as a new economic base. The radjadom also produced and exported superior fruits, especially oranges, and significant numbers of fine fat pigs, sleek beautiful cattle, and sturdy little ponies. Forging and pottery-making offered promise, as did spinning and weaving of cotton thread. But real economic opportunity lay elsewhere, perhaps in distant, underpopulated Djembrana. The people of Karangasem would like to migrate to Djembrana, and some did in fact migrate to Buleleng, but the Dutch had as yet to establish any policy of deliberate and effective support.

The Radja seemed to understand the problems of his state and to be willing to accept advice. But when the Controleur suggested that he send an intelligent young prince, his nephew and heir apparent, Gusti Bagus, to attend school in Buleleng, the Radja pleaded that he could not afford the expense. His private revenue, Kol calculated, was approximately fl. 30,000 per year, derived mainly from taxes upon rice lands, license fees for cockfights, and duties on imports.

At the time of Kol's visit, Radja Gusti Djilantik was a man of well over sixty but still robust and active. He had once apparently been quite handsome and was certainly intelligent, but there was about him also an air of furtiveness which, Kol thought, scarcely befitted his reputation for forthrightness. Kol was especially disturbed by the sight of the Radja's constant companion, a malevolent-looking prince named Anak Agung Ktut Djilantik, who had inspired the early uprising against him and still quite clearly aspired to succeed to the throne, or to usurp it. Perhaps it was merely elementary prudence which prompted the Radja to keep this prince always within his sight, and since the young man himself seemed rather extravagantly fond of women, cockfighting, and the theater, the matter might resolve itself. The young Gusti Bagus promised much better and Kol hoped he would be chosen as heir, as in fact happened.

Kol's conversations with the Radja, which, as noted, often seemed more like the Radja's interrogations of Kol, were conducted under no little difficulty occasioned by the interruptions of others and the Radja's own rather inconsecutive physical and intellectual maneuvers. The Radja never sat still; he was on his chair and off again within moments, catching his visitor's hand in his own, then dropping it, drawing his visitor close to him, then moving away; he leaped quickly from subject to subject and answered only those questions which he chose to deal with. Although he evaded any mention of the Lombok war, his eyes lighted up and his voice grew vibrant when he talked of his exploits in the Karangasem invasion of Klungkung in 1891. His troops had invested the *puri* of the Dewa Agung and had had to withdraw, he said, only because the Radja of Lombok recalled his auxiliaries and the Dutch threatened to intervene. The Radja grew even more animated when he spoke of cockfighting. He would roll his headdress up into a tight knot in his hands and talk excitedly of his champions and his wagers; but then his eyes would begin to wander and his voice to drift off and it seemed almost as though he were going into a trance. He was always the generous and thoughtful host, however, and he especially pleased his guests with his farewell speech "We shall dedicate ourselves to ruling wisely; we must always stand by our white friends."

Rigors and Pleasures of Travel; Roads and Accommodations

For Heer van Kol, his subsequent visits to other parts of Bali, even those areas usually regarded as more scenic and cultured, could scarcely be expected to surpass or even to match the introductory exposure in Karangasem and in fact none did. He traveled indefatigably, however, visiting successively the radjadoms of Bangli, Gianjar, Klungkung, Badung, Tabanan, and Buleleng, missing only Djembrana, which he had already visited briefly in 1877 while serving with the colonial government. He called not only upon the radjas but upon the more important *punggawa*; he attended feasts and entertainments, religious ceremonies and court celebrations. He collected information about agriculture, industry, and administration, religion, manners, and traditions, taking notes of memorabilia and trivia such as few other visitors to Bali at the time either discovered or mentioned. After the luxury of Karangasem, he found conditions of transportation, lodging, and provisioning elsewhere in Bali a challenge both to ingenuity and endurance.

For travel in Bali, Kol noted, one needed first of all a *laissez passer* attainable only through the good offices of the Resident, who would have to approve any request in person and then advise the local rulers and get their concurrence. The process might consume many days if not many weeks or months and only rarely was it even attempted. He had set the wheels in motion by calling briefly in Buleleng on his way to visit Lombok. Upon arrival in Karangasem he was delighted to take delivery from Controleur Schwarz of the coveted passport. It was a great four-fold document on heavy paper impressively inscribed in Dutch and Balinese and even more impressively sealed.

One needed next to assemble and outfit an expedition—meaning riding horses and pack ponies; porters, interpreters, and servants; furnishings, such as a bed, or at least a mat; and equipment for preparing, cooking and serving food and drinks, not to mention miscellaneous provisions, since local supplies were likely to be bacteria-laden. In the course of any given journey one must expect the porters to lose part of the baggage, the saddle of the riding horse to be a torture, the stirrups to be too small for Western feet, and the leather straps on the pack horses to break. Roads, trails, and pathways were certain to be either rocky and dusty or muddy and slippery; ascents and descents were frequent and treacherous; bridges were likely to give way and apparently shallow fords to prove bottomless. Lodgings were almost always stifling, filthy, vermin-ridden, and stained with betel nut spittle. Disinfectant soap was a necessity and a tough skin the best protection against mosquitoes. Visits to radjas and other dignitaries had to be timed to correspond to the brief intervals between their sorties to patronize cockfights and their self-seclusion to smoke opium. "But I am ashamed of myself to speak of all this," he added, "when for all of these miseries my desire to repeat the journey is so very ardent."

Visit to Gianjar; Controleur Schwarz at Work

It was in the Radjadom of Gianjar that Kol came closest to recapturing the first fine exhilaration of Karangasem. In Gianjar he called upon Radja Dewa Gde Raka, who had just recently (1900) been made Dutch Viceroy and whose state, thanks to his own efforts and those of the new Dutch Controleur, Heer Schwarz, was beginning to recover from decades of disorders. The Radja received him in state with his high priest beside him and his *punggawa* gathered around. He replied patiently to questioning and provided a great deal of information, but more about the turbulent recent history than about immediate circumstances. Yet Kol could observe for himself that the *sawah* were now being planted with fine rice, new homes were being built, work was in progress on roads and irrigation canals, and the state was quite certainly not the scene of terror and desolation it had so recently been. And he had Controleur Schwarz to brief him regarding all that he, Schwarz, had learned since his arrival and to pose for him as the model Controleur performing his multiple and startlingly variegated tasks.

For the enlightenment of those who had never observed a Controleur at work, Kol recorded a few of the more or less urgent items of business of a typical day. "It was 7 July in Gianjar," he wrote, "in the course of our stop at the *pasangrahan* [government rest house for officials and other visitors] and two very wearisome trips to and from Ubud." Controleur Schwarz had to cope with the following:

Dutch cavalry at Sanur.

A religious service for Dutch troops inside a Balinese temple.

Dutch cavalry in front of Puri Tabanan.

Arrival in Gianyar of the Dewa Agung of Klungkung, central Bali, and his entourage on the the occasion of the signing of a new contract with the Dutch.

1. A question with regard to *sawah* boundaries disputed by Klungkung.
2. Protest from Klungkung with regard to the recent incident of Gianjar citizens casting the body of a deceased Klungkung citizen into a ravine instead of allowing it decent burial.
3. The complaint of a *punggawa* with regard to his runaway wife.
4. The protest of a Chinese market woman with regard to the confiscation of her possessions.
5. A dispute with regard to extradition of criminals from Bangli.
6. The Radja's perplexity with regard to appropriate action to take against one *punggawa* who imposed illegal assessment upon coffee and another who withheld certain tax monies.
7. Preparation of proposals for improvement in the state financial administration in order to prevent Chinese merchants from evasion of taxes.
8. Prevention of certain rash actions which would have stirred up trouble with Klungkung.
9. Consideration of plans for improvement of water distribution in a certain rice-growing area.
10. Clarification to the Radja of a certain recent property settlement and explanation with regard to punishment of misdemeanors.
11. Consideration of methods to combat the use of false weights by Chinese coffee buyers.
12. Consideration of the proper route for a new roadway.
13. Escort for a certain *punggawa* who feared being intercepted by agents of the Dewa Agung.
14. Rescue of a woman who had been guilty of breach of *adat* (customary law) and had fled to Buleleng, only to return and be threatened with punishment by death.

At the end of the day, he concluded his inventory, "A Gusti (warrior) came to complain that one of the *punggawa* was neglecting his sister, a report which brought a smile to our lips and provides good evidence of the boundless confidence which Schwarz inspires in the breasts of the people, great and small."

Kol acquired from Schwarz certain statistics with regard to the Gianjar population. Before the troubles started in the 1880s, the population was 150,000, inclusive of 900 Brahmans, 8,000 Ksatrya, and 1,500 Wesya. During the period when most able-bodied men had been recruited into military service and bands of enemy soldiers had wandered through the land, doing damage when and as they could, there had been great loss of life, but, by the year 1900, the population figure was up to 190,000. Controleur Schwarz could not provide much precise information about production and revenues, such facts remaining still to be accumulated. But he did mention that the normal tax on rice amounted to about 4 per cent in kind, which the Radja shared with the *punggawa*.

With regard to Dutch policy in Gianjar, evidently well coached by the Controleur, Kol wrote:

We remain true here to the well-proven tactics of our colonial policy and to this we owe our greatness. We grant the radja self-rule and we permit the people to observe their ancient laws and customs. We remove abuses, and those which remain will yet disappear. The rule of the radja replaces that of the *punggawa*, who are concerned only with their private satisfactions. The position of the once powerful *punggawa* is now reduced, as it should be, to that of servant of the radja under our watchful supervision ...we have brought law and order.

Dewa Agung's Arrogance; Resident's Protests

Kol's great disappointment on his journey was his visit to Klungkung to meet the Dewa Agung. The Dewa Agung ignored him. The Dewa Agung, in fact, was deliberately making himself difficult and in so far as possible also inaccessible to the Dutch. It was his intention, said Kol, thus to assert his great power and prestige, which, in fact, had all but vanished. The position of the Dewa Agung and his claim to being Susuhunan (Emperor) of all of Bali, Kol added, was now sustained not by his own vain pretensions or the meager tribute and homage of his presumed vassals but only by the tolerance of the

Dutch themselves. The Dutch had recognized him as Emperor in negotiating their mid-nineteenth century treaties, and in continuing to show special deference they provided what little substance there was to his claim to hegemony. The Dewa Agung himself seemed most ungrateful for Dutch support; he consistently delayed for a month or more in replying to any communication from the Resident and in his own messages to him assumed an air of arrogance. When a mere Controleur came to call, the Dewa Agung habitually feigned illness so sudden and severe as to be intentionally unconvincing. His realm, the smallest and poorest of the Balinese states, had a population of a mere 36,000 persons, many of whom actually lived not in Klung-kung proper but in widely scattered enclaves within adjacent states. The entire radjadom was obviously impoverished and retarded, in comparison especially with the Dutch-dominated areas. Kol hoped that the example of prosperity and progress elsewhere would exercise a sobering influence upon the Dewa Agung, but he placed more confidence in the salutary effects of Dutch official firmness and tactfulness, which had not recently been much in evidence.

An audience with the Dewa Agung being out of the question, Kol contented himself with an "eye-witness account" of an audience which the Dewa Agung and the Crown Prince had recently deigned to grant the Resident and the Controleur. The Resident arrived on a warship, which cruised ominously offshore; he traveled to Klung-kung with a marine guard, which was obviously tough; and he spared no other stage effects which would make it very clear that he was not to be trifled with. The Dewa Agung Putera, aged about 50 but still notably vigorous and handsome, richly dressed and with much of his regalia on display, languidly received his visitors, leaving it to the Crown Prince, equally elegant and striking in appearance, to do most of the talking, as he did with great eloquence and at times at great length. During the intervals when the Dutchmen were speaking, the two princes chewed betel nut, smoked tobacco, toyed with their jewels, and otherwise deported themselves as though the performance were exceedingly wearisome. The court interpreters and secretaries tediously clarified and transcribed in quite excessive detail just what it was the Resident had on his mind. What the Resident and the Controleur had on their minds and on their agenda was a long catalog of offenses and affronts for which they were resolved to get immediate satisfaction.

The Resident made formal charges that the Dewa Agung had deliberately obstructed the work of surveyors sent to determine boundaries and engineers sent to repair waterways; he had violated the land and water rights of his neighbors; he had harbored criminals and debtors and other fugitives from Dutch controlled states and had received stolen property which he refused to restore; etc, etc. If Klungkung did not make amends within fourteen days, announced the Resident, the Dutch would blockade its seacoast and reduce the state to submission. There had been no blockade and the Dewa Agung had neither repented nor reformed. He still had the effrontery, in fact, to demand that the Dutch themselves return—or purchase—the *puri* slaves who sought shelter and freedom in other states, and to make other equally outrageous proposals, doing so, the Dutch were certain, only to annoy.

Imports and Exports; Receipts and Expenditures

Kol proceeded from Klungkung through the states of Badung, Tabanan, and Buleleng, where he accumulated, among other information, the most recent figures on receipts and expenditures of the Residency. These statistics, which relate mainly to Buleleng and Djembrana, the only two states which had already been for any considerable period of time under full Dutch control, were as follows:

Receipts

Tax on *sawah*	fl. 149,600
Opium monopoly	102,200
Tax on dry fields	33,300
Trade tax	12,800
Posts	8,000
Tax on slaughter of beef	5,000
Sea passages	3,700
Tax on home grounds	3,500
Tax on houses	3,300
TOTAL	333,000

Expenditures

Administrative services	139,200
Public works	65,200
Justice	32,600
Finance	7,100
Marine service (ports)	7,000
Education	5,000
TOTAL	233,000

In making mention that the stated items do not add up the stated totals, it seems appropriate to point out certain other facts upon which Kol did not comment: (1). The largest source of revenue in the north was the tax on rice lands, calculated at about 12 per cent of the crop value, whereas in the newly controlled state of Gianjar the Radja's tax was only about 4 per cent. (2). Opium, the second largest source of revenue, brought in over fl. 100,000. (3). The outlay on education was a minute fl. 5,000, but in fact the government had already opened at least one primary school in Buleleng and an expanded educational program was clearly in prospect.

Admonitions and Predictions

Kol's experiences and findings in all of the states except Klungkung seemed reasonably reassuring. He wound up his trip to Bali convinced of the general efficacy of Dutch rule and the benefits which the Balinese derived from it. It was a conclusion which contrasted quite sharply with his categorical declaration with regard to Java, where, he said, the Javanese were being repressed, exploited, and impoverished. "In Bali," he wrote, "there is great and noble work to be done, and hail to the Dutch if we proceed with this beautiful task in a spirit of dedication and selflessness!"

The melancholy postscript to Kol's carefully conditioned prophecy should be his own. Kol returned to Bali in 1910 to resurvey the situation after what he regarded as a fair test period of Dutch rule over the island in its entirety. He was saddened to have to report that in this "Hellas under a tropical sun" his countrymen had created grave political, economic, and social problems. He concluded, less confidently but more oracularly than before, "It is our sacred duty so to conduct ourselves that the results of our rule will be beneficial to the people, as will happen only if we are guided by humanitarian rather than selfish motives. Then, sooner perhaps than many persons think, the time will come when our own task will be completed, our own pledges will be fulfilled, and the Balinese will regain their freedom. May the Dutch in Bali work toward this end."

CHAPTER 12

Ethical Interlude
(1908–1930)

Reexamination and Reformulation of Colonial Policy

The punitive expeditions against Bali in the late 1840s passed almost unnoticed in the outside world except among the Dutch themselves, who were as greatly upset by their own reverses as they were gratified by their eventual victories. The Lombok Expedition and the *puputan* somewhat troubled the better informed and more compassionate sectors of the world public of the 1890s. Then came reports of the *puputan* of 1906 in Badung and that of 1908 in Klungkung. Certain private citizens, religious groups, and even official agencies in Batavia and The Hague were deeply disturbed by the massacres and the looting, and shock waves spread to London, Paris, and even, ever so faintly, to New York. Protests poured into the colonial office with regard to Dutch reprisals wildly disproportionate to any known Balinese offenses. The Dutch, who were under pressure also with regard to their policies in Java, Sumatra, and the eastern islands, resolved to make amends. They set themselves to reforms and reformulations which led to what they rather too sanctimoniously announced and acclaimed as the Ethical Policy.

Before, during, and after their open conversion to colonial ethicalism, the Dutch in Bali showed themselves to be genuinely in earnest about redefining and discharging their colonial responsibilities. Some of them became amateurs of professional quality in the new field of Bali studies, and upon these pioneering ethnologists, philologists, archeologists, and others almost equally receptive, Bali worked its native magic. There grew up a whole new generation of Residency administrators who regarded themselves not only as the agents of modernization in education, health, and administrative services but as the protectors of Bali's own traditional culture. It was a matter of at least equal significance that there grew up also a whole new generation of Balinese, among whom there were significant numbers of persons who were disposed to make the transition from a medieval to a modern society. What did not emerge, then or later, was a new Balinese way of life compatible with a new century.

Traditional Ruler as Radja and Regent; Role of Controleur

The Governor-General in Batavia continued to treat Bali along with Lombok as a separate Residency administered under a Resident and his staff in Buleleng in the north with a southern sub-office in Den Pasar. Each of the eight radjadoms had its Controleur, who personally embodied Dutch dignity and authority immediately alongside the throne. The Balinese ruler himself played the dual role of Radja and Regent, the rather subtle distinctions being at times lost upon both the incumbent and his subjects. The ruler, as Radja, retained most of the traditional responsibilities and perquisites insofar at least as those did not interfere with the proper functioning of the new Dutch Residency programs. As Radja, he was the venerated head of state, the ultimate authority in matters of *adat* (religion and custom), but an ornamental figurehead in matters relating to modern progress. He continued to perform the vital ceremonial functions upon which the welfare of the state traditionally depended, civil and religious ritual being as important to the Balinese as were protocol and administrative regulations to the Dutch. He lived in his ancestral palace, a complex of scores of more or less imposing and resplendent structures which constituted a walled royal village. Within the *puri* was always at least one *pura* (temple) for private and public ceremonies. There was an archive in which were kept manuscript copies of literary and religious works engraved on strips of lontar palm, some of them splendidly illustrated and great works of art and literature. There was also a treasure room in which were stored the sacred and magical articles of the royal regalia—lances, krises, rings, betel boxes, parasols,

High officials at a formal reading of lontar palm manuscripts in the library at the palace of Buleleng, ca. 1920. Second from left is the *Punggawa* of Sekaseda. Third from left is the *Patih* of Buleleng.

The *Patih* of Buleleng and his family in the Buleleng palace, ca. 1920.

and banners, often lavishly ornamented with gold and jewels. The Radja was surrounded by a retinue of dependants and retainers, who might number a hundred or more within the *puri* walls.

The Radja's *puri* was the focus of a civil and religious hierarchy of *punggawa* (chiefs) and *pedanda* (priests) who extended the royal influence into every village and every village temple. *The punggawa* made certain that the agricultural pursuits of the villagers proceeded smoothly; the *pedanda* made certain that all the proper rituals were observed; the *punggawa* and *pedanda* together resolved any serious dispute, perhaps by convening a *kerta* (court) over which the Radja might preside. Besides being the focus of civil and religious author-ity, the *puri* was also the center of arts and crafts, of which the Radja was always the chief patron. The Radja's *gamelan* (gong orchestra) was generally the finest in the kingdom, the instruments often being part of the royal regalia. The court dancers were the most accom-plished, and many of the pretty young dancing girls were destined to become royal concubines. Every *puri* had its craftsmen nearby— sculptors, painters, weavers, silversmiths and goldsmiths—whose products ornamented and enriched the court. The Radja and his fam-ily were the owners of large tracts of land from which they received rich revenue. Payment in cash or kind were occasions for visits of officials and farmers as well to the *puri*, so there was always a sense of public participation in *puri* affairs. The Radja was the personal pa-tron of various temples, upon which, particularly at festival time, he lavished gifts which thus constituted return royal tribute not only to the gods but also to the people.

The protocol-conscious Dutch and the *adat*-alert Balinese found it necessary very early on to work out a precise code of conduct for guidance of the Resident and the Regent in their official encounters so that neither would inadvertently give grave offense to the other. In accordance with a formal Residency ruling in which each Radja concurred, the Resident would give two days' notice to the Regent whenever he intended to pay an official call, advising him of the na-ture of his business, making arrangements for a rendezvous with the Regent's representative at the state boundary, and spelling out his re-quirements with regard to accommodations. Upon arrival at the state capital, he would notify the Regent of the day and hour he wished

The Radja of Karangasem, Gusti Bagus Djilantik, and daughter, dressed in rich hand-woven brocades, ca. 1918. In 1937, he took on the hereditary title of Anak Agung Ktut Karangasem.

A Dutch official being received by the Radja (Regent) of Karangasem. Strict protocol governed meetings between the Resident and Regent.

to set for an audience. The Regent would send a high court official to conduct the Resident from his lodgings, usually an official guest-house, to the main gate of the *puri,* the Resident clothed in full dress uniform with sword and plumes and walking under the royal golden parasol. The Regent would meet him ceremoniously at the gate, con-duct him to the audience *pendopo* (pavilion), seat him to his right— but never on a chair higher or more splendid than his own. At the end of the audience, the Regent would walk with the Resident to the steps of the pavilion, no further. It was necessary then for the Regent to call upon the Resident, who would send an aide to escort him, meet him at the door, seat him to his right, and escort him to the door again at the time of his departure. Any breach of this protocol was presumed to be a deliberate affront so serious that one was seldom made.

Much the same procedure applied in the case of the visit of a Controleur, up until the time, that is, that the Controleur took up his residence in the royal capital, when informality began to set in.

The Radja, in short, continued to reign in magnificence. But as Regent he ruled by the consent of the Resident and the Controleur, the latter of whom prompted his important decisions and relieved him of much routine by exercising control also over the *punggawa*. The Controleur very soon introduced the engineer who built the public works, the doctor who opened a clinic, the teacher who established a school, and eventually the military officer who recruited and trained a few soldiers. Perhaps as many as three or four Dutchmen settled into a given radjadom. But most of the Dutch officials lived in Buleleng or Den Pasar in little Dutch enclaves, populated by about 50 and 25 official families, respectively. One of the most important of the officials was the fiscal officer, who raised more revenue than the Residency in fact spent, his main sources being the opium monopoly and land taxes. With these revenues, and with enormous resources of unpaid labor, the Residency achieved an almost miraculous proliferation of roads, bridges, and dams, and also a few schools, clinics, and other modern facilities. Visitors to Bali very soon began to report that the island was just about the prettiest little exhibit in the whole of the Indies of Dutch efficiency and enlightenment.

European and Chinese Business Interests

Not the least of the evidence of ethical Dutch behavior and Balinese benefit therefrom was the absence of any conspicuous colony of Western residents. From the very beginning the Residency opposed all efforts of Dutch big business firms to open up rubber or tea plantations or sugar or tobacco estates such as flourished in Java. Only a very few Dutch business interests therefore found it either expedient or profitable to open up offices in Bali; the few that appeared were to be found in Buleleng and Den Pasar. The most conspicuous was K.P.M., the giant steamship line which linked Bali to Java and the

The Radja of Karangasem and his wife flanked by the Dutch Resident of Bali and Lombok and his wife, with various Dutch and Balinese colonial officials, the district heads of Karangasem (front left) and court priests (front right), ca. 1920s.

eastern islands and presently began to experiment with tourism. The firm Jacobsen van den Berg opened up an import–export agency, as did Reiss; Afscheep en Commissie Zaak, an affiliate of N.H.M. (which thus returned to Bali in about 1910), engaged in banking and shipping. Shell opened a Den Pasar office. That was the Western business community, which might include at any given time up to ten representatives and their families. There were also a couple of German planters, who had acquired leaseholds in Buleleng or Djembrana, and a few Arab, Armenian, Javanese, and Chinese who had similar holdings. These dated from the previous century or from short periods of years in the present century when the Dutch experimented with limited relaxation of their rules against alienation of land. They found themselves flooded with applications, mainly by speculators who somehow induced Balinese to join them in visionary schemes for opening up plantations. Those which existed rarely flourished.

The really important foreign enterprises in Bali were those of the Chinese, who acquired much urban property and a few coffee gardens and coconut groves, holding them generally in the name of a Balinese wife, but were rigorously excluded from acquiring other agricultural land. The Chinese merchant-traders, whose shops were to be found in all the larger towns, collected and shipped local produce and distributed daily necessities and seemed always to make good profits, no matter what restrictive measures the radjas—or the Dutch—adopted against them. They also constituted themselves the money-lenders and thus gained even greater wealth and opprobrium. By readily advancing much more money than the client could possibly pay back at their usurious interest rates, the Chinese burdened many a Balinese of high or low degree with debts which eventually cost him his lands. But these lands normally passed to another Balinese rather than a Chinese owner; iniquitous as the system was, it did not result in great tracts of Balinese land passing into the possession of non-Balinese.

Usury; Corvée; Taxes; Land; Production; Exports

Protection of the Balinese farmers against the exploitation of foreign merchants and planters and protection of the Balinese culture against sudden and disruptive impact of outside influences constituted the two great achievements of the Dutch colonial administration. There were also grave failures both of commission and omission. It is difficult to grade these shortcomings in order of magnitude, but one of the greatest was certainly the operation of the opium monopoly; another was the toleration of the evil system of Chinese usury; another was the neglect of education; yet another was the near passivity of the administration in the face of the very clearly analyzed problem of too many people, too little land, and too few job opportunities. Two which attracted remarkably little attention at the time but loom large in retrospect were the heavy reliance upon obligatory labor and the sharp increase in the effective rate of taxation. Both help to explain how the Dutch accomplished so much in so short a time with so little drain upon their own resources in improving the physical aspect of the island.

The Balinese were accustomed by long tradition to the performance of obligatory labor, which was endowed, indeed, with such social and religious significance as to seem virtually voluntary. The

A street in Den Pasar in the 1920s lined with the shops of Chinese merchant-traders. These merchants collected and shipped local produce and sold daily necessities to the local population. Many also acted as money-lenders.

A view of Gianyar in the 1920s. A *pura* (temple) within the walled royal palace complex (*puri*) was the site of private and public ceremonies. From the 1920s, high Dutch officials went about their business in motor-cars, not on horseback.

Dutch happily accepted and greatly expanded the scope of what they identified as *heerendienst* (the labor due to a feudal overlord) but never as corvée. The Balinese of the lowest caste (not of the three higher castes), which meant 90–95 per cent of the population, were subject to call for work on ordinary community projects such as construction and maintenance of temples and palaces. When the Controleur moved in, he quickly discovered that the best and ofttimes the only way to carry out new public works was to persuade the Radja and the *punggawa* to call up the farmers.

The new roads, dams, and ports, also the new offices and homes for the Dutch and the new palaces and temples for which the radjas felt an insatiable craving, required an enormous amount of labor. The Dutch supplied certain imported materials, but the people were expected to contribute not only their time and energy but also the very simple tools and materials upon which most of the work depended. Whereas in former times the people had devoted perhaps 15 days per year to the community and 15 days to the *pura* or *puri*, they were called upon to donate at least another 30 days to the colonial government. Many of the improvements, of course, were for their own good, but that was not exactly how they viewed it; a few weeks or even a few days of work on a new road could very seriously impair the prospects for their crops. Thirty to thirty-six days of labor per year for the state alone became the new standard, with provision that it should not interfere with harvests or festivals. Occasional little rebellions or threatened rebellions served to indicate that requirements became extremely onerous; but resentment was directed more against the *punggawa* than against the Radja or the Dutch. The *punggawa* often had other offenses for which to answer and were suspended or removed from office when they became especially unpopular.

According to the traditional system, the Balinese were subject to various direct and indirect taxes which might add up to about 4 to 6 per cent of an independent farmer's income. If he was a tenant farmer, however, the burden of taxation in addition to rent might become as much as 50 per cent of his harvest. Few Balinese had been tenant farmers in the past but great numbers became so in the late nineteenth century, when population pressures first began to make themselves seriously felt.

The Radja of Karangasem, Gusti Bagus Djilantik, and his wife in his palace, ca. 1930. To his traditional palace the Radja added new buildings and courtyards in the style of the courts of central Java, which he often visited. Furniture and carpets were frequently of European origin.

The Water Palace of the Radja of Karangasem, ca. 1930. Located near the coast, at Ujung, it was a large Dutch-style building, elevated to catch the cool afternoon breezes, and surrounded by water.

The traditional system of taxation was for the Radja to appoint a *sjahbandar* (harbor-master), a *pekaseh* (crop collector), and a *pachter* (opium monopolist). The *sjahbandar* and the *pachter,* who were usually Chinese, paid the Radja an annual fee of several thousand guilders or more for the privileges of an office of which he retained most of the proceeds. The *pekaseh*, who was almost always a Balinese, collected a portion of the crop for his own, the *punggawa's*, and the Radja's disposition. The *sjahbandar*, it was generally understood, would collect approximately 2 per cent on all imports and exports. He might sometimes make quite extortionate levies and accumulate enormous profits, but he was vulnerable to undermining and overbidding by rivals for the position, so that a system of checks and balances came to prevail. The *pachter*, whose calling was more dubious and therefore more hazardous, was subject to many pressures from the rulers, the smugglers, and the Dutch, and was put out of business in 1908 by the opium monopoly.

The *pekaseh*, the Radja's agent who became also the agent of the colonial administration, assessed various fees in various locations for land and water rights. In general his collections on behalf of the radjas had come to about 4 per cent of the crop, the assessment upon rice being by far his most important consideration. But the *pekaseh* and his assistants also tapped other sources of income, including the crops from dry fields and from all village agricultural and commercial activity. They might collect a royalty of 1½–3½ guilder cents on each coconut tree or coffee bush, ten guilders for each cockfight, and levy road tolls at the rate of 25 kopeng for a loaded pack pony, eight kopeng for a porter carrying two baskets slung from a shoulder pole, or four kopeng for a woman bearing a burden on her head. Under the radjas, in short, the assessment of taxes was well organized and the system was well understood. The tax burden was seldom crushing and seemed on the whole remarkably light.

As the Dutch established and extended their rule, they devoted themselves quite methodically to restructuring the tax system on a basis favorable to the colonial administration. One of their first moves was always to persuade or compel the ruler to relinquish control of customs (i.e. opium), which became a source of colonial rather than royal revenue, although in certain cases the Radja might be compensated by an annual pension. They then set about compiling a register of agricultural lands and a new system of assessment. The very compilation of the land register served, along with the sudden growth of population and consequent shortage of land, profoundly to alter Balinese concepts and practices with regard to land tenure. In early times the land was regarded as the property of the gods who made it available to the farmer for his use in accordance with his needs, his ability, and his performance of all the prescribed ceremonies with regard to planting, cultivating, and harvesting. Every man had the right to enough land to support himself and his family, and when his requirements for or his utilization of the land changed significantly there might be a reallocation; certain lands, furthermore, were held in common as community pasture or as fields of which the proceeds would be used for community purposes. The radjas acquired rights to extensive tracts of land by reason of the tradition that all property of a man who died without male heirs was theirs to dispose of, as, in the case of lands, they did by renting to landless persons.

In Dutch times population pressure and lack of new lands to be opened up, also the fact that the administration was compiling a very detailed register of who operated exactly what fields and therefore owed exactly how much in taxes, combined to convert rights of land use into rights of ownership and hence also of private transfer and sale. Good rice land (*sawah*) began to be valued at approximately fl. 1200 per hectare, a price which long prevailed.

The value of *sawah* was directly related to the value of crops and the level of farm income, whether of the owner or the tenant farmer. One hectare of good *sawah* in Bali would produce approximately double the rice crop of a hectare of *sawah* in Java, so rich was the soil and so skilled were the farmers. The commonly accepted crop figure was 150 *ikat* (300 *kati*, or 400 pounds) of rice per harvest, with two harvests each year and a total annual yield of 300 *ikat* valued at fl. 300. On this amount, ten *ikat* per harvest were reserved for taxes, ten for the harvesters, two for other labor, and one for seed, leaving the owner-farmer a quantity of rice worth approximately fl. 250. The tenant farmer, after payment of rent in kind, had approximately half that amount. Since the farmer had other sources of income, the normal income per farm family was something well over fl. 250 ($110, i.e. 50 per cent higher than the 1976 figure). And the landowner, whose hectare of *sawah* would yield at least fl. 120 after deduction of the Radja's tax and the tenant farmer's share, calculated that it had a sales value of ten times that amount, or fl. 1,200. Such was the tidy arithmetic of Balinese agriculture, at least until the Dutch tax assessor began adding on extras, which presently drove the total tax up to about 12 per cent.

The average farm holding in Bali at the turn of the century was about one hectare of good land, irrigated or dry, which would yield crop and income as indicated above, the produce from copra and coffee and other crops being about the equivalent of that from rice. There were many farmers who operated more than one hectare of land and thus earned more than the average income, but there were also an alarming number of tenant farmers. Rich as the rice harvest was, more and more of the population was coming to depend very largely upon other staples, especially sweet potatoes and cassava. But the island had an impressive quantity of rice available for export, to the value annually in the early part of the century of approximately fl. 500,000.

In the early twentieth, as in the nineteenth century, rice was always a major item in Bali's exports, but as the population increased, rice exports dropped. Copra and coffee, cattle and pigs came to surpass rice in importance as earners of export income, upon which the Residency itself realized approximately 3 per cent of the value in various duties. Cattle and pigs were of especial importance to the ordinary household economy, almost every family having at least one cow and several pigs which were intended, sooner or later, for sale on the local market and perhaps for export. In the year 1910 the total export of pigs from southern Bali came to 33,400 head and the total of cows to 9,500, the pigs fetching approximately fl. 20 each for the owners and the cows fl. 40–50 each.

Trade and commerce were to a serious degree inhibited by anomalous conditions with regard to currency. The money of the people and of the village market place was the kopeng or pitji, that is the small brass "cash" originally minted in Canton and later forged in Singapore, which had been introduced into the island by early foreign traders. The Balinese, characteristically, had endowed the kopeng with aesthetic as well as monetary significance, distinguishing at least eight types of differing artistic and therefore economic value, reserving one variety exclusively for ornamentation of ceremonial offerings. Large transactions, however, required resort to silver coins, which might mean Singapore dollars, Indian rupees, Spanish or Portuguese pieces-of-eight, Dutch guilders, or any other coin of precious metal, preferably attractive in mintage and convincing in pure metallic ring. The Balinese placed no confidence whatever in paper money and consistently refused to accept it. They were not even fully convinced about silver coins, preferring the bulk and reassuring weight of the strings of brass kopeng, several pounds of which were required to exchange for the rijksdaalder (2½ guilders). And much to the annoyance of the Dutch, they preferred the silver coins of almost any other nation to those of the Netherlands. The Willem II rijksdaalder, which the Dutch themselves thought so handsomely embossed with the distinguished features of the King, were known to the irreverent Balinese as the "dollar of the King with the long neck"; the Willem III coin, the pride of the Dutch mint, was disdained as "the dollar of the King with the cow-lick." These pieces would not exchange in Bali for their worth in silver, but the Chinese craftily bought up at cut rates all that somehow made their appearance and put counterfeits into circulation in order to ensure continuing lack of enthusiasm for any coin of Dutch provenance.

The kopeng were not only difficult to carry or to count; they also fluctuated wildly in value in relation to silver, the usual rate being between 600 and 800 to the Dutch guilder but sometimes touching 2,000. One kopeng was enough for a serving of rice, a drink of *arak*, or a few pieces of fruit; a loop of kopeng, strung through their square holes on cord made of palm fiber, would more than suffice for ordinary marketing; but the more important traders found the Balinese fixation upon the kopeng to be extremely awkward. So too did the Dutch administrators, who were frequently embarrassed to discover that no strong box or even strong room ever seemed sufficiently capacious for the safe-keeping of petty cash.

The cult of the kopeng gave rise to one further cause of confusion and also, frequently, of litigation. Among different states and even adjacent villages, there was no consensus on the exact number of coins which should be strung to constitute a standard loop, to make it easier, presumably, to give and receive payment without the laborious necessity of fingering every coin. In Gianjar the number was commonly 175 and in Karangasem 185 and there were various gradations in between. Certain traders, furthermore, made it their larcenous practice to extract one or more kopeng from a loop which was apparently intact. At times people carelessly entered into contracts for payment in a specified number of loops without stipulating exactly which loops and determining the so-called *long*, that is, the exchange rate between the loops of different villages. Disputes over kopengs led to such numerous court cases that at times the Radja's *Kerta* seemed to be concerning itself with little else. Certain foreign observers were under the distinct impression that the Balinese themselves rather enjoyed all the confusion and litigation and that they regarded deliberate obfuscation with regard to the *long* not as a swindle but as a gamble.

Opium and the Monopoly; Education and Medicine

Neither financial vagaries nor moral scruples ever much inhibited trade in opium, which, almost from the beginning, was a major item in Balinese commerce. Visiting merchants fetched opium to exchange for local produce, and in Balinese markets the standard unit, a ball of raw opium worth fl. 25, circulated as the equivalent of legal tender. The drug commanded a ready retail market among both Chinese and Balinese users, and it was a favorite investment for smugglers, who carried it to Java, Borneo, Celebes, and other islands in defiance of the Dutch *opiumregie* (opium monopoly).

Opium reached Bali from India, commonly by way of Singapore, packed into chests which could be purchased for fl. 1,550 wholesale to yield at least fl. 2,500 retail. Opium was a major source of revenue to the radjas, who always assessed import duty upon it and licensed the *opiumpachter* (opium farmer), generally a Chinese, who gladly paid a handsome annual fee for what amounted to a local dealership monopoly. Opium consumption by the Balinese themselves was originally confined mainly to the palaces, where court retainers and harem wives had money to spend and time on their hands. But in the late nineteenth century its use increased alarmingly among the common people, especially at festival time, when all manner of self-indulgence was encouraged and novelties were eagerly tested out. The radjadom of Bangli, which required only two chests of opium in the year 1860, consumed 15 in 1870. In 1873 the reported import of opium in the northern seaport of Buleleng, where the Dutch exercised close control and compiled careful statistics, came to a total value of fl. 2,250,000. The Chinese *opiumpachter* of Badung at the turn of the century was paying the Radja fl. 3,600 annually for his privilege and other radjas were realizing even more. But opium addiction was obviously becoming a curse upon the island. The Dutch, who felt that in Bali, as elsewhere in the Indies, outright prohibition of opium would be both unrealistic and profitless, decided to regulate it. While earnestly advising the radjas and the people against its use, they promulgated the *opiumregie* which had already afforded them great moral and financial comfort in Java.

The *opiumregie* went into effect throughout all of Bali on January 1, 1908. It immediately induced certain more or less predictable consequences. In Gelgel in particular there occurred a series of disorders and outrages which provoked a punitive expedition which, in turn, resulted in the Klungkung *puputan* of 1908 and the total submission of the last of the states to resist Dutch rule. Government regulations provided that no one under the age of eighteen would be permitted to make purchases and that all adult users must register with one of the 100 official outlets. But opium was packaged in a manner which lent itself to easy and widespread sale to the common people; the popular "two drop" dosage, for instance, retailed for six guilder-cents. Later, when opium prices were increased by 50 per cent and more, the "two drop" dosage was largely replaced by the "one-half drop," which sold for a mere three cents, the equivalent, to be sure, of 5 to 10 per cent of the daily wage of the manual laborer, who found it a solace. Adult users who failed to make their habitual purchases over any period of a few weeks' duration were subject to fine for patronage, it was presumed, of an illegal market. Purchase of opium was made especially attractive, furthermore, by acceptance of payment in the popular coin of the people, the brass kopeng, at a more favorable rate of exchange against the guilder than that which prevailed in the public market. In the year 1910, the average outlay for purchase of opium throughout the whole of Bali worked out at about fl. 12 per household. This was almost exactly enough for one half drop daily for every adult male.

In 1908, the first year of the operation of the monopoly, when large stocks of pre-monopoly opium were still on hand, the *opiumregie* itself reported the import of stocks valued at fl. 273,000. In 1909 the value was fl. 894,000, of which about 90 per cent would be net profit. Sale of opium accounted, in fact, for about 75 per cent of the administrative budget and assured the Residency each year of a very gratifying surplus which was often larger than total expenditures.

While actively and profitably marketing opium through the state monopoly, the Dutch were conducting a campaign to combat its use, especially in the royal families where the habit had become a vice which interfered quite seriously with affairs of state. As early as 1870 the Resident himself had persuaded the Dewa Agung and the Dewa Manggis to renounce the use of the drug, at least for the moment. The Dewa Agung, upon pronouncing himself cured, had dispatched his silver opium pipe to the Governor-General as a gift of gratitude, receiving in return a fine Damascene sword. But the use of opium was always especially difficult to combat because many of the Balinese regarded it as a cure-all even more efficacious than the long-popular Chinese medicines, of which it might also be an ingredient.

In the year 1910, when the Dutch realized well over fl. 1,000,000 from the sale of opium in Bali, they expended less than fl. 20,000 on schools, increasing their educational budget only very modestly and gradually thereafter. Heer van Kol, the visitor of 1902 and 1910, an outspoken critic of his country's colonial policies, was almost equally censorious with regard to the opium monopoly and educational neglect. He pointed out that the Balinese were avid for learning and that despite the lack of any formal school system in the past, many could read their own language and some were familiar with *kawi*, the archaic language of religion and literature. The ordinary Balinese, it seems, sometimes achieved literacy by understudying the highly trained temple priests and then proudly introduced his friends to his own new accomplishment. The Dutch themselves had begun building *inlandsche schoolen* (primary schools for indigenous children) as early as the 1890s, first in Buleleng (two schools), later one each in

Badung, Gianjar, Bangli, and Tabanan, the total enrollment being about 600. Kol complained, however, not only that the schools were far too small but also that they were modeled upon those of Java; rather than teaching Balinese literature and the practice of agriculture, as would have been appropriate, they adhered to a sterile and unimaginative Dutch-prescribed curriculum derived from Dutch texts and taught mechanically by Javanese teachers, even the vacation period corresponding not to any Balinese festival but to the Muslim fasting month. Such schools seemed to Kol to be conducive only to the creation of "imitation Dutchmen" or "bastardized Javanese" who would be supercilious toward other Balinese but incapable of earning a living. Kol urged immediate rethinking as well as expansion of the program, which in fact occurred over the next several decades. Even then only a small minority of Balinese actually achieved even lower primary level education although a select few, the children of royal families, received special attention and were taught in Dutch so that they might, if they chose, continue their education in Java or Holland.

Heer van Kol was less uncomplimentary to his countrymen in Bali when he reported upon the medical services which they provided. The Dutch, he said, had already made great progress in the control of smallpox, cholera, venereal diseases, leprosy, and other more or less common maladies. The Residency had established four clinics, all predictably packed with patients, and the offices of the Controleurs were frequently visited by persons seeking the simple remedies which they too dispensed. A certain Dr. Kroll treated 150 persons each day in the Karangasem clinic and other foreign doctors were soon to be introduced to manage other clinics already built or contemplated. A Chinese "Java Doctor," that is, a trainee of the medical college in Batavia, was in private practice in Den Pasar and others were expected. In the decades after Kol's visits, the medical services, like the schools, were to be much expanded and improved, and the Balinese population seemed to later visitors to be notably bright and healthy, as, indeed, it had been before.

Balance of Benefits and Burdens; *Kerta* Courts

Assuming that it was inevitable that Bali should pass through a colonial period and that it is fruitless to repine, it seems admissible to suggest that the benefits and burdens of Dutch rule almost counterbalanced. The Dutch did grave damage to Balinese political and economic self-sufficiency and also to Balinese pride and self-confidence. But the evils of the colonial era—opium, taxes, corvée and usury, to mention only some of the worst—were none of them new; nor were any of them likely to have decreased rather than increased even had the Dutch not intervened. It served in part at least to offset these evils that the Dutch introduced clinics and schools, abolished slavery and suttee, built roads, bridges, dams, and other important works, and quite definitively imposed law and order. The feuds of the radjas, which had resulted in much turbulence in pre-Dutch times, did not die out, but they no longer climaxed in widespread violence. And the radja's *Kerta*, the court of final appeal, undoubtedly meted out justice with less regard than ever before for caste, creed, or cash.

The *Kerta* enjoyed, in fact, the reputation of being a reasonably impartial and objective court even before the Dutch Controleur joined or replaced the Radja as the presiding dignitary. The accused, upon being brought into court, had the privilege of calling in spokesmen and witnesses. The jury, which consisted of learned *pedanda*, listened in total silence but checked all proceedings against remembered and recorded precedent and in the end validated or invalidated the judge's verdict. The Controleur made sure that the sentence did not involve cruel punishment, such as blinding and maiming, and that fines were collected and prison terms served. The majesty of the Radja, the prestige of the Controleur, the dignity of the judge and jurors, the sanctity of the oaths to which all witnesses were called upon to subscribe, and the awfulness of the maledictions which were pronounced upon malefactors: all combined to make the *Kerta* a body in which something close to the truth generally came out and something close to justice would prevail. One especially memorable curse of the *Kerta* went as follows:

> Wherever they may be, let them [the perjurers] be overtaken by all evils. If they go into the forests, let them be entangled by creepers, let them be lost, running hither and yon without finding the way out, let the tigers pursue them and drive them against the rocks where their skulls will be cracked and their

brains dashed out. On the roadway between villages, let them fall to the earth or be crushed by a falling tree. In the fields, let the lightning strike them from a clear sky, let them be bitten by venomous serpents, let them be gored on the horns of the water buffalo. Let them fall into the river bed on rough rocks so that their breasts are pierced, their bones are broken, their veins are drained of blood, and their corpses are lost in the depths of the water. If they put out from land, let them be attacked by crocodiles, let the sharks and the barracuda attack them, let the venomous lamprey bite them, let the marine monsters devour them. When they are in their homes let them be afflicted with all maladies, let them die unnatural deaths, let no one attend them. Let it be even so whether they are standing or sitting, eating or drinking. Let not them nor their children nor their grandchildren nor their great-grandchildren be reincarnated as human beings on the face of the earth. Let them be reborn as maggots, snails, worms, serpents. Such is the malediction upon perjurers. Let the great Gods attest it, the Gods of the North, East, South, West, and Center, and the Thirteen Divine Revelations. Let them and their children and their grandchildren and their great-grandchildren enjoy no good from this day hence.

CHAPTER 13

Euphoria and Trauma
(1930–1955)

Recurrent Problems of Christian Missions and Converts

The aspect of their Bali policy in which the Dutch take greatest pride and for which the Balinese give them greatest credit was their protectionist and conservationist stance with regard to the island's culture. In certain quarters at the time this policy aroused severe criticism— among Dutch Christian missionary bodies, for instance, which eyed Balinese Hinduism as an especially abandoned brand of hedonistic paganism. Certain Balinese leaders themselves felt at times that more rather than less Dutch intervention would be desirable, especially in helping to rebuild shrines and temples which earthquakes and volcanic eruptions, not to mention customary Balinese standards of maintenance, caused to fall into ruins. Certain Chinese and Western business interests, furthermore, felt that the Resident and the Controleurs were unduly vigilant in excluding them from potential profits.

The question of Christian missions recurred again and again after the doleful 1881 incident of the murder of Rev. de Vroom by his disciple, Nicodemus. Powerful church groups, both Protestant and Catholic in Java and the Netherlands, put pressure upon the colonial government to relax its ruling against missionary activities, claiming at times that it was not the Balinese themselves but the Resident and the Controleurs who were hostile to Christianity. In 1891 the Jesuits received permission to establish a post in Bali, this order being thought to be more sympathetic to Balinese ritualism than other Christian bodies; but the Jesuits lacked the personnel at the time and the per-

The Kerta Gosa (Hall of Justice) in Klungkung, the place for the administration of traditional juctice in pre-colonial times, as it was ca. 1920.

The original ceiling paintings in the Kerta Gosa, which tell of the punishments awaiting evil-doers in Hell, and of the delights of the gods in Heaven. The paintings were restored and modified in 1960.

mit lapsed. In 1920 the Apostolic Prefect of the Lesser Sundas, who was in charge of a very active program in Flores, negotiated with the Resident to convert one of the two new government secondary schools into a private church school, but again lack of personnel caused the project to be dropped. In 1924 the Apostolic Vicar for Java revived the plan, then modified it to propose the establishment of a new church school in Klungkung, a proposal which caused such grave offense to several of the radjas and other prominent Balinese that it had to be withdrawn. The Balinese decried the possibility that Klungkung, the center of traditional Balinese culture, should become the base of mission penetration and challenged the concept which the church then entertained of building both clinics and schools in various parts of the island. The radjas were stirred, in fact, to raise money for a school of their own in Klungkung and the government made amends for the distress they had suffered by granting the school a subsidy.

Missionary enterprise took a new departure in 1930 with the appearance in Bali of representatives of an American fundamentalist sect, the Christian and Missionary Alliance, which had long been active in Celebes and more recently in Lombok. Rev. Jaffray, the head of the mission, visited Bali and assigned one of his catechists, an Indonesian Chinese named Tjang, to live there to work with the minute Chinese Christian community. The Resident gave his reluctant approval, and Tjang, taking advantage of contacts arranged for him by the Balinese wives of certain of the Chinese, promptly extended his work into certain Balinese villages in Mengwi and Djembrana. In 1932, after less than two years, he reported that he had made some 300 converts. This piece of ecclesiastical and evangelical intelligence electrified the missionary world of Java and the Netherlands. It profoundly shocked the Balinese radjas and the Dutch Controleurs, who immediately began to receive or to accumulate complaints from converts and non-converts alike. It was alleged that Tjang had promised his prospective converts that Christianity would bring relief from taxes, corvée, and all the community obligations to which the Balinese Hindus were subject; also cures for all illnesses and other afflictions. The wages of conversion proved instead to include the branding of all Christian apostates from Hinduism as community outcasts, already dead from the point of view of their villages and disqualified from any traditional village benefits, forbidden even cremation. It was also said that Tjang had inflated his statistics by counting as Christians all members of the household of any individual who could be persuaded to repeat after him the sentence, "I believe in Jesus Christ."

The Resident expelled Tjang, whose presence had posed a threat to the "peaceful calm" which all administrators were expected regularly to report. But he still had to deal with the conflicting pressures of other church groups which argued for admission of Dutch missionaries to undo or redouble the work of the Americans, and that of the radjas, who demanded that all missionary activity be banned in perpetuity. He adopted the compromise solution of announcing that one Catholic priest and one Protestant pastor might settle in Bali to minister to the European, the Chinese, and now also the minute Balinese Christian communities, on the strict understanding that they were not to evangelize.

The Catholic priest, J. Kersten (S.V.D.) was the first to arrive (September 1935). On Easter Sunday, 1936, he baptized his first two Balinese converts—young men from the town of Toeka, Mengwi, who had sought him out for spiritual guidance. They had already been converted by Rev. Jaffray and Tjang; after the expulsion of the Christian and Missionary Alliance, they had declined to affiliate themselves with the East Java Church, which sought to create one new Protestant body in Bali by uniting the Mengwi converts with Javanese Christians living in Buleleng. By 1940 Father Kersten could report 250 converts, made not by himself, for he observed the prohibition upon evangelism, but by his two original disciples and the 20 other ex-followers of Tjang whom they soon brought with them. The East Java Church could claim about the same number of Protestants.

Soon the Christian and Missionary Alliance cautiously resumed its work and made a few more converts. The new agent was Rev. Brill, who traveled periodically from Lombok to Bali and became a familiar figure in Den Pasar and Mengwi, from the Dutch point of view half sinister, half ludicrous. Rev. Brill trudged about under the hot tropical sun clad always in a heavy black coat, which quite unmistakably distinguished him from the white-jacketed Dutch colonial officials and made it all the easier for them to trace his movements through the reports of the observant Balinese. Rev. Brill's deportment seems to have been discreet, as was that of the very few other foreign mission representatives who appeared in Bali in pre- or post-war days. Deliberate proselytizing has been both officially and privately discouraged, but the Christian population has increased nevertheless to a total of about 100,000 persons, preponderantly non-Balinese, although allegations are still heard about wooing the poor with promises of rice and jobs.

Cultural Conservationism and Continuity

The Dutch policy of cultural conservationism resulted in large part from the circumstance that in preparing themselves better to fulfill their functions, certain of the Dutch colonial officials became distinguished scholars and appreciative connoisseurs of many aspects of Balinese life. Diligent Dutch research refreshed the Balinese memory with regard to traditions and customs which might otherwise have begun to lapse. Whether Dutch policy and practice did or did not have anything much to do with it, Balinese culture seems to have experienced a quickening influence which made the early part of the

The inner courtyard of the palace at Den Pasar, ca. 1920s. A monumental covered gateway, the Padu Raksa, leads into the courtyard. Inside the gate is the aling, a screen wall to impede the passage of evil spirits, who are deflected to each side.

present century an era of quite distinguished achievement in art and architecture and in all the cere-monial manifestations of Balinese life, which the greatly increased wealth of the radjas could the more readily finance.

The Balinese culture is a self-contained, self-renewing system which, like the human body, regenerates its own vital tissues, but, unlike the human body, does not—or did not—as a whole perceptibly age. Balinese temples are built in the expectation that they will be rebuilt a generation later. The stone, like the timber, disintegrates in a tropical climate under conditions of very little if any maintenance other than sweeping of the grounds. The extravagantly ornamented tufa, which is worked when freshly cut and easy to carve, hardens into apparently impervious stone upon prolonged exposure to air; but after a decade or two it begins to scale and flake. The wooden superstructures and the thatch roofs are good for half a century to a century at most before they too have to be extensively repaired or replaced. Each new generation of craftsmen and artists, therefore, recreates the masterpieces of its predecessors with variations which may spell either decadence or refinement. The same is true to a lesser degree of the workers in metal and bone and ivory, whose media are more durable but whose traditions are constantly revitalized. It is even more true of the actors, the musicians, and the dancers, who take great pride in innovation. No such sweeping generalization can be made about the writers and the thinkers, who were also the priests, but in an era when the temples flourished as never before, so too did the whole religious and intellectual establishment.

Reports began filtering out to Europe and America that Bali, not Fiji or Samoa or Hawaii, was the genuine, unspoiled tropical paradise, known as yet, even by reputation, only by the cognoscenti, a category with which all of the more affluent world travelers sought to identify themselves, as did a certain few more or less learned scholars. The Dutch colonial establishment in Bali was flattered by the attention which the island was beginning to receive and by the generally favorable notices regarding Dutch altruism; but it entertained grave misgivings about the effect upon Bali and the Balinese.

The Residency had sheltered Bali from missionaries and merchants. It now sought to shelter it from world travelers. It undertook also to

A Balinese girl at a temple gate, photography by Thilly Weissenborn, ca. 1923, a typical image from "the island of bare breasts."

shelter the travelers from exposure to what might be the irresistible temptation to settle in and to stay, perhaps to corrupt, or to be corrupted by, the presumably innocent but hedonistic Balinese. It was not President Sukarno, as has frequently been stated, but pre-war Dutch officials who, whether out of consideration for Balinese dignity or Dutch prudery, first required the women of Den Pasar to cover their breasts when they ventured out into the streets. In both pre- and post-war days the Dutch administrators several times rounded up and deported a few foreign nationals who were thought to be misleading the island's youth. But foreign anthropologists, archaeologists, ethnologists, artists, musicians, dancers, and actors, eventually sociologists, economists, and political scientists of more or less reputable professional credentials, not to mention numerous drifters and occasional diplomats, inevitably and eagerly sought out Bali on missions ofttimes indistinguishable from tourism. Pre-war numbers never became genuinely significant, and the Dutch themselves were spared any painful decision on control of tourism by reason of World War II and the Indonesian national revolution.

Tourism and Tourist Agents; Artists, Writers, Expatriates

Tourism came to Bali in the 1920s. By 1930 as many as 100 visitors a month were experiencing the delights of the island. These early pioneers reported so happily to others that by 1940 the total had climbed to about 250 per month. This figure does not include the passengers on the *Stella Polaris, Lurline, Franconia, Empress of Britain, Reliance,* and a few other cruise ships which advertised and delivered a day or two in Bali as the high point of their winter schedules. Except on days when the cruise ships put in and some one hundred carloads of sightseers careened about the island, tourism never caused much stir. The cars were hired mainly from private Balinese or Chinese owners; the itinerary was virtually the same as it is today, except that it included luncheon—always a 20-course *rijstafel*—at the Bali Hotel in Den Pasar, instead of Bali-burgers at the Bali Beach, and the cost per person was only about $3.50 instead of $35.00. For the other tourists, those who stayed a full two days, or long enough to be counted in the statistics, a visit to Bali meant a much more leisurely round of scenic and cultural attractions. Their travel agents

A group of tourists in the 1930s, photographed by Robert Koke. Bali was promoted as an up-market tourist destination by the Dutch colonial powers, and by the 1930s was regularly being visited by cruise ships and the yachts of millionaires.

provided motor cars (Essex or Hudson five- to seven-passenger touring cars or sedans, which rented for $10–15 daily); accommodations (ranging from an austere government rest house at $2.50 to the luxury Bali Hotel at $7.50 double, tout compris); and advice and assistance on all incidental problems (for instance, comfort facilities, then, as now, frequently meant "the rice paddies for the ladies," "the coconut trees for the gentlemen.")

Bali tourism began, to be quite precise, when K.P.M., the Dutch steamship line, decided to attract passengers to fill up the cabins of the ships which it sent to Buleleng to load copra, cattle, coffee, and pigs. But K.P.M. was almost scooped by the activities of an enterprising clique of friendly rivals. These included a Balinese "princess," Mah Patimah; a Persian-Armenian entrepreneur, M. J. Minas; an American adventurer, André Roosevelt (son of Cornelius by a French wife); and later an Anglo-American romantic, Miss Manx (eventually to become famous first as Surabaya Sue, a World War II radio propa-

Legong dancers in Den Pasar, ca. 1920. Said to have been created by the King of Sukawati, I Dewa Agung Made Karna (1775–1825), who during meditation saw two celestial angels respendent in glittering gold costumes, the Legong is an ex-quisite abstract dance performed by two young girls.

Balinese girls performing the *Janger* folk-dance in the 1930s, photographed by Robert Koke. Performed by groups of girls and young men, the *Janger* comprises a mass flirtation: provocative singing of nonsense rhymes by the seated girls provokes an excited reaction from the male dancers.

gandist for the Japanese, and then as Ktut Tantri, author of a highly imaginative autobiography, *Revolt in Paradise.*)

Mr. Minas was a kinetic cinemast who introduced Western moving pictures to enraptured Balinese villagers by traveling with a portable projector and soon made himself the wealthy theater king of Buleleng (one house). He was also the first really to perceive the tourist potential. In about 1920 he started picking up passengers off the K.P.M. ships who had been put ashore by rowboat at Buleleng with a little advice and repeated admonitions to avoid Mr. Minas' attentions. Mr. Roosevelt, who arrived in Bali in about 1924 with very little money but very good connections, threw in with Mr. Minas and brought American Express and Thos. Cook patronage with him. K.P.M., in riposte, opened a tourist office of its own in Buleleng (1925), bought the government rest house in Den Pasar and rebuilt it as the Bali Hotel (1928), which it soon expanded with de luxe wings and an annex, while also acquiring the Kintamani rest house as a mountain resort adjunct. After Mr. Roosevelt's departure in the mid-1930s, K.P.M. wooed and won American Express and Thos. Cook. K.P.M. thereafter dominated the tourist scene, experiencing some discomfiture but no serious damage from the activities of Mah Patimah, Miss Manx, and a few later comers.

Mah Patimah was romantically reported to have been a wife of the late Dewa Agung and to have escaped from his funeral pyre just as she was about to be forced to commit suttee, a story which she did not contradict. She was known to be from Karangasem, to be married to a Buleleng Armenian, and to have built up a profitable business in silver and an impressive fleet of taxis. She was given to having herself rowed out to sea to meet all ships, armed with flowers and a bottle. She tended at times to become a bit forgetful about business while dallying with the officers and the crew, so her personal fleet of half a dozen vehicles was generally available to K.P.M. on hire. Miss Manx was somewhat more worrisome. She joined an American named Robert Koke in operating a small beach retreat at Kuta, then built a much more exotic resort of her own, on a spot close by and made it her practice to visit the Bali Hotel bar to lure K.P.M. clients with visions of her seaside Eden. But by pre-war standards tourism was booming and there were visitors enough for all. If there was any

The official government guest house at Klungkung, ca. 1930, one of a dozen such establishments built to accommodate traveling or newly assigned Dutch officials. They also accommodated the overspill of tourists from Bali's hotels.

Residence of the Dutch Controleur, Gianjar, c. 1925. The gambrel roof (a hipped roof with gable-like ends), central porch, masonry columns, and tiled roof show Dutch influence.

overflow from the hotels, there was always space in one of the dozen or so little government guest houses which had been built to accommodate traveling or newly assigned officials, of whom there were still only a very few.

Pre-war tourists came to Bali almost always by sea—K.P.M. ships putting in at Buleleng, or in the event of heavy seas, at more sheltered spots nearby, the cruise ships calling at Padang Bai in the south. Travel by motor-car from Java became possible in the mid-1930s, when a ferry service was started up between Banjuwangi and Gilimanuk by a pair of energetic German beachcombers, and a road was put through from Gilimanuk to Den Pasar by a Controleur who surveyed it by occasional reference to a compass and built it by reliance upon hand labor. But the trip was strictly for the adventurous. The car ferry might take days to arrange and then, if current, wind, or waves proved unfavorable, the one-mile crossing might take not half an hour but half a day, and by night the Gilimanuk road was infested with tigers. Air travel also became possible in the 1930s, but it was never very highly recommended. The first survey flight (August 16, 1932) of the K.L.M. affiliate, K.N.I.L.M. (Royal Netherlands Indies Airways), crashed into Gunung (Mt.) Batu Kau (without serious casualties), and the first airport, built in Bukit, was much too risky for landing except in the calmest weather. With the completion in 1938 of a new airport at Tuban, the site of the present airport, Bali became an overnight stop on the weekly K.N.I.L.M. flights to Australia and to Makassar. This added only very modestly to the monthly number of visitors.

The tourists came to Bali for a few days of romantic escapism; an assortment of artists and writers, aesthetes and expatriates, came to stay. The most famous and almost the first of them was the German musician and painter, Walter Spies, who moved to Bali in 1926 after having already spent a few years as bandmaster in the court of the Sultan of Yogyakarta. Walter Spies, who was interned in 1940 and perished when a Japanese submarine torpedoed the ship on which he was being transferred to Australia, built himself a simple house on the edge of a scenic ravine just outside the town of Ubud, Gianjar. He proceeded to produce two or three paintings a year of such radiant and revealing beauty that he established a new esthetics which the Balinese have since made their own.

Walter Spies was joined in the early 1930s by the German novelist, Vicki Baum, who wrote *Tale of Bali*, a story sufficiently romantic, tragic, exotic, and authentic to rate as one of the classics of Balinese studies. The Mexican artist-ethnologist, Miguel Covarrubias, and his American wife, Rose, moved in nearby to produce the great study, *The Island of Bali*, which remains unrivaled in English as an exposition of the Balinese culture. There came also Colin McPhee and his wife, Jane Belo, who wrote *A House in Bali* and *Trance in Bali*, respectively, and Margaret Mead and her husband, Gregory Bateson, who carried out important anthropological inquiries. The painters, however, usually outnumbered the writers. These included the Dutch painter, Rudolf Bonnet, who has returned on short visits in the 1970s; the Swiss, Theo Meier, who now lives in Thailand but visits Bali frequently; and the Belgian, Le Mayeur de Perpres, who died in 1958, leaving his home with its splendid murals to his Balinese dancer wife, Polak, the property eventually to revert to the state. All of these early European painters and most of their successors accepted Balinese understudies who have created their own schools of painting which now flourish throughout the island. There were also dancers and photographers, among them Jack and Katharane Mershon. Almost all of these early cultural colonists established reputations for insight and empathy which later comers have rarely matched.

Life in the 1930s; Japanese Occupation

Life in Bali in the 1930s was agreeable not only for affluent foreigners but also for the Balinese. The foreigner could and did live very comfortably on an income of about $150 per month, which was the average for the official and the expatriate. It was quite sufficient to allow for a home and a car, a staff of half a dozen household servants, and a bountiful table. The large and numerous Balinese royal families were wealthy and privileged, enjoying every Balinese amenity and imported luxuries as well. Their *puri* were equipped not only with comfortable living quarters but with splendid reception pavilions, and their treasuries were well stocked with gold and jewels. The ordinary people had on the whole plenty of rice and relatively few complaints. Many of their troubles they attributed to the Chinese money-lenders rather than to the Radja or the Dutch, a circumstance which may help to explain why the Chinese were officially tolerated. The radjas themselves, thanks to a much acclaimed and self-acclaimed Dutch administrative reform, the *Zelf Bestuurs Regelen* of 1938 (Rules of Self Government), recovered what seemed almost like autonomy by reason of separation and division of powers between the central and the regional government and the demotion of the Controleur to status of consultant. The very small element of the population which made up the emerging Balinese middle class—the employees, for instance, of the government offices—might earn no more than about fl. 25–50 per month ($10–20), but they were treated with respect and they could live quite well. They had to pay only a few guilders in rent for a decent house, and 25 guilder cents would easily buy a day's provisions for an entire family.

Among the foreign residents at least, the only really serious cause for concern in Bali of the 1930s was the prospect of war in the Pacific, a threat which suddenly became a reality in December 1941. Japanese troops then began their march down the Malay Peninsula to capture Singapore, the key to the whole of the region, including the dangerously exposed and weakly defended Indonesian archipelago. When war broke out most of the European population of Bali sought refuge in Java and onward passage to Australia. As the Japanese moved ever closer, the Dutch officers of the small Balinese-manned military garrison joined the civilian exodus, in fact deserting their posts and exposing themselves to post-war court martial. A small Japanese expeditionary force appeared off Bali on February 14, 1942, and soldiers landed at Sanur on February 18. The demoralized garrison surrendered without offering any resistance. The Japanese occupation of Bali began several weeks prior to the occupation of Java and ended in 1945 without having caused any great bloodshed or destruction such as occurred elsewhere.

The victorious Japanese administered Bali in accordance with the system already established by the Dutch, reverting, in fact, to the situation prior to the 1938 administrative reform. Japanese military government officials occupied the offices vacated by the Dutch, and a Japanese District Officer (*bunken*) was attached to each of the royal courts with powers at least equal to those formerly exercised by the Dutch Controleur. The Radja of Gianjar proved to be intransigent; he was deposed and exiled to Lombok, his elder son replacing him on the throne. None of the other radjas invited the same treatment, and only Gianjar, where the new young Radja was not exactly sub-servient, suffered much deliberate Japanese retribution. To a very lim-ited extent, not by any means as notably as in Java, the Japanese put the Balinese themselves into relatively responsible positions to re-place the Dutch.

For the most part the Japanese did not very actively intervene in Balinese affairs because there was little reason to do so. The small modern segment of the island's society and economy continued to function mainly on momentum, gradually running down, and in the end grinding to a halt when the few public services of the larger towns all but disintegrated. The most serious effect of the occupa-tion resulted from the requisition by the Japanese of rice and other foodstuffs and their failure to supply textiles, pharmaceuticals, man-ufactured goods, and replacements or spare parts for such modern machinery as had already been introduced. By the time the war ended the Balinese were experiencing severe privations and were faced with the very immediate prospect of famine and epidemic. It was not until four months after the end of the war that the first representatives of the victorious allies appeared—a small party of British and American officers who arrived, it seems, by submarine in late December and spent only a couple of days on the island. They had come to accept the surrender of the Japanese and to look out for Dutch and other prisoners of war who might have been interned on the island. But there were no internees and the Japanese had in effect already sur-rendered to the Balinese, willingly or unwillingly turning over to them most of their weapons.

Return of the Dutch; Nationalist Revolution

The Dutch returned to Bali in early March 1946, first as a small party of civil administrators together with the Gadjah Merah (Red Ele-phant) Regiment of ex-K.N.I.L. (colonial) soldiers, mainly Ambonese, under Dutch officers recently released from Japanese prison camp in Burma and Siam. In re-establishing their political and military authority in Bali the Dutch encountered relatively little resistance, which is not to say that they were welcome or that there was not a strong Balinese independence movement. The Balinese were for the most part distant and detached bystanders with regard to the Indonesian nationalist revolution, which centered on Muslim Java, with which Hindu Bali felt little sense of identity. Very few Balinese felt any special attraction toward the Republican revolutionary leaders, of whose policies and personalities they had very little knowledge. Nevertheless, a Balinese liberation movement had already started, had aligned itself with the newly proclaimed Indonesian Republic, and had established a rudimentary administration of its own staffed by former understudies of the Dutch or the Japanese. It was backed by a fledgling army made up of men who had been trained by the Dutch or the Japanese military contingents, plus numerous inexperienced but fiery young volunteers, all of them eager for combat.

The movement dated from the summer of 1945, when the Japanese assembled in Batavia a representative group of Indonesians from all parts of the archipelago in order to prepare for the establishment of an independent state under Japanese sponsorship. Bali sent two representatives, who remained in the capital after the end of the war and the declaration of independence and became members of the national parliament. The new Indonesian government regarded Bali as a province of the Republic and named a prominent Balinese, I Gusti Ktut Pudje, as Governor. It was under his leadership that local self-government began to develop. A Balinese military officer, Colonel Ngurah Rai, meanwhile converted the Prajura Corps, or island defense force, into the Balinese army, recruiting also various volunteers. When the Dutch returned, many of the civilian officials were jailed, together with a small clique of intellectual élite who had joined them. But the Prajura Corps under Colonel Ngurah Rai withdrew to the hills, from which the members emerged at times to create small incidents and to indoctrinate or intimidate certain influential citizens. Within a very short time, however, still in early March, they encountered a much stronger body of Dutch troops in the neighborhood of Tabanan. In what seemed in certain respects like a modern *puputan*, that is, self-immolation in a battle already clearly lost, the Colonel and most of his followers were killed, to be buried on the spot, which is now a heroes' cemetery marked by a shrine. All organized resistance to the Dutch collapsed with the elimination of the army. Small-scale disorders continued until the end of the year, sometimes directed against the Dutch, more often, however, Balinese fighting Balinese. No few of the islanders seemed willing to seize the opportunity in troubled times when arms were readily available to settle old scores relating more to personal, family, and village feuds than to revolutionary politics. But Bali was virtually pacified well before the outbreak of the more serious and sustained fighting in Java.

The return of Dutch colonialism, destined as it was to be of brief duration, resulted in Bali both in restoration of old forms and experimentation with new ones. The island became again a Residency administered by a Dutch official and his staff, with new headquarters not in Buleleng, however, but in Den Pasar, close to the airport. The staff was much larger than ever before and it included many professional personnel—doctors and teachers, engineers and agronomists, economists and political scientists and propagandists, all of them backstopped by a regiment of troops. A Dutch District Officer, no longer endowed with the power and prestige of the Controleurs of pre-1938 days, was assigned to each of the eight radjadoms. The radjas themselves ruled their little kingdoms again in their own right in accordance with the colonial reform regulations of 1938, but they cooperated closely and on the whole willingly with the Dutch Residency authorities.

Bali as Member of Federal System and New Republic

In 1946 the Dutch constituted Bali one of the 13 administrative districts of the Republic of East Indonesia (capital: Makassar) which they were sponsoring as a rival state to the revolutionary Republic headed by Sukarno and Hatta. They also created the *Dewan Radja-Radja*, or Council of Radjas, a consultative and advisory body with which the Dutch Residency officials regularly conferred and to whose judgment they frequently deferred. In 1948 Bali became an autonomous state within the Republic of East Indonesia and the *Dewan Radja-Radja* succeeded the Dutch Residency as the overall authority. The Dutch administrators, remaining thereafter as advisors to their Balinese successors, set themselves to complete the rehabilitation of the island. They sought to make Bali the show-piece state of the Republic of East Indonesia and thus the conclusive evidence of the possibility and the advantages of genuine Indonesian–Dutch cooperation.

It seems a fair objective judgment in which most Balinese would concur to state that the post-war Dutch administrators, starting in 1946 and redoubling their efforts in 1948, achieved a great deal more success in Bali than anywhere else in Indonesia. They shipped in adequate quantities of food, clothing, pharmaceuticals, and other supplies, inclusive both of daily necessities and luxuries—more than enough to put Bali back in good operating order. Roads and irrigation systems were repaired; agricultural services were restored and extended. Particularly urgent attention was given to schools, clinics and hospitals, all of which were soon much more numerous and much larger than ever before. Bali even began again to export rice, a sure sign that conditions had dramatically improved, although the export was dictated more by Dutch propaganda considerations than by any genuine agricultural surplus.

The Dutch succeeded so well in Bali that the Balinese themselves were genuinely disposed to collaborate in the demonstration that fruitful Dutch–Indonesian cooperation was possible and that Dutch-sponsored states could peacefully coexist with the Indonesian Republic. Balinese leaders—and other leaders of the Republic of East Indonesia—proved willing to work with the Dutch up until the point where the Dutch attempted not just to compete with the revolutionary leaders but to wipe out the Republic by resort to military action. They then helped to tilt the balance against the Dutch in favor of the Republic. Their influence was especially important before and during the Round Table Conference in The Hague (1949), which resulted in Dutch recognition of Indonesian independence. In the newly emerging Republic of the United States of Indonesia (R.U.S.I.), a union under the Dutch Crown of the Republic and the onetime Dutch-sponsored states, Bali was still the leading member of the Republic of East Indonesia. But R.U.S.I. was not fated to last, nor was the union with the Dutch. The unitary Republic of Indonesia, inclusive of all the onetime members of R.U.S.I., was created in mid-1950; it renounced the Dutch union in 1956; soon it embarked upon the highly adventurous Sukarno-guided course which led to civil war, international disrepute, and economic and political catastrophe. In no part of Indonesia was the transition from colonialism to independence an easy one. In Bali it was even more difficult than elsewhere by reason of mutual suspicion on the part of Jakarta and Den Pasar.

The reasons for suspicion and lack of cooperation were as numerous as they were dolorous. The Republican leaders in Jakarta resented the fact that the Balinese had not very actively participated in the violent phases of the revolutionary struggle but had collaborated with the Dutch and had greatly benefited thereby. They regarded the radjadoms as fossilized feudal states, artificially resuscitated by the Dutch, which perversely refused to relax their traditional hold upon their people's loyalty even when they were officially dissolved, as happened upon the creation of the unitary state. The Republic, furthermore, has always been Javanese-dominated, and despite their common ancestry and cultural antecedents, the Muslim Javanese do not understand the Hindu Balinese and two-way communication is likely to become badly blurred. As the years went by and national troubles multiplied, the Javanese-dominated, Jakarta-centric Republican establishment fell into disrepute throughout the nation for its incompetence and corruption. This was especially true in Bali. President Sukarno, his cabinet ministers, his state guests, and his chosen civilian and military cronies paid all too frequent and well-publicized visits, making such unseemly spectacles of themselves as to prove that they were morally and spiritually unfit to rule. The Balinese Hindu concept of the just and therefore the legitimate ruler is that he is one who conforms to the laws of man, nature, and the gods, as, within a decade of his achieving the presidency, Sukarno quite certainly did not.

CHAPTER 14

Decade of Disaster
(1955–1965)

Nationalists, Communists, and the Later Sukarno Years

During the late Sukarno years (1955–1965), Bali underwent profound political, economic, social, and cultural change which seriously troubled many of its people. A clique of Sukarnoists, civilian and military, more of them Javanese than Balinese, dominated the island, competing vigorously with one another for power and wealth. They exercised administrative authority mainly to reward themselves and their friends and to punish their enemies, a category of persons which came to include many of the island's leading citizens. Their offices were packed with badly trained and badly paid bureaucrats who demanded bribes before performing even the most routine services. After having been one of the best administered regions of the archipelago in the late colonial period, Bali became one of the worst neglected and most exploited provinces of the new Republic.

The one most significant political development of the period was a process of massive and sinister politicization. Prior to the mid-1950s the Balinese were not much interested in national politics and not much attracted to the national parties. Regarding themselves primarily as Balinese and only secondarily as Indonesians, they remained aloof from the great Nationalist Party (P.N.I.), whose ultra-nationalistic leaders in fact regarded the Balinese as anachronistically non-revolutionary. As Hindus they were not much disposed to associate themselves with the major Muslim parties, either the ultra-orthodox N.U. or the liberal Masjumi. The Communist Party (P.K.I.) seemed to them to promise only the desecration of all their cultural institutions. Their leaders tended to affiliate themselves, if at all, with the Socialists (P.S.I.), the small clique of intellectual élite headed by Sutan Sjahrir. But in the 1950s the Balinese Socialists, like their counterparts in Java and Sumatra, were much too rational for their own comfort or even safety under an irrational regime increasingly dominated by the P.N.I. and the P.K.I., the chosen instruments of the demagogic Sukarno.

In the 1950s, as economic conditions very seriously deteriorated, the P.N.I. began to win many Balinese converts, and so too, soon afterwards, did the P.K.I. The P.N.I. was able to offer the quick, easy profits of official appointment or favor, and there proved to be many Balinese who were happy, as new P.N.I. loyalists, to acquire goods and properties at artificially cheap prices, and to exercise influence on behalf of their friends and to the dismay of their enemies. The P.K.I. adopted subtler tactics. It patronized the arts and the artists, employing as its early vehicle of penetration the cultural foundation LEKRA, upon whose members were bountifully bestowed the paints, canvases, musical instruments, dance costumes, and other goods which were otherwise almost unobtainable. Both the P.N.I. and the P.K.I. thus undermined public and private probity, at the same time posing as benefactors of the people and advocating the very reforms which their own activities made the more vitally necessary. In Bali in the early 1960s, virtually no village was without its conspicuously identified P.N.I. office and its P.N.I.-sponsored activist movements of peasants, women, and youth, all of which the P.K.I. duplicated and not always by any means in a spirit of fraternal cooperation.

Politics in Culture and Land Reform

Thanks to LEKRA, the P.K.I. succeeded remarkably well in injecting politics into culture and making political capital of cultural change. Balinese actors, renowned for their skill at improvisation, began lauding the Sukarnoists and attacking their opponents, frequently doing so with such polished wit that they commanded an amused hearing even from those persons who most deplored what was happening. Dancers performed propaganda-packed people's dances which might have been choreographed in Moscow or Peking. Painters adapted the verbal slogans of the Sukarnoists as visual symbols. To those who knew and loved the genuine traditions of the island these manifestations were quite frightening. What was most disturbing of all was that Bali, the island of religion and culture, was being drenched with the most poisonous of politics. The mystical Balinese were being converted into political zealots, mouthing the Sukarno slogans about death to all demons and monsters, suddenly no mere mythical creatures but actual living persons.

What LEKRA was to the arts, land reform was to agriculture—a fraudulent promise of the fulfillment of the people's wishes. In Bali ever since the turn of the century, the pressure of a rapidly expanding population upon an inelastic supply of land had resulted in a great annual increase in the number of landless persons who had to eke out a living by combining tenant farming with day labor. Perhaps as much as 15 per cent of Bali's land had come into the possession of landlords, mainly the scions of the high caste families whose own numbers had increased so remarkably that holdings were generally small and income modest. These were precisely the persons who were most likely to have acquired education and position in colonial days, to have been associated politically with the Socialists rather than the Sukarnoists, and to have eyed the P.N.I.–P.K.I. rise to power with gravest misgivings. They were easily targeted as feudalists, colonialists, and counterrevolutionary conspirators whose properties should be distributed forthwith among the people. The landlords were therefore deprived of their land, sometimes receiving token payment years later in rupiahs which had lost at least 90 per cent of their value. The lands were more or less parceled out among the people—the people, that is, who had proven themselves most loyal and active in the P.N.I.–P.K.I. cause. This redistribution of lands, rewarding some and victimizing others and ignoring both the agrarian and the social consequences, lighted delayed-action fuses which ignited demolition charges throughout the island in 1965 and 1966, when the fall of Sukarno and the eclipse of the P.N.I. and the P.K.I. signaled that the time had come for retribution.

Economic Manipulation; Rice Supply
The Balinese economy, meanwhile, suffered set-backs at least as serious as those which occurred in other Indonesian provinces. The

central government had rejected the conventional and hence reactionary and nonrevolutionary concepts that income should equal outgo, exports should balance imports, and expenditures should be contingent upon calculation of resources and returns. Political favorites, civilian and military, plundered the island by taking advantage of ruinous economic controls. They were able to buy up produce or property at a small fraction of its value, sell it at enormous profit, and repeat the cycle as frequently as opportunity presented itself. Labyrinthine economic regulations made it possible, as inflation escalated and foreign exchange operations became more and more fanciful, to buy an automobile for Rp. 10,000, sell it for Rp. 10,000,000, then use the rupiah profits to buy up coffee and copra at low official prices for export to foreign countries against payment in good hard currency. Or one could merely pocket official funds and abscond with official equipment, for which accounting procedures were rudimentary and easily obscured. While the few became very, very rich, the many suffered hardships which began to remind them of the evil days of the Japanese occupation.

Rice, the one most essential commodity, was in short supply at inflated prices despite—or rather because of—government efforts at control; and the politicians rather than the farmers reaped the rewards of the flourishing black market. Clothes, medicines, and all other necessities were so scarce that much of the island reverted to barter. The transportation system deteriorated so desperately and all conditions became so unsettled that even tourism almost came to a stop.

Sukarno's Visitations and Affronts

The frequent visits to Bali by President Sukarno and his entourage did nothing to dispel but served only to intensify the apprehension of many of the Balinese that the island had fallen under a curse. President Sukarno, whose mother was Balinese but whose father was Javanese, made Bali his favorite retreat and built himself a showy palace and guest house. He chose the site of an earlier Dutch official rest house on a superbly beautiful hilltop site above the especially sacred Tampaksiring Temple. It gave special offense to the Balinese that he built his private quarters to overlook the temple springs and baths. Sukarno frequently called upon the priests to stage ceremonies of welcome

President Sukarno, his mother, who was Balinese, and other members of his family. Bali was his favorite retreat.

for himself and his guests when they landed at the airport or arrived at the palace. He called command performances anywhere and everywhere of the actors, musicians, and dancers. For his own collections he appropriated the finest works of the painters, the sculptors, the woodcarvers, and the other artists and craftsmen. In his palace he staged night-long parties which deteriorated into orgies.

Sukarno affronted the Balinese by converting their sacred ceremonies into government theatricals and by requiring tens of thousands of common people to line the roadways to wave, smile, sing, and shout as he passed. He outraged them even more by dispatching his aides to collect the prettiest young girls to be delivered to the palace, there to be debauched by himself and his party. The President, his state guests, who included many of the world's notables, his one hundred ministers, his very numerous generals, and his male and female camp followers, were not welcome in Bali except among those who profited enormously from their visits. This category did not include many of the common people. The ordinary Balinese can recall all too vividly the occasions on which an advance party of military personnel would shoot the pigs and the dogs which the Hindu Balinese love. They did so in order to avoid any possibility of giving offense to a fastidious Muslim visitor for whom any contact with a pig or a dog was a contamination and even the sight distasteful. Most Balinese preferred pigs and dogs to state visitors.

Premonitions of Evil; Plague of Rats

In Bali, to an ever more marked degree than in the other parts of Indonesia, there was premonition of disaster. Prevailing circumstances were so unusual as to seem ominously unnatural. The supernatural powers, it was feared, were being provoked to some truly dreadful visitation and retribution. Human beings would somehow be compelled by acts of nature or the gods to revert to the standards and the values of the past and to impose order upon the present. The first unmistakable signal that the divine powers were seriously displeased, and that their displeasure would be even more disastrously manifested unless there were indications of human repentance, came in 1962 when a plague of rats infested the fields and the granaries. Rats by the thousands and by the millions, huge, insatiable rats such as had rarely been seen before, feasted upon the ripening grain and then upon such grain as remained to be harvested. The destructive hordes seemed to multiply rather than to diminish as a result of the efforts to destroy them. The government proved totally incapable of rising to the emergency. It promised but could not provide rat poison, which was not a commodity in which the corrupt economic operators chose to deal. Eventually the farmers and their families engaged in a war of extermination which terminated the affliction. They then piled up token mounds of corpses and gave them symbolical cremations in order to atone for taking even rodent lives, the rat being regarded in fact as the familiar of the rice goddess. But the conviction persisted that the gods were displeased. The conclusive and awful evidence came in 1963 with the first eruption in modern times of the sacred Mt. Agung.

Eka Dasa Rudra Celebration and Eruption of Mt. Agung

In late 1962 and early 1963 the people of Bali began to prepare for the celebration of the Eka Dasa Rudra, the most sacred of all Balinese temple festivals, which occurs only once in a hundred Balinese 210-day years. The Eka Dasa Rudra is held in what is regarded as the most ancient and hallowed of the island's shrines, the magnificent Besaki temple complex on the slope of Mt. Agung. It still evokes the prehistoric animistic worship of the spirits of the great volcano which dominates the island and signals the attitude of the gods toward the people by its own serene or violent aspect.

In Bali in 1962 and 1963 there was abundant reason to fear that the original tutelary deities of the island were far from pleased with recent developments. There was great consternation on the part of the priests as they made their calculations to determine on exactly which days the festival should be held—or whether it should be held at all. The learned authorities differed widely in their readings of the omens, and casting and recasting of the horoscope led only to greater confusion in its interpretation. It was a matter of especially grave concern when the high priest, as was required by custom, made his ceremonial ascent to the very brink of the crater to draw lustral water from a sacred spring. He discovered that the spring had gone dry and that the fumes from the crater itself were alarmingly pervasive.

Bali's religious authorities went into prolonged and agitated consultation regarding postponement or even cancellation of the ceremonies and how such an unprecedented decision could be justified on the basis of divine revelation. The signs, they feared, were not auspicious, and to schedule the island's most sacred festival under unpropitious circumstances would constitute a sacrilege. But everyone knew that the time was nearly at hand for the observance of the sacred centennial. The civil if not the religious authorities were determined that the celebration must be firmly scheduled. The prestige of the state was at stake, since even hesitation seemed to be an admission of lack of confidence in Sukarno's much acclaimed new era. President Sukarno had already publicly announced his intention of attending and of participating; in one of its sporadic attempts to promote tourism the government had invited travel agents from nearby countries to hold their annual conference in Jakarta and to attend the Eka Dasa Rudra as the climax of their visit. The priests were constrained to defer to official ukase. The Eka Dasa Rudra was scheduled to begin on March 8 and to continue for about one month as a sort of command performance for President Sukarno and his state guests.

On February 18, just as the preparations at Besaki were getting well under way with the construction of a special archway honoring President Sukarno and other works of ornamentation at the temple site, Mt. Agung suddenly began to emit smoke and ash, and occasional earth tremors could be clearly felt. In the course of the next several weeks volcanic activities continued and intensified. Again the religious authorities argued for reconsideration; again they were overruled. On March 8, therefore, although swirls of smoke and a dusting of volcanic ash were perceptible in the immediate Besaki area, the ceremonies began. But the priests were fearful of profanation of the sanctuary; the crowds were apprehensive rather than festive; Sukarno himself failed to show up. The Eka Dasa Rudra, which started as a disappointment, turned into a disaster.

On March 12, while the ceremonies still continued, Mt. Agung began to throw out mud and rock. By March 17 great rivers of molten lava were pouring down the mountainside. Flames leaped higher and higher into the sky; smoke and volcanic ash blotted out the sun and darkened the countryside. The Besaki temple complex, situated on a sharp ridge and bracketed by deep valleys through which the lava flowed, escaped the main line of destruction. But it was covered deep in hot ash; the palm fiber thatch of the shrines was set ablaze, as were some of the wooden superstructures. The main sanctuaries themselves were miraculously spared, but the very first casualty was the ornamental gateway built to honor Sukarno. By then not only Bali but the whole of the nation was aware that Mt. Agung had terminated the ceremonies which Sukarno had ordered. Javanese as well as Balinese interpreted this as a divine judgment upon the Sukarno regime. Not only the island of Bali but the eastern end of Java, including the city of Surabaya, was darkened at midday by dense clouds of smoke and ash such as no one could remember ever having experienced before.

The volcanic eruptions of early 1963, which had been preceded by a frightening plague of rats, were accompanied by scenes of horror and terror and followed by widespread famine and disease. The year 1963 is indelibly engraved upon Balinese memory as the worst in historic times—at least, that is, up until the even more dreadful years of 1965 and 1966. Entire villages were wiped out, and thousands of hectares of rich farmlands were covered deep in lava, boulders, and ash. One hundred thousand refugees were driven from their homes and farms. Many of them died of asphyxiation when trapped by blocked paths and roadways; others died later of injuries, exposure, or starvation. For many months famine prevailed over wide areas and epidemic was a constant threat. National and international bodies attempted to mount relief operations, but the agencies came into serious conflict. Personnel and supplies sent from abroad were not properly utilized and often did not reach Bali at all, Indonesian agencies of the Sukarno period being both jealous of prerogative and corrupt in handling valuable medicines, foodstuffs, and other relief goods. During the worst of the crisis, Jakarta officials authorized planes, which were desperately needed for relief, to fly the visiting tourist agents to view the scenic spectacle by moonlight and firelight.

GESTAPU Coup and 100,000 Killings

The island's disasters of 1962, 1963 and 1964 were still fresh in Balinese memory in late 1965 when disaster very suddenly, but so far as the Balinese were concerned, not unexpectedly, struck the entire nation. The Sukarno regime had obviously long since passed the point of no return on the road to self-destructive folly. During the night of September 30, 1965, a clique of conspirators—Communists, Air Force officers, certain Army units, and rabid Sukarnoists—inspired to an as yet undeterminable degree directly or indirectly by Sukarno himself, Peking, and sheer mischief-makers such as Foreign Minister Subandrio, staged an abortive coup d'état. The most gruesome aspects of GESTAPU (an acronym for the September 30 incident) were the kidnapping, torture, mutilation, and murder of five top army generals and one lieutenant (mistaken for General Nasution, the Commander-in-Chief). It was a tactical blunder which provoked popular revulsion and military vengeance so prolonged and widespread that the conspirators themselves were virtually wiped out and the Sukarno regime collapsed. But it required the better part of a year after GESTAPU for the nation really to begin to steady itself with the clear emergence of Suharto as Sukarno's unchallenged successor. In the meantime there had occurred a nation-wide bloodletting, nowhere more frightful than in frightened little Bali.

At the time of GESTAPU, Bali was under the control of a Balinese Communist Governor of the royal family of Negara and a strongly P.K.I. and P.N.I. infiltrated and indoctrinated clique of civil and military officials, all of them deeply implicated in the excesses and the extravagances of the Sukarno regime. The Governor himself fled from Bali to Jakarta together with all of his immediate family. In Jakarta President Sukarno provided him with shelter, assigning him a house within the well-guarded Senayan sports complex, then virtually a military cantonment. It was only a few weeks, however, until the Governor vanished—picked up by a party of Balinese activists, according to well-informed report, and taken off to a nearby rubber plantation to be executed.

The events of late 1965 and early 1966 in Bali have never been fully reported and perhaps need not and should not be. A total of some 100,000 persons were killed, thousands of homes were burned, and immense damage was done to the island's economy and its morale. One of the special causes of convulsion in Bali was that the P.K.I. and the P.N.I., the two strong political parties which had maintained an uneasy but mutually profitable alliance during the late Sukarno period, turned upon one another, and everyone who had a grievance to settle settled it then. After years of wretched misrule and exploitation, Balinese grievances were numberless. The military supplied logistic support for vigilante squads which rounded up persons informed upon by the P.K.I. or the P.N.I., also other persons accused of being Sukarnoists, communists, corrupt, or mere sympathizers with the coup. Truckloads of victims were lined up on the river banks to be machine-gunned or beheaded. The bodies were buried in shallow graves or merely rolled into the river. These very numerous Balinese dead, having never been cremated, have no chance of reincarnation in human form. In Bali the thought frequently occurs that the spirits of the guilty and the innocent alike cannot be expected to submit indefinitely to such impious neglect, and that the island may not even yet have atoned sufficiently for its sins, including the 100,000 recent killings. The divinities, who have already visited a series of catastrophes upon the island, may still be unappeased.

After the events of the early and middle 1960s, times in Bali could scarcely have grown worse and they have in fact improved. The new government of President Suharto has undertaken and achieved major reforms of administration and minor miracles of rehabilitation. The government offices have been purged of the more incompetent and corrupt of the Sukarnoists, and a new spirit of responsibility has been infused into the civil service. The government has undertaken a program of development which already enables the economy and the society to function at least as well as in the 1950s. This is far from good enough for the 1970s, but it is much better than might have been anticipated in 1965. One of the most significant achievements of recent years, the result as much of the people's initiative and energy as of government assistance and encouragement, is the repair of much of the damage wrought by the 1963 eruption of Mt. Agung.

A visit to the state of Karangasem, which Mt. Agung dominates, is no longer the dismaying experience of a few years ago when one traveled over ruined roads across a blighted landscape. The road to Besaki, happily, reveals very little evidence of the volcanic action save that a fine new bridge, one of the most important provincial construction projects, crosses a river bed deeply overlaid with lava. The temple complex itself has been largely restored to its earlier state, and the view from the temple terraces is again one of scenic splendor unmarred by evidence of devastated fields. Other areas much more adversely affected by the eruption cannot now be said to be beautiful, but life is much more than faintly stirring in the ruins. The town of Karangasem is being so rapidly rebuilt that new structures mask old houses and shops which now stand a meter or two below ground level. On the edge of the town it is still possible to see the dramatic contrast between rich rice fields and an adjacent expanse of what seems like pock-marked moonscape. Such contrast is not so sharply apparent in the more distant rural areas where the transitions are much more gradual. With the help of the patient farmers, the eternally verdant life forces of Bali are vigorously reasserting themselves. It is prophetic, one trusts, of triumphs over other and even graver problems that the Balinese are surmounting a natural disaster of major dimensions. In Bali to a much greater degree than anywhere else in Indonesia, recurrent natural convulsions such as volcanic eruptions and earthquakes have conditioned the people to rely for re-generation upon divine favor and their own vigorous efforts. Both will be required to the fullest degree for the island to meet the all too pre-dictable emergencies of the late twentieth century, in which, as yet, productivity cannot keep up with population nor achievement with aspiration. The new formula for restoration of Bali's former fortunes is the vigorous promotion of international tourism, a prescription which may poison the rich but ailing culture it is meant to preserve.

CHAPTER 15

Royalty Updated
(1856–1976)

Five Generations of Gianjar Royalty

The most distinguished Balinese today is Ide Anak Agung Gde Agung, recently the Indonesian Ambassador in Vienna, whose previous high offices have included that of Radja of Gianjar; Minister for the Interior and later Prime Minister of the Federal State of East Indonesia; and Minister for the Interior and later Foreign Minister of the Republic of Indonesia. Ide (the honorable) is the title of a ruling prince (or one who has ruled); Anak Agung (great child) is a title of the Ksatria caste; Gde (illustrious) is an added honorific; and Agung is the given name. With this name and title, Ide Anak Agung Gde Agung and members of his family, whose titles are equally sonorous, have adopted Agung as a surname for reasons of convenience in the outside world, where they spend much of their time. His friends, the press, and the general public usually refer to him merely as Anak Agung, or even more familiarly as Agung, and although there are many Anak Agungs in Bali, there is never any doubt but that he is *the* Anak Agung.

Anak Agung's life story very tidily encapsulates the history of Bali in his generation, but then, so too does the story of his father epitomize the Bali of his times, and that of his grandfather and his great-grandfather; it may well be that his four sons, all of whom are studying or have studied abroad and are headed for careers in the professions, will be equally representative of the new Bali of today and tomorrow. For these various reasons the family history which includes much Balinese and national history, seems well worth tracing, beginning with Dewa Manggis VII and his successor, Dewa Gde Raka, to whom recurrent reference has been made in the foregoing chapters.

Dewa Manggis VII; His Conflicts with His Peers

Dewa Manggis VII came to the throne of Gianjar in 1856, not long after the Balinese–Dutch wars of the 1840s which had seriously shaken all of the radjadoms, including his own. These wars had also gravely impaired the position of the Dewa Agung of Klungkung, who had not for a century or more been able to impose his will upon the big distant northern states of Buleleng and Djembrana or even adjacent Karangasem and was unable thereafter to retain much more than the pro forma allegiance of the five smaller southern states of Gianjar, Bangli, Tabanan, Mengwi, and Badung. The Dewa Manggis, being the ruler of the state in which much of the traditional culture still centered, was especially restless under Klungkung's evanescent authority. Neither his powers nor his borders being very clearly defined, he came into sharp conflict not only with Klungkung but also with his other neighbors, especially Badung and Bangli, when he tried to assert what he held to be his historic rights. He also came into conflict with his own *punggawa*, some of whom, notably those of the border areas, were prepared to collaborate with the other rulers in defiance of their own. Eventually he found his position so insecure that he attempted to effect a reconciliation with the Dewa Agung by renewal of declarations of allegiance in return for protection. But the allegiance of the Dewa Manggis was no more unequivocal or immutable than was the Dewa Agung's protection, and the arrangement was not even confirmed before it collapsed, thus triggering open warfare which continued for the better part of two decades.

Dewa Manggis VII, under whom the long-smoldering feud between Gianjar and Klungkung burst into an open blaze, seemed to foreign visitors at the time rather a mild and inoffensive figure to be the center of so much intrigue and violence. Dr. Julius Jacobs, who visited Gianjar in 1881 as a member of a party headed by the Resident, described him as pleasant in appearance, cultivated in manner, forthright in speech (in Balinese and broken Malay), and very well preserved for his years, being aged then about sixty-five. The Radja had recently been quite ill, said Jacobs, but acting upon the advice of his high priest he secluded himself for 11 days in the family temple, and when he emerged he was completely cured. He seemed to Dr. Jacobs to be a wise ruler, readily assenting, for instance, to the suggestion that at his own expense he should send a promising youth to study in Banjuwangi in order to return and serve the state as professional vaccinator.

Dr. Jacobs reported, furthermore, that Gianjar was then by far the most prosperous and promising of all the states of Bali. He made special note of the presence of an unusual number of Chinese, a sure indication of commercial activity. He himself and the other members of the party put up in fact in the home of a wealthy Chinese resident which had been requisitioned by the Radja as an occasional guest house for visiting Dutch officials. In contrast to the quarters in which the party stayed elsewhere, especially Klungkung, the Gianjar *pasanggrahan* was conspicuously clean, neat, and well run, and the owner had left a full staff of servants and everything needful to the visitors' comfort. The Dutch flag flew over the house during the visit, and on the walls of the guest rooms were color prints from Europe—one portraying Potiphar and Joseph, another Boas and Ruth with texts in French and Dutch.

Dewa Manggis VII, whose state seemed to the Dutch visitors of 1881 so remarkably peaceful and prosperous, was in such precarious circumstances in 1885 that he took the risk of paying a personal visit to Klungkung to seek a settlement with the Dewa Agung. Accompanied by his four sons and numerous members of his court, he crossed the heavily guarded river ravine which constituted the state boundary and presented himself at Puri Klungkung, only 11 kilometers distant from Puri Gianjar but the stronghold of his enemies. The Dewa Agung treacherously converted the audience into a royal razzia, causing the Dewa Manggis, his sons, and his followers to be seized and incarcerated under watchful jailers in the village of Satrije, five kilometers distant from Klungkung town. The Dewa Manggis remained in exile in Satrije until his death in the year 1892. But his four sons meanwhile contrived to make their escape and return to Gianjar, where they immediately stirred up insurrection against the Dewa Agung.

The Dewa Agung had not been content merely to exile the Dewa Manggis; he also caused the Puri Gianjar to be looted and burned, thus signaling the apparent demise of the radjadom which he then proceeded to partition. He reserved the larger portion for himself but assigned one large stretch of territory to his brother-in-law, the Radja of Bangli. In the process of partition he aroused the cupidity of other rulers, some of whom craved certain of Gianjar's rich rice lands for themselves. The return to Gianjar of the sons of the Dewa Manggis and their efforts to recover their father's lost domain occasioned the outbreak of widespread warfare. Mengwi, the most tractable of the Dewa Agung's vassals, sent an army into Gianjar to dislodge the young claimants; Bangli and Badung sought to protect and advance their own interests by doing the same. Karangasem thereupon intervened for the dual purpose of sharing the spoils and inflicting humiliation upon the Dewa Agung, whose authority it habitually flouted. The most immediate, curious, and tragic results of this five-way head-on collision were: first, the massacre of Sassak troops from Lombok in the service of Karangasem, thus precipitating a Sassak insurrection at home which Karangasem tried to help repress by transfer of its own troops to Lombok (1891); second, a war between Badung and Mengwi (1891); and third, the redefection of some of the Gianjar *punggawa*, thus leaving the radjadom even more exposed than before to its many enemies.

Dewa Manggis VIII and Controleur Schwarz

For the state of Gianjar the decade of the 1890s was a period of ruinous turbulence. Bands of soldiers roamed the land, killing, burning, looting, interrupting normal village pursuits. The *punggawa*, who appropriated to themselves such of the royal revenues as could still be collected, were not always eager to see order restored. But Dewa Gde Raka, the second son of the old Radja, proved to be a vigorous leader and shrewd tactician. He gained the support of Tjokorda Gde Sukawati, the especially prestigious *Punggawa* of Ubud, rallied the demoralized fighters, imposed reverses upon the armies of his neighbors, and thus gradually won the confidence and allegiance of the other *punggawa*. After the death of his father and a brief interim rule of Dewa Pahang, his elder brother, Dewa Gde Raka gained recognition as Radja (1892), rebuilt the *puri*, and began to rule as well as to campaign in the field. But he was still surrounded by hostile neighbors who refused to concede his right to the throne. He therefore set about convincing his *punggawa* that there was in fact only one realistic measure which would preserve the state. It was to apply to the Dutch Resident in Buleleng for Dutch protection, that is, conversion of the radjadom into a Regency on the model of the states in the north. In fact it was a plan which Dewa Manggis VII had entertained in the early 1880s, but the original Dutch response both to Dewa Manggis VII and to Dewa Gde Raka was curiously evasive. The Dutch were reluctant to make any move which might provoke anti-Dutch outbreaks in Bali until they wound up a long and costly war in Atjeh and then a shorter but even costlier war in Lombok. In 1900 their hands were again free. When Dewa Gde Raka reverted to the subject, sent Tjokorda Gde Sukawati to Buleleng to visit the Resident, and invited the good offices of the Radja of Karangasem, the Dutch quickly agreed. The Resident visited Gianjar on March 8, 1900, to install the Radja as *Stedehouder* (a more prestigious title than that of mere Regent), and Controleur H. J. E. E. Schwarz, who accompanied him, took up residence within the *puri* itself. The Dewa Agung protested, but Dewa Gde Raka, with Controleur Schwarz always by his side, began rehabilitating and developing the state, which became once again the most pleasant and prosperous in all of Bali.

In 1908, the Radja-Stedehouder Dewa Gde Raka held an especially sacred ceremony, the *Mabiseka*, in which he was declared the Dewa Manggis—the last ruler of Gianjar so to be designated. Dewa Manggis VIII, like his father before him, impressed foreign visitors as being highly intelligent and cultivated, but save for the foregoing outline of events, there is little evidence on which to base an appraisal of his personality or his capabilities. There is little, that is, save for the very considerable record of progress in his state in the twelve years of his rule as both Radja and Stedehouder (1900–1912). How much of this is to be attributed to the ruler and how much to Controleur Schwarz is a matter which historians will not soon settle, if, indeed, they devote their attention to the problem at all. But Controleur Schwarz quite certainly established himself with the Radja on terms of mutual respect and was one of the most accomplished and energetic Dutch officials ever assigned to Bali. He became fluent in the Balinese language, even the "high" court Balinese, gaining thereby an insight into the Balinese character which only long and intimate association can bring. He collaborated, in fact, with the Radja's heir in compilation of a Balinese dictionary which, unfortunately, has never been published. He was a man of indefatigable energy and astonishing versatility, his position as court advisor implying also ser-vices as surveyor, engineer, judge, teacher, medical practitioner, in fact, general handyman and trouble-shooter. He lived and worked in Bali for a period of several decades, retiring to Bogor, Java, in the 1930s, where the then Radja of Gianjar was pleased to pay him a visit.

Radja Ngurah Agung as Feudal Relic and Man of Vision

The then Radja was Ide Anak Agung Ngurah Agung, who was born in 1892, succeeded to the throne in 1912, ruled until 1943, and died in 1960. He grew up in a royal court in which the Western impact was just beginning to make itself felt. He was a much pampered prince who, as eldest son of the Radja, was destined to be heir to the throne and was expected, therefore, to understudy his father in all the court ceremonials and to be carefully instructed by the household priests in all the religious rituals. He received no Western style schooling—that was for the next generation. He spoke no Dutch—although he came to understand more than he chose to admit; he became competent in modern Indonesian but his real linguistic skills were in Balinese, the ordinary Balinese of the people as well as the high Balinese of the court and the archaic language of literature and religion. He became a connoisseur of music, dancing, and acting. He was a highly discriminating patron of the sculptors, the carvers, the painters, the weavers, and all the other artists and craftsmen for whom the court was a magnet. Naturally be became a devotee of fighting cocks and cockfighting, never missing a big match and never hesitating to lay heavy wagers on his own entries and those others which caught his fancy. As he grew up he acquired 24 wives who bore him a total of only nine children, of whom four survive.

Radja Ngurah Agung made his court one of the most splendid in Bali, consciously competing with his peers in display of lavishness. Even though his state was relatively small in area, it included some of Bali's richest rice fields and its people were celebrated for their achievements in all the arts. The Radja himself owned great tracts of land and received large revenues from them; he could afford not to be frugal in his outlays for court ceremonials and temple festivals. His regalia included lances with golden heads, jeweled krises, gold and silver ceremonial vessels, many of them richly worked and endowed with magical properties which, together with the wisdom of the ruler, were thought to preserve the realm.

Radja Ngurah Agung deliberately set himself to be a wise ruler, both just and firm. While there were divergent views with regard to the degree to which he succeeded, there was agreement that this was no easy self-assignment in a period when all values were changing and there was confusion with regard both to the responsibilities and the privileges of royalty, the traditional and the modern outlook being wide apart on such questions, for instance, as the appropriateness of concubinage. Probably the soundest judgement on his rule was passed by his own people when they accorded him the one great triumph with which he hoped his reign would be climaxed. It was a royal cremation in the great tradition of unstinting labor to create the huge and gorgeously ornamented bier and tower, and of long sustained feasting and other entertainment, not, of course, in celebration of his demise, but of his passing into another cycle of incarnation. The cremation was attended by half a million persons, including virtually the total population of his state and scores of national dignitaries. It was an enormously costly as well as a totally satisfying spectacle, and the modern economist might calculate with some dismay the outlay on the part of the family and the state.

The more empathetic, including all Balinese, reckoned it a tribute to a still vital tradition, no few, including the old Radja himself in his later years, mourning not the expense and labor of preserving it but the cultural danger inherent in its loss.

The old Radja was almost the last survivor of Balinese royalty who lived in the grand manner of Balinese feudalism—autocratic, eccentric, extravagant, but also, at least those who survived on the throne, far-sighted and shrewd enough to dedicate themselves to the welfare of the state. He acquired the reputation among the Dutch of being headstrong and hard to handle, but he also established cordial personal relationships with his Controleurs, who recalled their service in Gianjar with nostalgia. The Radja himself made a point at times of baiting the Dutch in order to see just how far he could go. He practiced, in fact, a policy of mystification. He was given, for instance, to reading the omens for victory in cockfights from the exact minute of arrival and the minutiae of costume of a certain Controleur, who never was able to understand why he was sometimes made most effusively welcome and at other times not, or why he was frequently summoned when there was no apparent business at hand. When his Controleur at one point advised him that in preparing for the visit of a high official he should do something about the palace plumbing, complaining also about the smell of fresh paint in the guest rooms, the Radja had walls everywhere sprayed with a cheap but powerful Eau de Cologne, which, as he may have expected, proved even less agreeable. In his old age, when he was seriously ill with diabetes and confined for years to his private quarters, he confounded his Western-trained physicians by following their advice and taking their prescriptions only as suited his whim and as conformed also to the advice of his native practitioners. He might cut down on sweets for a few days before the impending visit of his physician, but a satisfactory test always signaled new self-indulgence. In both personal and official matters, the Radja demonstrated such strong individuality that he had troubles with the Japanese which far exceeded his difficulties with the Dutch. The Japanese deposed him, exiled him to Lombok, and placed his eldest son on the throne; after the departure of the Japanese he was restored to his *puri*, but he never really ruled thereafter. State affairs were then rapidly passing into the hands of a new set of officials as the radjadom itself was being transformed into an administrative district of the new province in the new Republic.

Radja Ngurah Agung's great rival for local fame, wealth, and power was the Radja of Karangasem (d. 1968), who outdid him in such matters as construction of palaces and accumulation of treasure. Karangasem had a fixation upon water palaces and kept building ever larger, more expensive, never completed or inhabited follies, set in artificial lakes which bred mosquitoes and ornamented with cheap imitation carvings in molded concrete. Gianjar contented himself with rebuilding the historic *puri* after the great earthquake of 1917 and restoring, among other features, an especially beautiful tower and fountain. Karangasem also outdid Gianjar in the number of his wives and offspring, continuing to marry and sire children when he was already many times a great-grandfather. He may even have surpassed him, although witnesses differ in their appraisal, in the magnificence of his cremation (1969). Neither the Karangasem nor the Gianjar cremations is likely ever again to be matched. No one can now afford the expense.

Gianjar clearly prevailed over Karangasem in certain equally if not more significant competitions. When both radjas were encouraged by the Dutch to design new state uniforms for themselves in the Western manner, Gianjar's proved the more imaginatively gold braided and frogged and the more magnificently bejeweled. When distinguished foreign visitors began visiting Bali, among them Charlie Chaplin, it was to Gianjar rather than Karangasem that the Dutch escorted them for truly royal entertainment. Gianjar had had the inspiration to import a French chef to train two of his wives in an innovational and much relished non-Dutch European cuisine which complemented the already distinguished dishes prepared by other wives skilled in the Chinese, the Javanese, and the Balinese traditions. His dining pavilion was surrounded by an ornamental pond into which, on one occasion at least, he tossed one lady of the harem whose deportment as wife or as cook seems to have displeased him.

One of Gianjar's greatest triumphs was his Fiat Grand Phaeton, which he had had refitted to suit his tastes and his station. This was one of the very first motor vehicles to be seen in Bali and what it lacked in power it more than compensated for in panache. The Radja had the windshield so heavily bordered in gold that the driver had to peer around rather than through it; even at that he had difficulty seeing over the radiator ornament, which was almost a life-size Garuda cast in pure gold. The Fiat had power enough to proceed at a stately pace on level ground, but the royal subjects were summoned to push when it ventured uphill and were well advised to flee when it sped down. This resplendent vehicle, unfortunately, has now vanished without a trace, but the connoisseur of classic cars can get the general idea of its splendor by visiting the *kraton* of the Susuhunan of Surakarta, Java, which preserves one of just about the same vintage but more restrained in decor.

Anak Agung Gde Agung as Western Educated Heir

Radja Ngurah Agung was well aware that he himself was a figure of the past, but he was determined that his children should be prepared for the world of the future. He concentrated his greatest attention upon his eldest son, the heir to the throne, whom he caused to be trained in both the Balinese and the Western tradition; but he also educated his two daughters, one of whom was the first Balinese girl to study in Java and the first also to study in the United States. The young Anak Agung himself was carefully initiated into all of the ritual and ceremony of the radjadom; but he was also sent to Western-style schools and inducted into the modernized civil service. He attended Dutch language primary school in Klungkung and was then sent to secondary school in Malang, Java, where he lived in the home of the Dutch principal and acquired Western manners at the same time that he acquired Western learning. In 1939 he was sent to Batavia, where he entered law school, but he did not actually take his degree until the mid-1950s, his professional education having to be suspended because his father required his services in Bali at the time that the Pacific War was imminent. On his return to Bali, where, as a result of recent Dutch administrative reforms, the Radja had just recovered autonomy in state affairs, Anak Agung served his father as District Officer. When the Japanese invaded and occupied the island and presently exiled his father, he succeeded as Radja. As District Officer and Radja he paid court to one of his Malang schoolmates, the daughter of Tjokorda Gde Raka Sukawati of Ubud, whom he married on August 27, 1944. The wedding ceremony and celebration, which went on for 42 days and nights, requiring continuous serenade by singers and gamelan players among other formalities, was the one great state occasion in Gianjar during the period of the Japanese occupation.

Anak Agung and his bride, Vera, both of them the products of a Balinese *puri*, were equally the products of the Dutch schools which gave them, among other accomplishments, fluency in Dutch, French, German, and English, to add to their Balinese, Javanese, and modern

Indonesian. They were not fated, however, to have quite the carefree, luxurious, royal life which their horoscopes indicated. The *pedandas* (priests), who cast and read the horoscopes, had sagely foreseen, of course, that there would be troubled as well as happy times. The first great trouble was that of the Japanese occupation, which worked special difficulty for Gianjar because the Japanese retaliated for the old Radja's refusal automatically to accept instructions. The end of the Japanese occupation, the return of the Dutch, and the outbreak of the nationalist revolution brought political complications which spelled the end of life in the *puri* and the beginning of a new career which has been both turbulent and brilliant.

Federalist Leader; Participant in Round Table Conference

Anak Agung came into prominence nationally and internationally as the leading figure, alongside his father-in-law, Tjokorda Gde Raka Sukawati, in the emerging Negara Indonesia Timur, or State of East Indonesia, of which he became successively Minister for the Interior and Prime Minister, Tjokorda Gde Raka Sukawati being the distinguished but not very active President. At the Linggadjati Conference (November 1946) between Dutch and Indonesian leaders under British auspices, the Dutch–Indonesian military conflict had apparently been resolved by Dutch recognition of *de facto* Republican sovereignty over Java, Madura, and Sumatra, and Republican consent to the creation of the Dutch-sponsored Negara Indonesia Timur. The latter state was to include the Lesser Sundas, Celebes, and the Moluccas (but not Irian Barat, or Dutch New Guinea, always a prickly issue); it was scheduled eventually to join the revolutionary Republic of Indonesia in a federal union with the Netherlands under the Dutch Crown. Anak Agung was a delegate to the Den Pasar Conference of December 1946, in which the Dutch colonial representation, headed by Governor-General van Mook, accepted the main proposals regarding the nature of the new Negara Indonesia Timur but rejected renewed proposals for the inclusion of Irian Barat, thus creating the problem which was eventually to wreck Dutch–Indonesian cooperation. The Negara Indonesia Timur was duly constituted and the Republic granted it formal recognition. Nevertheless, the Republic was always suspicious of federalism and the federalists, especially when the Dutch began creating other states as well as the one which had been agreed upon.

The Negara Indonesia Timur achieved a reasonable degree of progress in working out its own great problems of integration and development of its widely scattered island territories. Anak Agung himself earned the reputation of being a vigorous and enlightened official. The State played an important role in the resolution of the continuing Dutch–Republican conflict which manifested itself in two Dutch Police Actions, i.e. armed invasions of Republican-held areas. It took its most drastic step in mid-1948, immediately upon the outbreak of the Second Police Action. Headed by Anak Agung, the entire cabinet resigned in protest, thus demonstrating to the Dutch the impossibility of genuine Indonesian–Dutch cooperation until the Republic was reconstituted and peaceful negotiations were resumed. When the Dutch yielded, Anak Agung was instrumental in calling an Inter-Indonesian Conference (July 1949) in Yogyakarta to work out an agreed-upon Indonesian position for subsequent negotiations. He himself led the East Indonesian delegation to the Round Table Conference in The Hague in which the Dutch agreed to transfer sovereignty. At this conference his delegation was very much concerned with the Irian Barat issue. The Dutch were refusing to transfer sovereignty over Irian Barat on the grounds that it was not naturally a part of the new nation. Had Anak Agung and his delegation not insisted upon inclusion of a clause on Irian Barat in the final agreement, the other Indonesian leaders might, for the time being at least, have relinquished this particularly delicate claim.

The Round Table Conference worked out, as a last resort, a compromise clause calling not for the actual transfer of Irian Barat but for the settlement of the issue between Dutch and Indonesian negotiators within the calendar year 1950. It was an ill-omened failure of resolution which poisoned Dutch–Indonesian relations for over a decade. Irian Barat gave Sukarno and the Sukarnoists an irredentist cause which, while neglecting matters of much greater importance, they could and did repeatedly escalate into a national and international crisis. It cost the Dutch unilateral Indonesian repudiation of all existing political and economic agreements and eventually it cost them the whole of Irian Barat as well, plus massive subsidy for its development. Anak Agung, who was present at the hatching of this albatross but had argued for immediate, not delayed or obscured attention to it, was himself doomed later on to try to shoot it down.

Foreign Minister; Negotiator of Irian Barat Dispute

During the first few years of Indonesian independence Anak Agung served successively as Minister of Interior and as Ambassador to European countries, first Belgium, later France, with concurrent assignment to Luxembourg and Portugal. In 1954 he attended the Geneva Conference on Vietnam as Indonesian observer. In 1955 he returned to Indonesia and soon thereafter became Foreign Minister in the Burhanudin Harahap Cabinet (August 15, 1955), a caretaker body appointed to prepare for the first national elections, which were expected to resolve but only worsened the debilitating conflict between the right and the left. It was a weak coalition of the right and center with a few strong individuals who adopted an unpopularly rational position at a time when fanatical Sukarnoism was coming into the ascendant. The Masjumi (liberal Muslim) and the Socialist Party (Anak Agung's) were its main support; but in the elections which it supervised, the Masjumi lost millions of votes to the very conservative (many thought reactionary) N.U., while the Socialists were virtually demolished. The P.N.I. (Nationalists) and the Communists (P.K.I.) demonstrated great strength, and Sukarno opportunistically inspired and then amplified their most extreme demands. Meanwhile, laboring under the impossible burden of Sukarno's open animosity, attack from the extreme left and right, and internal friction and betrayal, the Harahap Cabinet set itself the priority task, in the midst of elections, of resolving the inflammatory Irian Barat issue. This thankless mission fell to Anak Agung, the Foreign Minister.

Three previous efforts at Indonesian–Dutch negotiations had failed completely (1950, 1952, and 1954); attempts to achieve a settlement through the United Nations had also miscarried. Sukarno and the Sukarnoists were shouting for ever more massive political, economic, and military reprisals against the obstinate Dutch. Anak Agung persuaded the Dutch to agree to a preliminary meeting of representatives in The Hague to work out the agenda for a full-scale conference to focus on Irian Barat. The Dutch sought to include almost all of their other grievances—especially the arrest of Dutch citizens in Indonesia and the violation of economic and financial guarantees—and could only with great difficulty be persuaded to include the major issue. The Indonesians, to be sure, wished to negotiate on the basis of prior commitment to transfer sovereignty, which seemed to the Dutch like unlocking the barn door to let the horse be stolen. Anak Agung himself headed the Indonesian delegation, which met with the Dutch first in The Hague (December 6, 1955) but soon transferred the venue to cooler, calmer Geneva.

From the first the sessions were highly disputatious and disruptive. Indonesian politicians in Jakarta kept detonating land mines which were calculated to destroy the negotiations and the negotiators. The Dutch, at once bewildered and relieved by the sabotage in Jakarta, which seemed to spare them any necessity for laboriously working out an agreement which probably would not outlive the Harahap Cabinet, seemed disposed to let the demolition process take its course. Concession of sovereignty over Irian Barat would have been politically indefensible in Holland, just as any other arrangement would have been intolerable in Indonesia.

Jakarta several times suddenly called the conference off, then on again, and between February 12 and 14 things just fell apart. Anak Agung hurried back to Jakarta to try at once to comprehend and to explain what had been happening. The Cabinet abrogated all existing Dutch–Indonesian agreements and reasserted its irreducible claim; the opposition, meaning Sukarno, the P.N.I. and the P.K.I., declared the abrogation itself unconstitutional and blamed the failure of the conference upon the Cabinet. The Cabinet submitted an abrogation bill to Parliament for validation, achieved a Parliamentary victory, despite challenge on procedural grounds and a walk-out by the P.N.I. and P.K.I. members; then, in response to further challenge, it won a Supreme Court decision that the abrogation procedure had been unquestionably legal and constitutional and therefore valid. Nevertheless, Sukarno refused to sign.

The Harahap Cabinet wearily and gratefully returned its mandate (March 3, 1956), to be succeeded by the new Ali Sastroamidjojo Cabinet of the P.N.I. and associated parties of the extreme left. Sukarno, the P.N.I., and the P.K.I. (which did not yet hold cabinet post) launched themselves upon the highly adventurous course which led to acquisition of Irian Barat in 1962 by simultaneous threat of invasion and manipulation of U.N. mediators. But it was a collision course with national disaster, preceding the hysterical endeavor to "Crush Malaysia," climaxing in political, economic, and social collapse, the GESTAPU coup, and the fall of Sukarno. For Anak Agung it was almost a collision course with oblivion. Sukarno refused to confirm his subsequent appointment as Ambassador to Sweden and not long afterwards clapped him into jail.

Political Prisoner of Sukarno; Ambassador and Author

Anak Agung originally incurred the animosity of President Sukarno by reason of association with federalism, a policy which the Republican leaders, after earlier acceptance, angrily rejected as a Dutch formula of divide-and-rule. To Hindu Bali and the Balinese, who are always suspicious of Javanese Muslim schemes to monopolize power and in fact experienced Javanese domination and exploitation during the late Sukarno years, federalism looked different. It seemed to provide for genuine local autonomy without necessity for revolutionary warfare, but with benefit of visible, valuable Dutch contributions in goods and services to island development. It seemed to lead to the same objective of a loosely federated United States of Indonesia in an intentionally nebulous union with the Netherlands under the Dutch Crown. But both the Dutch and the Republicans violated the preliminary and subsequent agreements. Sukarno could never tolerate the fact that Anak Agung at various times played a key role—much more creditable than his own—in the more or less successful attempt to bring Dutch–Indonesian relations back into at least a semblance of harmony.

Anak Agung's greatest political triumph in the 1950s—his persuasion of the Dutch to negotiate at all with regard to Irian Barat—was a set-back to Sukarno's ambition to resolve the problem by demagogic tactics. It was clearly an abortive triumph almost from the outset, an unwelcome reminder to Sukarno of the accomplishments of other Indonesians than himself. Reasoned federalism regarding the State of East Indonesia and reasoned patriotism regarding Irian Barat combined to make Anak Agung a twice-marked man on Sukarno's list of personal and political enemies. He earned other black marks by reason of his close personal and political association with Vice-President Hatta and Sutan Sjahrir, the leaders respectively of the Masjumi and the Socialist parties and the most prominent and outspoken critics of Sukarno's policies. As the Sukarno regime grew more and more corrupt and authoritarian, everyone knew that Anak Agung and his friends were slated for serious trouble. It came in early January 1962, when Anak Agung, Sjahrir, Harahap, and half a dozen others (but not Hatta, who had resigned and retired and was much too venerable to touch) were suddenly picked up from their homes in the middle of the night and thrown into jail.

The arrest and detention without stated charges or court trial of this distinguished party of prisoners occasioned much excitement and speculation, but the Sukarnoists merely branded them traitors to the revolution and their friends were virtually powerless to help them. The most plausible explanation of their arrest was that the Sukarnoists suspected them of conspiracy, having heard a rumor that they were plotting to overthrow the regime. The venue of the conspiracy, it was alleged, was the Puri Gianjar, where the whole group had been guests of Anak Agung at the time of the cremation of his father (August 1961). The most heinous aspect of the crime, perhaps, was that Anak Agung had only belatedly and unenthusiastically extended an invitation to Sukarno himself to attend. Sukarno, who was piqued at being thus slighted, decided in the end not to attend but to schedule at the very last minute a command party in his Jakarta palace which detained reluctant guests who would much have preferred to be in Bali. No evidence of conspiracy was ever produced, but the prisoners remained in jail until May 1966.

Anak Agung and his fellow jailbirds constituted as illustrious a coterie of intellectual élite as has ever been assembled in Indonesia for any protracted period, and they succeeded, characteristically, in converting their prison commons into a continuous salon. They read omnivorously in many languages on many subjects, sharing the books which friends were permitted to send, and they discussed everything which they read. They wrote long letters, which reached their friends by more or less legal courier. These letters were often analyses not only of their own condition but that of the nation, which they were eminently qualified to judge, their collective views being conditioned by attentive auditing of many radio broadcasts and assiduous reading of the press. They also taught one another new languages, learned to play various musical instruments, experimented with arts and crafts, competed in tennis on escorted trips to nearby courts, and practiced yoga. In order to glorify their meager prison fare with ingredients included in food packages from home some made themselves proficient in cooking. Once each month their wives and families were permitted to pay them visits, a dispensation which worked both pleasure and hardship, for the trip from Jakarta to Madiun was long, difficult, and expensive, and treatment of visitors by prison authorities was unpredictable.

Anak Agung received regular monthly visits by his wife, who spent much of her time between visits trying to determine the prospects for his release, or, more productively, preparing packages to take to Madiun on her return. His wife was permitted to share his cell for a month while she nursed him through what was nearly a fatal attack of misdiagnosed typhoid; she was as graciously permitted to stay for another month when she, in turn, fell ill and he nursed her. On a happier occasion, half a dozen of his friends from Gianjar arrived at the prison with all that was required for celebration of the *Galungan* festival—food, decorations, costumes, and musical instruments. The prisoners invited the wardens to be their guests; the wives and families were also present; the exercise grounds was converted for a day into a Balinese temple courtyard, and the New Year was auspiciously launched. It was not to be the new year of Anak Agung's release, but Balinese optimism was duly recharged.

The curious treatment of the prisoners, which alternated between severity and laxity, was to be accounted for in part by changing political circumstances, in part by the inclination of the Javanese wardens and other responsible officials to be able later on to point to evidence of whatever sort of treatment it might seem expedient to claim. Originally the prisoners were held incommunicado without any clue to their future state; when they were moved to Madiun their treatment was generally more considerate. On one occasion they were briefly paroled for visits to their families in Jakarta but were quite unnecessarily held overnight in the grimmest of Jakarta jails alongside the toughest criminal element. They were permitted, as noted, to have monthly visits by members of their families, but no one could anticipate how long the visit might last or what might be the degree of severity of screening presents. They were permitted to have radios, books, papers, and the like, and they were given the daytime use of a commons room, but for the most part the prison authorities did very little for them except supply a most inadequate ration of food and a dreary suite of cells. In the end, when the Sukarno regime collapsed and their lives were obviously in danger in Communist-dominated Madiun, they were transferred to Jakarta. But it was six months before the government managed to process the papers for their release. It might have been six months longer save for one tragic and dramatic circumstance, the death and vindication after death of Sutan Sjahrir.

Sjahrir fell seriously ill in Madiun and was transferred to a military hospital in Jakarta, where his condition worsened. On urgent appeal of important national figures, his family was permitted to transfer him to Switzerland for medical treatment, and there not long afterwards he died. When Sjahrir's body was returned to Jakarta, the Indonesian public manifested its genuine affection and attachment in a manner which made Sukarno's monster political demonstrations seem, as they were, artificially contrived. Anak Agung and his fellow prisoners were released from jail just long enough to attend the funeral. It was their first appearance in public after their arrest and they were lionized by the crowds. The recent shock of the GESTAPU coup and of the series of appalling revelations which followed made people regard those who had long been anti-Sukarno as foresightedly pro-Indonesia. As Sjahrir went to his grave in the Jakarta Heroes Cemetery, with Sukarno failing to put in an appearance to pronounce the eulogy, the other prisoners became symbols of enduring courage and principle in times when many one-time revolutionary leaders, including Sukarno, were being repudiated.

Anak Agung and his friends were released in May 1966, but restoration of freedom did not automatically imply professional reinstatement. It took another two years for Anak Agung himself to work his way back to prominence. Meanwhile he spent a year in Honolulu as a Senior Specialist at the East–West Center, preparing a manuscript dealing with Indonesian foreign relations; he spent the subsequent three months in the Netherlands on a study grant from the Dutch government for continuation and completion of the project. The finished study was published in English in The Hague in December 1973, under the title *Twenty Years of Indonesian Foreign Policy* and has been very favorably received. After his return to Indonesia he became special advisor to the Foreign Minister until he received new assignment in 1970 as Ambassador to Austria, an office which he held until December 1974, when he again returned to the Foreign Ministry in Jakarta.

During his four years in Vienna, Anak Agung was much engrossed in representing his country in Austrian and other European functions of many types, including international conferences, while also supervising a very busy Embassy. He played host to relays of distinguished Indonesian visitors, among them, in 1973, President and Madame Suharto and their entourage, for whom he entertained in Indonesian and Balinese fashion, with decorations, food, and entertainment which were a sensation even in a sophisticated city. Whenever possible he returned for short visits to Bali, where his presence in the *puri* is always a signal for scores of Balinese to show up at all hours, bringing gifts, seeking favors, paying social calls, much in the manner that prevailed in the *puri* in the time of his father. At the present time he devotes part of his attention to the Jakarta ministry, part to the Bali *puri*, and part to official missions overseas.

Four Sons as Students Overseas and Young Professionals
Anak Agung and his wife Vera—his only wife, his father's example notwithstanding—have a family of four sons, all of whom have grown up in the new Balinese tradition of internationalism. The eldest, also Anak Agung Gde Agung, a graduate of Harvard Business School and the Fletcher School of Law and Diplomacy, has recently returned to Jakarta to become the representative of a multinational corporation. The second son, Raka, to skip the titles, having graduated from Carleton College (Minnesota) and the Institute of Social Studies (The Hague), has returned to Bali to engage in various commercial and cultural activities, to teach in Udayana University, and to maintain the continuous family presence in the *puri*. The third son, Putere, is a medical student in Leyden; the fourth, Oka, is studying architecture in Aachen.

CHAPTER 16

Basics of Balinism

Elements of Balinese Hindu Beliefs

At the bottom of everything there is magnetic iron, but in the beginning there was nothing, all was emptiness; there was only space. Before there were the heavens, there was no earth, and when there was no earth, there was no sky. Through meditation the world serpent Antaboga created the turtle Bedawang, upon whom he coiled two snakes as the foundation of the world. On the world turtle rests a lid, the Black Stone. There is no sun, there is no moon, there is no night in the cave below (the underside of the stone); this is the underworld, whose gods are the male Batara Kala and the female Setesuyara. There lives also the great serpent Basuki....

Kala created the light and Mother Earth, over which extends a layer of water. Over this again are consecutive domes or skies, high and low; one of mud (which dried to become the earth and the mountains); then the "empty" middle sky (the atmosphere), where Iswara dwells; above this is the floating sky, the clouds, where Semara sits, the god of love. Beyond that follows the "dark" (blue) sky with the sun and the moon, the home of Surya; this is why they are above the clouds. Next is the Perfumed Sky, beautiful and full of rare flowers, where lives the bird Tjak, whose face is like a human face, the serpent Taksaka, who has legs and wings, and the *awan* snakes, the falling stars. Still higher in the sky is *gringsing wayang*, the "flaming heaven of the ancestors." And over all the skies live the great gods who keep watching over the heavenly nymphs.

* * *

After Siwa had created the insects, Wisnu the trees, Isara the fruits, and Sanbu the flowers, Batara Guru discussed with Brahma the creation of human beings to populate the new world. Brahma admitted that he did not know how and asked Batara Guru to try first. The latter made four figures, four men out of red earth, and went into meditation so that they would talk, think, walk, and work. Brahma remarked that if those were human beings then he could make men, and taking some clay, he proceeded to make a figure that resembled a man. Batara Guru was annoyed and made the rain, which lasted for three days, destroying the figure Brahma had made. When the rained stopped, Brahma tried again, this time baking the figure. On seeing the man baked of clay, Batara Guru boasted he would eat excrement if Brahma could give it life; but Brahma succeeded in making it alive by meditation and demanded that Batara Guru make good his boast. Batara Guru took some clay and made images of dogs that became living dogs, and wished that forever after they should walk, whine, bark, and eat excrement.

* * *

After the world, the mountains, and the cardinal directions were created, and there were trees, fruits, and flowers, a god made four human beings out of red earth, whom he provided with utensils to work with and houses to live in. Batara Siwa, the Supreme Lord, next made four mature girls for wives of the four men. The god of love, Batara Semara, made mating a pleasure so that the women would be fertilized and eventually the four couples had many children: 117 boys and 118 girls, who grew, became adolescent, married, and had children.

These three citations, taken from Miguel Covarrubias' classical study, *The Island of Bali* (New York, 1937), are excerpts from Balinese legends regarding the creation of the universe (Bali) and of human beings (the Balinese). Through the meditation of the serpent Antaboga the island of Bali was metamorphosed out of magnetism in the void. The serpent created the turtle Bedawang upon whose shell, supported by two inter-coiled snakes, rests the world and its waters. Below Bedawang lies the black underworld presided over by Batara Kala, the Lord Avenger, who created Mother Earth. Over the earth, in multiple and successive domes, rise the various skies. In the "empty sky" dwells the great god Siwa (or Iswara, or Brahma), the manifestation and reconciliation of all opposing natural, human, and divine forces—good and evil, fire and water, matter and nothingness, male and female, the seeker and the sought. In the "floating sky" lives Semara, the God of Love, and in the "dark sky," Surya, the God of the Sun. Yet further beyond, among the falling stars in the Perfumed Sky, live the great man-bird Tjak and the winged serpent Taksaka. Last, in the "flaming heaven of the ancestors" are to be found the ancestral spirits and everywhere the great gods keeping guard over the heavenly nymphs.

When the world was ready for human habitation, Batara Guru (the Great Teacher) debated with his other self, Brahma (or Siwa) the need and nature of man. The two-in-one then engaged in a sportive competition, fashioning figures of men out of red clay and by process of meditation infusing the figures with life. From these four—or five—first males and the female mates with whom they were provided sprang the Balinese people and their civilization.

The account of the creation, with its curious echoes of the Sutras, the Bible, the Koran, and various other scriptures and folklore of East and West, is at once synoptic and syncretic, philosophical, scientific, poetic, and quite characteristically and whimsically Balinese. The concept of the evolution of the universe out of the void through process of meditation is not far removed from modern scientific theory. The byplay between Batara Guru and Brahma is indicative of the spirit of inventiveness and earthiness with which the Balinese endow their drama. The catalogue of imported and indigenous deities, great and small; the invocation of magical names and mythical creatures, good and evil; the celebration of the ancestors and of nature and of both sacred and profane deeds and thoughts: all these key elements of the above brief extracts pervade the highly eclectic Balinese thought. Philosophy and theology, superstition and mysticism, animism and *adat* (custom or tradition which constitute in fact uncodified law): all combine to inspire the unique Balinese culture. It is commonly identified merely as Hinduism and sometimes more accurately described as an archaic form of much modified Hinduism. Certainly it is not a Hinduism which any Indian Hindu, ancient or modern, would recognize as approximately his own system of beliefs, values, and dogmas. It can only be identified with any precision by the purist by calling it simply Balinism.

Miguel Covarrubias, to revert to the great Mexican master of modern Balinese studies, summed up the elements of this distinctive "Balinese Hinduism" as follows:

The conglomerate of religious principles manifests itself in elaborate cults of ancestors and deities of fertility, of fire, water, earth, and sun, of the mountain and the sea, of gods and devils. They are the backbone of the Balinese religion, which is generally referred to as Hinduism, but which is in reality too close to the earth, too animistic, to be taken as the same esoteric religion as that of the Hindus of India. Since the earliest times when Bali was under the rule of the great empires that flourished in the golden era of Hinduistic Java, the various forms of Javanese religion became in turn the religions of Bali; from the Mahayanic Buddhism of the Sailendras in the seventh century, to the orthodox Sivaism of the ninth, to the demoniac practices of the Tantric sects of the eleventh century. In later times Bali adapted the modified, highly Javanized religion of Madjapahit, when Hinduism had become strongly tinged with native Indonesian ideas. Each of these left a deep mark upon Balinese ritual; to the native Balinese cults of ancestors, of the elements, and of evil spirits were added the sacrifices of blood, the practices of black magic of the Tantric Buddhists, the Vishnuite cult of the underworld, Brahmanic juggling of mystic words and cabalistic syllables, the cremation of the dead, and so forth, all, however, absorbed and transformed to the point of losing their identity, to suit the temper of the Balinese.

In Bali there is no creed, no dogma, no scripture, no conviction about salvation or damnation by reason of adherence to any metaphysical doctrine. But there is an immense deposit of mystical and spiritual manifestations which the villagers constantly re-experience in daily life, always aware of the living presence in nature of the ancestral and divine spirits. Under the guidance of the priests who plan the temples and conduct the temple ceremonies, these manifestations assume substance and names and significance. This arrangement proves philosophically gratifying to the learned and symbolically satisfying to the unlettered. And there is a rigid code of conduct which conditions every contact between human beings or between men and the immortals.

Reverence for Custom and Ceremony

The ordinary man in his daily life must be aware of caste distinctions (now of rapidly diminishing importance) inclusive of levels of language and permissible contracts of marriage. He must adhere to rules of etiquette with regard, for instance, to seating arrangements and presentation of food and gifts. He must be thoroughly knowledgable about division of labor between men and women and among villagers and much else which classifies as *adat*. A breach of *adat* is regarded as evidence of lack of breeding and it necessitates, in extreme cases, a trial before the village elders or an elaborate ceremony of purification.

When he visits a temple the Balinese must be correctly dressed (always with a scarf tied about his waist); he must take an appropriate offering (the most beautiful he can contrive); he must show proper deference to the priests as they chant, pray, strew flowers, and sprinkle lustral water. He must be able, if he proceeds very far into the more esoteric rites, to go into a trance or to assist in bringing someone else safely into or out of one, an art which implies a more or less sophisticated knowledge of applied psychology. Above all else he must cultivate some special skill which will enable him to contribute to the temple and to the village community as a craftsman, an artisan, an artist—or at least as a good farmer providing at the end of each harvest season (his womenfolk carrying it) a splendid ornamented specimen of his crops to offer to the gods. After wafting the "essence" toward the altar, the worshippers pragmatically carry the offering back home again for household consumption. But the Balinese need not, and unless he is a high priest he does not, read and study sacred writings, perform prescribed prayers, or reflect very profoundly upon virtue and vice. It is enough to make daily offering of a few grains of rice and some flowers at the shrines within his home compound and perhaps at certain village shrines as well and always to participate in village and temple affairs—actively to participate, that is, rather than merely to profess. Balinism therefore is not a systematized philosophy or theology but an artistically stylized way of life.

Search for Harmony and Self-Fulfillment

To define Balinism as an artistically stylized way of life is not to imply that it is a "life-style" in the modish modern sense of "liberation" but rather that it is a life-order in which each individual naturally finds his place, and the community, as much as the person, becomes a living, evolving, creative entity. What the Balinese seeks is to be and to feel Balinese; conversely, what he most fears is to be or to be deemed un-Balinese, that is, an outcast pronounced "dead" by his own community by reason of such grave offenses as profaning or pillaging a temple, committing an act of incest or bestiality, conversion to Christianity, Islam, Buddhism or some other alien religion, or (in former times) the contraction of leprosy. The Balinese seeks harmony with his family, his community, his ancestors, the world of nature, and the world of the gods and the demons. He does so in the belief (his one real dogma) that correct conduct in this life will ensure his reincarnation in the next, not as a serpent or a monster, but as a happier, nobler order of being. Such reincarnation is only possible if he participates in the proper works and rites. Of these latter, the last and most crucial, a ritual which only a devoted family can or will arrange for him, is cremation. In cremation the body, the mere shell of the spirit, is purged through fire and the soul is set free to seek and find a better vehicle for its entry into the next cycle of existence. Cremation, therefore, is the ceremony supreme within the family and village system—an occasion for joyous feasting and entertainment in celebration of a human being's triumph in death over life itself.

The Balinese first discovers his true role in his own home. As a child he is treated with the most loving care as a gift of the gods. In contravention of much modern theory of child care, he is not only overindulged by his doting parents but he responds by being affectionate, obedient, respectful, and nonquarrelsome, conspicuously eager to understudy his elders in any labor and to care for and teach any younger child. Until fairly recent times he discovered his true identity—indeed, his true name—only with the birth of his first child. Thus Bedug and Koman, having a child whom they name Alit, become known thereafter in the community as Pan Alit and Men Alit; even more confusingly, since they prefix the name of the first child with Wajan (and the second with Nengah, the third with Njoman, the fourth with Ktut), which may be used instead of the given name, they become, like many other parents in the village, Pan Wajan and Men Wajan. This seems to cause the Balinese little or no concern, so interchangeable is the individual with the community identity.

Childlessness, which can be corrected by borrowing or adopting the child of another, has always been regarded in Bali as the worst of all possible fates except only that of becoming an outcast. Childless women are doomed in the underworld to suckling a huge worm and childless men and women alike cannot be certain of cremation and hence a happy reincarnation. Fear of childlessness has been a major factor in perpetuating the practice of polygamy. Two or more wives may mean two or more quarrelsome wives, notwithstanding the pride which the Balinese place upon domestic harmony; but it provides insurance against becoming an ancestor without descendants and hence without roots outside the empty spirit world.

Just as the Balinese individual immerses himself in the family, so the family merges into the community and the community into the *desa*, that is, the village or group of villages. In former times the patriotism of individual Balinese was limited mainly to the *desa* or at most to the radjadom. But the community organization has been so pervasive and the linkages between communities on the basis of court and temple ceremonies have been so clear that there has long existed an almost homogenous Balinese society. Social similarities did not preclude political animosities which, in former times, frequently made life in Bali quite turbulent. But being recruited into the military service of a radja or *punggawa* was far from being as significant a factor in Balinese life as was voluntary participation in community labor and ritual.

The Balinese family lives in a spacious, walled compound which is part of an enclave of compounds occupied by related or closely associated families, perhaps a village in itself, perhaps a distinct segment of a village made up of two or more such enclaves. The heads of the households, who hold hereditary rights to certain lands, elect a *klian*, or headman, to preside over community activities. Such activities relate especially to the upkeep of roads and waterways, the performance of rites and ceremonies, and the maintenance of shrines and temples. Each village is likely to have three different temples: the *pura puseh*, which memorializes the founding of the community; the *pura desa*, in which most village ceremonies are held and in which may often be found the *balai agung*, or village meeting hall; and the *pura dalem*, the temple of the dead. The major community activities are the preparations for the planting and harvesting of crops (preferably always rice), and the staging of the *odalan* (temple anniversary festivals), or other ceremonies such as cremations. These agrarian and religious undertakings require not only rituals at the shrines, but cockfights, music, dance, and drama performances, and invariably feasting. They occasion processions of all the villagers, accompanied by musicians, dancers, and actors, carrying the *artjas*, or guardian images, to a nearby river for symbolic bathing.

Each individual Balinese finds himself and his place in the community as he learns to plant rice and perform other labors, to prepare the ornamental offerings, to quarry, place, and carve the moist tufa of which the temples are built, to participate actively in the entertainments and ceremonials. The ordinary Balinese peasant, who labors by day in the fields, may appear in the evening, handsomely costumed and completely self-possessed, as a musician, a dancer, an actor, and so may his wife, his son, and his daughter. Or he may be a skilled sculptor or wood carver. His wife will almost certainly be able to weave the palm leaf *lamak*, patterned banners several meters

A topeng (mask) dance being performed by Ida Bagus K'tutu from the village of Mas, Gianjar, 1949. His white mask denotes royalty.

long, hundreds of which hang from swaying bamboo poles along the roadways at festival times. She may also be able to weave splendid textiles. The husband may prove to be not just a farmer but also a priest but not the highest of the Brahman priests, who are men of great erudition and often great arrogance, scorning the humbler practitioners as mere witch-doctors.

Among the 90 per cent of the Balinese population which belongs to the Sudra, the lowest of the four castes, the incidence of great artistic skill and accomplishment is amazingly high, much higher, in all probability, than among any other people. Among the 10 per cent of the aristocracy—the Brahamana (priests), the Ksatria (rulers), the Wesia (warriors)—the incidence is even higher. It has been elicited and refined by the social obligation to participate creatively in a communal system such as the artistically impoverished international Communists have never yet dreamed of. In fact, during the period in which they sought and almost achieved political power in Bali, the Communists attempted to convert the vital island artistry into a sterile, propagandistic tool of a cheap new people's culture.

Characteristic Features of Temples and Dance Dramas

The Balinese temple, which is the focus of village life as well as ritual, is an architectural and artistic monument to the local artisans and artists. They lavish labor and skill upon it, rebuilding it every few decades, always inventing and improvising certain distinctive elements of their own while still adhering to fairly standard principles of layout, design, and ornamentation. According to the findings of Miguel Covarrubias and Walter Spies, who surveyed scores of temples to divine the typical plan, the prototype would consist of two courtyards, the outer essentially a service area with pavilions for preparation of feasts and for putting up pilgrims, with space also for entertainments, the inner being built up with various shrines.

The outer courtyard is approached through a high split gateway, the *Tjandi Bentar*, which looks like a massive and elaborately carved tower which has been precisely bisected and the two halves pushed apart to allow for entry over a high, steep stairway through wooden gates into the temple compound. The *Tjandi Bentar*, which is commonly ornamented with arresting carvings of mythical and monstrous creatures, is sufficiently overpowering in itself to awe the common man. To the erudite it may suggest the eternal duality in unity of the mystical universe or even the divine trinity of Brahma, Vishnu, and Siva, the twin pillars being sometimes regarded as symbols of the latter pair. It calls to mind also the legend of the splitting of Mahameru, the cosmic mountain and abode of the gods, to form Bali's Mt. Agung and Mt. Batur. The *Tjandi Bentar* and its carvings lend themselves to as many readings as there are students of Balinese architecture and theology. The tower in the front right-hand corner lends itself only to one, which is reassuringly simple in contrast. It is the *Kukul* tower sheltering the great wooden gong which calls the villagers together for any temple ceremony, village meeting, or other event of importance, including emergencies such as flood or fire.

The inner courtyard is approached through the *Padu Raksa*, a monumental gateway which is covered rather than split; it is guarded in front by a pair of stone *raksa*, or giants, and in back by the *aling*, a screen wall to impede the passage of evil spirits, which have difficulty always in negotiating a right angle turn. In the center of the inner court stands the main shrine, the *Pepelik*, dedicated to a local deity, in which are preserved certain relics and treasures, sometimes a stone with an ancient inscription, sometimes the village theatrical costumes, sometimes a lingga. In the court will be found at least one *meru* (a pagoda built of wood with thatched roofs) dedicated to Mahameru, the mountain center of the universe. There will be various small shrines, always including one dedicated to Mt. Agung, the most sacred mountain of Bali, and one to Mt. Batur. The most conspicuous feature of the inner court is often the *Padmasana*, a towering stone chair dedicated to the sun god Surya and placed in the corner of the courtyard with its back to Mt. Agung. The *Padmasana* is carved to represent the cosmos. The base is the turtle Bedawang; above the turtle are two stone snakes; above the snakes, the various tiers represent the earth, the seas, and the skies. Two of the smaller, less elaborate shrines are reserved for Ngurah Alit and Ngurah Gde, the bookkeepers of the gods, who are stationed below to make sure that all rites are properly performed, all offerings come up to divine standards, and all worshippers are discreet in deportment. In one corner of the compound is a stone niche for Taksu, the divine interpreter, who enters into the body of the temple mediums and through them pronounces curses and prophecies, inspires trance dancers and exorcizes evil spirits.

The outer courtyard of the temple is the preferred and the ideal scene for entertainments, rivaled in beauty only by the royal palaces.

Center stage back is usually the *Padu Raksa*, sometimes the *Tjandi Bentar*, the sudden apparition of the brilliantly costumed, dramatically posed performer within the monumental gateway being the most effective of theatrical entries. The gateway is ornamented with flickering oil lamps set in the deep carvings to cast light and shadow upon the areas immediately in front and to the sides of the gate in which the *gamelan* is placed and the dances or dramas are performed. The bright electric notes of the *gamelan* gongs are synchronized with the appearance of dancers or actors, and what follows is often a performance of consummate artistry. Even when transferred to drab theater stages in New York, London, and Paris, it is still a sensation, although never the genuine experience, which can be achieved only within the true Balinese ambiance of temple or palace courtyard. The setting is equally appropriate to the contest between Rangda the witch and Barong the lion, to the *Legong* dance (of pre-adolescent girls), the *Baris* (warrior dance), the *Ketjak* (monkey dance), the *Kebiyar* (the modern invention of the great dancer Mario), the *Topeng* (mask pantomime), the *Wajang* (puppet show), or any other of the numerous theatrical arts.

The Balinese audience is at once casual and critical. Everyone in the village, man, woman, and child, turns out for any given performance. People move idly about, children fall asleep, their elders chat with their neighbors, and the performances may continue for most of the night. But always some are watching attentively; almost everyone becomes alert when a dancer or actor turns in an especially inspired performance; and expressions of disapproval are audible if anyone misses his cues or seems clumsy. If the villagers' own troupe is performing, everyone knows every musician, actor, or dancer and obviously has his favorites. If the troupe from a neighboring village has been invited over, people are interested in making comparisons, ofttimes highly critical; if something both novel and effective is introduced, the local performers take note for later emulation. Balinese theater is a highly professional chain of theaters which combine the best aspects of summer stock company and city arts group without any of the artificiality which in the Western world attaches to both.

Every Balinese can identify the musical, the choreographic, and the dramatic motifs as readily as he can recognize the gates and shrines and sculptures of the temple compound. He is familiar not only with his own temple and its ceremonies and entertainments but also with every other temple within walking or bicycling distance of his village. But he is likely to become confused between and among the innumerable *batara* (great gods) and *dewa* (lesser gods), who appear sometimes in one guise, sometimes in another; he realizes that one divinity may go by various names but he becomes a bit vague about which at any given point is which and may take resort in facetiousness. He knows them not only as they appear in the ceremonies but also as they appear in the entertainments, conducting themselves, from his point of view, as indicated in the legend quoted above, very much like confused mortals. The *pedanda*, or high priests, know the literature, the theology, and the legends by heart; they can chant long prayers in *kawi* (an archaic Sanskrit–Javanese–Balinese); they can also pronounce frightening incantations. The ordinary Balinese is more impressed by the latter than the former. For to him, as indeed to the élite as well, it is almost equally important to appease the evil spirits as to propitiate the good.

Demons and Monsters; Rangda the Witch; Barong the Lion

Beautiful, tranquil Bali is the home not only of the gods but also of demons. Of these there exist an almost infinite number and variety who set themselves deliberately to trap, trick, and torture the unwary. The most evil of all is not Kala, the Lord of Darkness and the Underworld, but Rangda, the witch. Rangda is identified by legend with a Balinese queen, Javanese by birth, the mother of Airlangga, the first great Balinese hero. For having dabbled in magic in her earlier years, the queen was eventually turned into a witch and driven into the jungle. She engaged thereafter in the abominable practice of feeding upon the blood of pregnant women and the entrails of unborn infants, thus inducing pestilence and other disasters upon any home or village which she visited. Rangda is still held guilty today of many of the misfortunes which befall the ordinary islander.

The dramatic confrontation between Rangda, the witch, and Barong, the beneficent lion—the contest between good and evil—is one of the most celebrated and exciting of Balinese temple dramas. The mere appearance of Rangda sends some of the participants into a trance in which they turn their krises violently but harmlessly upon themselves and one another, bite off the heads of chickens and engage in wild antics dangerous to the bystanders. To play the role of Rangda—or the two-man role of Barong—requires actors of skill and also of extraordinary physical and spiritual powers. A man of weak physique or character is likely to be exhausted to the point of permanent diabolical possession in merely attempting the role.

The witch Rangda—her hideous face and bestial fangs shrouded in madly disarranged sepulchral hair, her pendulous breasts dragging below her waist, her fingers sprouting gigantic nails—appears awesomely in the split gateway after a dramatic build-up of gamelan music in the courtyard and incantations at the shrine. Barong, the bold and sportive lion, prancing and dancing, advancing and retreating, rolling its enormous eyes and loudly snapping its wooden teeth, seeks to drive her away while the kris dancers whirl and shout and attack. Eventually Rangda is vanquished and vanishes, but every Balinese knows that she will reappear at the next temple festival or even sooner, at a time, perhaps, when he is walking alone by night along a deserted pathway.

Leyak and Other Mischievous or Malign Spirits

Besides Rangda, the Balinese have to cope with the ubiquitous *leyak*, sometimes mere mischievous sprites, sometimes malicious and malign spirits, which manifest themselves in mysterious balls of fire in the night or by day as grotesque shapes in the *waringin* (banyan trees), the favorite haunts of evil spirits, or as dimly perceived monsters in the depths of the forests. A *leyak*, seen or unseen, may be responsible for any sudden pain, slip or a fall, the disappearance of valuables, the loss of a crop, possession by a demon, or death through mysterious violence. One deals with *leyak*, also with Rangda or other evil creatures or spirits, by patronizing a dealer in magic and spells. Some of the most accomplished are priests of high or low degree—the venerable and learned *pedanda* or the humble keeper and sweeper of a village temple, the *pemanku*; others are professional *sunguhu,* who are at least as likely to deal in black as in white magic. One also makes offerings: not the beautiful offerings which are carried to the temples, but a filthy mess of decayed foodstuffs which one dumps contemptuously on the ground and then hurries away, leaving it to the *leyak* or the village dogs and pigs to devour.

Both black and white magic flourish along with witchcraft and exorcism, defilement, and purification. It is a rare Balinese who has not at some time sought out a practitioner for treatment of an ailment, real or imaginary, for advice in matters of love, for retrieval of some lost object, for procurement of a potion or a charm or indeed an antidote to one which is already in the possession of someone else. If a young man wishes to win a beautiful girl, he may send her a comb which has been enchanted to order. If a wife wishes to preserve a husband from a predatory rival, she may present one or both with a ring of which the stone has been treated to repel. Practice of black magic is regarded, however, as extremely dangerous; there builds up within the body of the practitioner himself an accumulation of magical impulses which may eventually prove to be toxic, or, as in the case of the unhappy queen who is now Rangda, transform the adept into some creature which inspires loathing and horror. The role of magic in Balinese society has never really been explored by an outsider. The starting place for some bold acolyte scholar might be one of the small temples dedicated explicitly to witchcraft, the location and function of which Balinese seldom mention.

Calendars; Horoscopes; Cremations

The Balinese live by a complicated calendar, or rather by two ingeniously synchronized calendars, having succeeded in meshing the Indian lunar year of 12 months with the Balinese *wuku* year of 210 days, the latter being divided into ten sequences of one-to-ten day weeks. Each day can thus be identified by a dozen more or less well-known names, and the correspondence of certain days between the two calendars makes for arcane interpretations of great significance. The calendar automatically lends itself to the casting of horoscopes, for which the ordinary Balinese feels an insatiable need. One of the prime functions of the calendar and of the priests who read it is the determination of the propitious days for the planting and harvesting of rice and for the scheduling of the frequent celebrations, such as the *selamatan* in honor of a new home, or the cremation of a deceased relative, or the temple festivals. Since rice is planted and harvested throughout the year, the climate allowing it to mature either at the two main harvest seasons or in between seasons, and since every village has at least three temple festivals of its own each year and is very much interested in those of its neighbors, the study of the calendar becomes an esoteric art in which many, many persons engage.

The cremation ceremony, the most important festivity which is arranged by the family rather than by the community, although the whole community is sure to participate both in the preparations and the celebrations, requires the most meticulous services of the horoscope-casters to determine the day and hour of each event. Once the correct horoscopes are cast, the ceremonies seem to assume a momentum and direction of their own, especially in the case of a royal cremation, when the bodies of many deceased subjects may share the glorious and expensive rites. It becomes at once a major private, state, and religious event. At the time of death the body is bathed, covered with spices, wrapped in white cloth and a mat of split bamboo, and then either buried, or, in the case of a royal family, retained in the *puri* until the family has accumulated the necessary money for the cremation expenses and has determined from the priests what will be a propitious day and hour. Once the cremation is arranged the remains are removed from the temporary coverings, re-wrapped with various charms such as coins and jewels, and placed in a bier which is fashioned usually like a gigantic cow. The bier itself is deposited in an elaborately ornamented funeral tower, the tower is burned, and the ashes are collected and cast into the sea for final purification. This chain of events, which may require many days for completion, involves a series of spectacular processions and much feasting and entertainment. Splendid cremations still occur in Bali, but very few families are now able to afford anything approximating the regal scale of many of those of the past.

Great Festivals of *Nyepi* and *Galungan–Kuninggan*

The major island-wide festive events of the year are *Nyepi* and *Galungan–Kuninggan*. *Nyepi*, or the Spring Equinox Festival, ushers in the Balinese New Year with the exorcizing of evil spirits; *Galungan*, climaxing in *Kuninggan*, succeeds it, when the ancestral spirits return to earth for celebration with their descendants. *Nyepi* lasts for two days. The first day is given over to the most elaborate of celebrations: presentation of offerings at the temples; ceremonies of worship and purification; staging of feasts, cockfights, and entertainments. All is made as noisy and colorful as possible in order to excite the curiosity of the evil spirits, all of whom crowd into the temple compound to see what is going on only at the climax of the festivities to be quite suddenly and violently exorcized by the priests. The second day of the festival is dedicated to total silence and rest in order to deceive the spirits into thinking the island has been abandoned by its people and to trick them into taking up their own new abode elsewhere. On the second day no one stirs from the home, no food is cooked, no work is done, no light is lit; nothing visibly moves about except the livestock. The evil spirits seem never to be deceived for long, but each year, at the Spring Equinox, the Balinese try again—or at least they now try insofar as it is still possible as modernity intrudes.

The *Galungan* festival is even more impressive and enjoyable, mainly because it lasts longer—ten days—and allows the Balinese to consort with their revered ancestors. The spirits of the ancestors arrive five days before the actual *Galungan* date, in order, it seems, to determine whether the offerings, feast, and entertainments will be worthy of them and hence warrant lingering to enjoy. Since the Balinese spare no effort or expense to make the *Galungan* as physically and spiritually satisfying as is humanly possible, the ancestors always remain for the full ten days. The *Galungan* climaxes in the almost equally elaborate *Kuninggan*, which is intended to speed the ancestors so happily back to the spirit world that they will not in the course of the following year be moved to return uninvited or linger about to haunt their descendants.

The period of the *Galungan* and *Kuninggan* festivals is the time of year par excellence for a visit to Bali. Everywhere the women are staging their processions bearing on their heads towering and artistically arranged offerings, everywhere the temples are crowded with celebrants; there is a cockfight every morning in every village; there are gamelan performances which last most of the day and dance and dramatic performances which last most of the night. It is tens days of pageantry which, of course, is repeated, although on a less ostentatious scale, 10 or 20 more times a year within any given village area. This ensures for the Balinese that whatever calendar they reckon by, whether the Indian, the Balinese, or now the Western, at least one day and night in ten will be occupied with festivities for which in other countries, radio, television, moving pictures, sports events, political rallies and demonstrations, even folklorica, offer no remote equivalent.

Vulnerability and Durability of Balinese Culture

The Balinese, in short, really lives his culture, which compresses into one aesthetic package his life, his work, his social involvements, his religious practices, and his artistic self-fulfillment. For a thousand years or more this culture came as close as possible to satisfying all of his needs. It seems, in fact, according to the witness of various eminent anthropologists, artists, writers, and other observers, to have been a culture of gem-like beauty and value such as has rarely if ever been matched by any other people. The vulnerability and fragility of any such anachronistic system in the chaotically changing modern world is altogether self-evident.

It is some comfort to think that the more empathetic Dutch colonizers of the late nineteenth and early twentieth century feared and predicted that the real Bali could not long survive the impact of the Western world. It did survive, and the forebodings of the present generation of Balinese and Western cultural conservationists may prove, happily, to be no more accurate than those of their predecessors. But it is no comfort at all to recall certain salient facts: there were only one million Balinese in 1900, whereas there are over two million today; there were no more than 100 Western visitors per year in 1900 but there are now 100,000; the material base of the culture—the rice crop—is shrinking in proportion to the number of consumers; and the spiritual base, the once vital and valid Balinism, is being processed into synthetic bait with which to lure world tourists.

Bibliography

Arntzenius, J. O. H., *De Derde Balische Expeditie in Herinnering Gebracht*, 's Gravenhage, 1874.

Begin ende Voortgangh van de Vereenigde Neederlantsche Geoctroyeerde Oost-Indische Compagnie, Amsterdam, 1646.

Bloemen Waanders, F. L. van, "Aanteekeningen omtrent Bali," *T.B.G.*, Dl. V, 1855, pp. 431–447; Dl. VII, 1857, pp. 73–77.

—— "Aanteckeningen omtrent de Zeden en Gebruiken der Balinezen, inzonder-heit die van Boeleleng," *T.B.G.*, Dl. VIII, 3e Serie, Dl. II, 1859, pp. 105–279.

—— "Bijdragen tot de Kennis van het Eiland Bali," *T.N.I.*, Dl. VIII, 13e Serie, Dl. II, 1859, pp. 370–410.

—— "Dagverhaal eener Reis over Bali in Juni en July, 1868," *T.N.I.*, 3e Serie, 1870, Dl. I, pp. 415–441; Dl. II, pp. 12–38.

Blom, Govert, *Lotgevallen op mijne Reis naar Java*, 1841.

Boogaard, F. H., *L'Expédition de Lombok*, Paris, 1896.

Booms, P. C., *Précis des Expéditions de l'Armée Néerlandaise des Indes Orientales contre les Princes de Bali de 1846–1849*, Breda, 1850.

Carnbee, P. Melvill de, "Essai d'une Description de Bali et de Lombok," *Le Moniteur des Indes Orientales*, 1846-47, Ire Partie, pp. 87–92, 169–180, 252–262, 280–294, 331–338.

Cool, W., *De Lombok Expeditie*, 's Gravenhage, 1896. (Also published in English in an abbreviated version as *With the Dutch in the East*, London, 1897.)

Covarrubias, Miguel, *Island of Bali*, New York, 1936.

Eck, R. van, "Een en ander over Bali," *De Indische Gids*, 1880, II, pp. 544–562.

—— "Schetsen van het Eiland Bali," *T.N.I.*, Nieuwe Serie, VII, 1878, Dl. II, pp. 85–130, 165–213, 325–356, 405–438; VIII, 1879, Dl. I, pp. 36–60, 104–134, 286–305, 365–387; IX, 1880, Dl. I, pp. 1–39, 102–132, 195–221, 401–429, Dl. II, pp. 1–18, 81–96.

Friederich, R. H. Th., "Voorloopig Verslag van het Eiland Bali, *V.B.G.*, XXII, 1849, pp. 1–63; XXIII, 1850, pp. 1–57. (Also published in English as "An Account of the Island of Bali," *Journal of the Royal Asiatic Society*, N.S. Vol. VIII, 1876, pp. 159–218; Vol. IX, 1877, pp. 59–120; Vol. X, 1878, pp. 49–97.)

Gerlach, A. J. A., *Neerlands Heldenfeiten in Oost-Indië*, 1876. (Also published in French as *Fastes Militaires des Indes Orientales Neerlandaises*, Paris, 1859.)

Helms, Ludvig Verner, *Pioneering in the Far East*, London, 1882.

Hoëvell, W. C., van, *Reis over Java, Madura, en Bali in het Midden van 1847*, Amsterdam, 1849–54, 3 vols.

Jacobs, Julius, *Eenigen Tijd onder de Baliers*, Batavia, 1883.

Kemp, P. H. van der, "Verslag nopens het Eiland Bali," *O.T.O.I.*, I, 1835, pp. 158–236.

Kielstra, E. B., "Het Eiland Bali," *De Indische Gids*, IV, 1893, pp. 468–491.

Kol, H. H. van, *Dreimaal Dwars door Sumatra en Zwerftochten door Bali*, Rotterdam, 1914.

—— *Uit Onze Kolonien*, Leiden, 1903.

—— *Weg met het Opium*, 1913.

Lauts, G., (De Hoogleeraar) *Het Eiland Bali en de Balienezen*, Amsterdam, 1848.

Lekkerkerker, C., *Bali en Lombok: Overzicht der Litteratuur omtrent deze Eilanden tot Einde 1919*, Rijswijk, 1920.

—— *Het Voorspel der Vestiging van de Nederlandsche Macht op Bali en Lombok*, 1923.

Leupe, P. A., "Het Gezantschap naar Bali onder den Gouverneur-Generaal Hendrik Bouwer in 1633," *B.K.I.*, 2e Reeks, Dl. I (Dl. V), 1856, pp. 1–71.

Liefrinck, F. A., *Bali en Lombok: Geschriften*, Amsterdam, 1927.

—— "De Residentie Bali en Lombok na het Jaar 1894," *V.I.G.*, 1902, pp. 137–166.

Lingensz, Hernout, "Bali 1597," (Copie van 't gheene ick aen Jan Jansz. Kaerel overgegeven hebbe), *B.K.I.*, 2de r., Dl. I (Dl. V), 1856, pp. 203–234.

Medhurst, W. H., "Short Account of the Island of Bali, Particularly of Bali Bailing," in J. H. Moor, *Notices of the Indian Archipelago and Adjacent Countries*, Singapore, 1837.

Nielson, Aage Krarup, *Leven en Aventuren van een Oostinjevaarder op Bali*, Amsterdam, 1928.

Nieuwenkamp, W. O. J., *Bali en Lombok*, Edam, 1906–1910.

Nijpels, G., *De Expeditiën naar Bali in 1846, 1848, 1849, en 1868*, Haarlem, 1897.

Raka, I Gusti Gde, *Monografi Pulau Bali*, Djkarta, 1955.

Rietschoten, C. H. van, *Algemeen Verslag van den Chef van den Staf der Expeditie naar Bali, 10 September–30 October, 1906*, 1910.

Schwartz, H. J. E. F., "Aanteekening omtrent het Landschap Gianjar," *T.B.G.*, XIX, 1900, pp. 166–189.

Swellengrebel, J. L., ed., *Bali: Studies in Life, Thought, and Ritual*, The Hague, 1960.

Swieten, J. van, *Krijsverrigtingen tegen het Eiland Bali en 1848*, 's Gravenhage, 1849.

Utrecht, E., *Sedjarah Hukum Internasional di Bali dan Lombok*, Bandung, 1962.

Verster, J. F. de Balbian, *Een Amsterdammer als Pionier op Bali*, Amsterdam, 1911.

Vlijmen, B. R. F. van, *Bali in 1868*, Amsterdam, 1875.

Weitzel, A. W. P., *De Derde Militaire Expeditie naar het Eiland Bali in 1849*, Gorinchem, 1859.

Zollinger, Z. H., "Verhal eener Reis over de Eilanden Bali en Lombok Gedurende de Maanden Mei tot September, 1846," *V.B.G.*, Dl. XXII, 1849, 9e Stuk, pp. 1–15.

B.K.I.: Bijdragen van het Koninklijke Instituut voor de Taal-, Land-, en Volkenkunde van Nederlandsch-Indie

O.T.O.I.: De Oosterling Tijdschrift van Oost-Indie

T.B.G.: Tijdschrift van het Bataviaasch Genootschap

T.N.I.: Tijdschrift voor Nederlandsch Indie

V.B.G.: Verhandelingen van het Bataviaasch Genootschap

V.I.G.: Verslag der Algemeene Verhandelingen van het Indische Genootschap